WEAL.   .THY

Exploring   ities
between rich and poor

Karen Rowlingson and Stephen McKay

First published in Great Britain in 2012 by

The Policy Press
University of Bristol
Fourth Floor
Beacon House
Queen's Road
Bristol BS8 1QU
UK
Tel +44 (0)117 331 4054
Fax +44 (0)117 331 4093
e-mail tpp-info@bristol.ac.uk
www.policypress.co.uk

North American office:
The Policy Press
c/o The University of Chicago Press
1427 East 60th Street
Chicago, IL 60637, USA
t: +1 773 702 7700
f: +1 773-702-9756
e:sales@press.uchicago.edu

www.press.uchicago.edu

British Library Cataloguing in Publication Data
A catalogue record for this book is available from the British Library.

Library of Congress Cataloging-in-Publication Data
A catalog record for this book has been requested.

ISBN 978 1 84742 307 8 paperback
ISBN 978 1 84742 308 5 hardcover

The rights of Karen Rowlingson and Stephen McKay to be identified as authors
of this work has been asserted by them in accordance with the 1988 Copyright,
Designs and Patents Act.

Cover design by Robin Hawes
Front cover: image kindly supplied by istock.com
Printed and bound in Great Britain by TJ International,
Padstow
The Policy Press uses environmentally responsible printers

For Vince
And for Lilian

Contents

List of tables and figures

Tables

Figures

Acknowledgements

We would like to thank our colleagues at the University of Birmingham for their support when writing this book, not least for agreeing to give Karen Rowlingson study leave during the autumn 2010 term and covering some of Karen's teaching and tutoring during that time. Thanks also go to colleagues for providing ideas and comments on drafts of certain parts of the book. Particular thanks here go to John Doling and Stephen Gorard. Thanks also to the team at The Policy Press, particularly Karen Bowler and Laura Vickers, for all their support through the writing and production process. An anonymous reviewer also provided some very useful comments that helped us to tighten up the arguments in the book, so thanks are due to him/her also. Last but not least, we would like to thank Adrian Sinfield for all his encouragement over the years to pursue this area of work.

This report includes new analysis of four large-scale datasets:

- Data from the *Wealth and Assets Survey* (WAS) (ONS, 2010) were supplied by the UK Data Archive. We thank the Office for National Statistics (ONS) (the data collector) and the funders for the availability of this data.
- Data from the *Family Resources Survey 2008/09* (FRS) were supplied by the UK Data Archive. We thank the ONS and the National Centre for Social Research (NatCen) (the data collectors) and the Department for Work and Pensions (DWP) (the funders and designers) for the availability of this data.
- Data from the *British Social Attitudes Survey* (BSAS) were supplied by the UK Data Archive. We thank NatCen (the data collectors and designers) for the availability of this data.
- Data from the *Citizenship Survey* were supplied by the UK Data Archive. We thank the Department for Communities and Local Government (CLG), Ipsos MORI and BMRB (the data collectors and designers) for the availability of this data.

The usual disclaimer applies – all remaining errors are the responsibility of the authors.

About the authors

Stephen McKay is Professor of Social Research at the University of Birmingham, UK. He has research interests in the welfare state and in methods of analysing large-scale datasets.

Karen Rowlingson is Professor of Social Policy at the University of Birmingham, UK. She has particular interests in poverty, wealth and inequality, and in mixed research methods.

Introduction

In recent years there has been increasing academic, policy and public interest in personal assets, and in the growing gap between rich and poor. This book brings these two issues together. Although they are conceptually distinct, they are also strongly related, with the rich having significant levels of assets while people at the bottom of the economic distribution have very few, if any. It is aimed at a wide audience, including students, academics, policy makers, journalists and members of the general public. It draws on debates from a range of disciplines including sociology, economics, politics and philosophy, and it touches on policy issues in relation to taxation, housing, pensions and education. It is therefore an ambitious book and one that we do not see in any way as definitive, but as a contribution to an important debate on wealth and the wealthy.

But why should we be interested in wealth and the wealthy rather than in the seemingly greater social problem of poverty and low income? We are not arguing that poverty and low income are unimportant, but these issues have received a great deal of attention from academics and policy makers for decades; there has been much less discussion of wealth and the wealthy. The first two chapters in the book consider why wealth and the wealthy are important issues for social science and, in particular, for social policy. We argue that wealth is an important issue because there has been increasing emphasis placed on personal assets by both Conservative-led and Labour governments in recent years. This shift towards personal assets and more individual responsibility for welfare has, however, failed to achieve its aim of greater individual financial security and wellbeing and so, we argue, a new settlement is needed. We also argue that wealth, in the form of personal assets, is important because it plays a different role in people's lives than income. There is growing evidence that wealth might have an independent effect on people's health, prospects and general wellbeing. Chapter One considers the evidence here.

The wealthy are an important subject for social science for a number of reasons. First, there is increasing discussion about whether or not the gap between rich and poor causes various social and economic problems. Second, there is also discussion about the *process* by which some people become wealthy and the extent to which this is based partly on luck of birth rather than merit. And finally, there are strong arguments to suggest that the *extent* of the gap between rich and poor cannot be justified even if those who accumulate large amounts of wealth did so largely through merit rather than birth. These points are discussed in Chapter Two.

Chapter Three provides a more detailed discussion about what we mean by the terms 'wealth' and 'wealthy' as these are often used in different ways, and there has been too little discussion of their conceptualisation, definition and measurement. In this book we focus on 'wealth' in the form of personal assets, particularly housing, financial and private pension wealth. The term 'wealthy' is more complex and we discuss a range of perspectives, particularly from sociology, on social class and elites. We draw particularly on the work of John Scott to define the wealthy (or rich) as those who can afford more exclusive and private lifestyles.

Chapters Four and Five review current empirical data and provide some new analysis of data on wealth and the wealthy. The Wealth and Assets Survey (WAS) was a major step forward in terms of data on wealth, and we present various statistics from this but also draw on other datasets where appropriate. When looking at the wealthy we divide this group into the 'rich', the 'richer' and the 'richest'. Our 'rich' group comprises the most affluent 10 per cent by income and by assets. This group appear quite distinct from other groups in terms of their levels of income and assets and their characteristics and lifestyles. Most people in this group would probably not see themselves as rich as they do not realise how far above the average they are. The 'richer' group comprise the top 1 per cent and this group are more likely to appreciate their privileged position. They have certainly seen their income and wealth grow faster than other groups in recent years. The 'richest' group are the top 1,000 and we see how their wealth decreased in 2009 but recovered again by 2011.

Having provided empirical evidence on wealth and the wealthy, our last two chapters review the policy implications of recent trends in this field. We conclude by arguing for a fundamental review of policies towards assets to take into account the appropriate balance between: assets, incomes and services; accumulation and decumulation of assets; and different forms of assets (housing, pensions and savings). We also consider the goal of asset policy and whether it is to reduce poverty and/or inequality, or to help people achieve financial security and/or to make citizenship a more meaningful concept. The respective roles of the state, the individual, the employer and the private sector more generally also need to be considered.

As far as the wealthy are concerned, Chapter Seven discusses three main areas of policy: equal opportunity policy, taxation policy and original income and wealth policy. All three are needed in order to reduce the gap between rich and poor to more justifiable levels. We also discuss what level of inequality we might aim to achieve given that we, like most members of the general public, accept that some degree of inequality is justifiable as a reward for hard work and effort. However, we argue that, at present, those who have the highest levels of income and wealth have not necessarily achieved this through individual merit, and even if they had, the nature of the effort rewarded and the level of the rewards at the top cannot be justified on the grounds of relatively limited differences in effort or skill.

ONE

Why wealth matters

Introduction

Wealth in the form of personal assets[1] has received increasing attention in recent years from researchers and policy makers. This is for two main reasons. First, in the UK there has been an increase in policy emphasis on personal asset holding since the 1980s and a growing proportion of the population now own some kind of personal wealth. For example, 70 per cent of households are owner-occupied. This shift has been the result of deliberate policy change, from 1979 onwards, aimed at reducing state provision of welfare and collective ownership of wealth. We have seen this in the state withdrawing from providing social housing and instead encouraging people to become home owners. The state has also reduced levels of entitlement to the state retirement pension and encouraged people to take out their own private pensions – although the success of this policy has not been as great as with home ownership. And the state has privatised a number of industries and companies, selling off shares to individuals. This decline in the collective ownership of wealth and the corresponding rise in personal asset holding is part of a broader shift from collective forms of responsibility and risk through the state to more individual forms of responsibility and risk. These are significant trends, affecting the lives of us all. They demand analysis of the causes, consequences and policy implications of such trends as while some people have benefited from these trends, others have been left behind.

The second reason for social policy to focus on assets as well as income is that income is not the only important economic resource. It certainly plays a vital role in relation to people's livelihoods, but assets play their part. Some research suggests that assets have a positive effect on people, independent from income, and if this is the case, then social policy should not only concern itself with discussing ways of increasing incomes for those in poverty but also ways of increasing their assets.

This chapter discusses each of these reasons in more detail.

From collective welfare to individual assets

The year 1979 was a major turning point in British history. The new Conservative government hit the ground running with a range of policies designed to 'roll back the frontiers of the state'. In 1980 a Housing Act was introduced, giving people the 'Right to Buy' their council homes with a large discount. Changes in the mortgage market in the following years contributed to a major increase in home ownership in the 1980s (see Figure 1.1) (Stephens et al, 2008b; see also Forrest et al, 1990, 1999; Stephens, 2007; Williams, 2007; Doling, 2010).

Although the Labour Party had originally opposed the Right to Buy Act 1980, New Labour embraced home ownership wholeheartedly and eventually stated, in government, that their aspiration was for 75 per cent of households to be owner-occupied (CLG, 2007). In 2005, the Labour government argued that it was important to encourage:

> ... more people to share in increasing asset wealth: homes are not just places to live. They are also assets.... Support for home ownership will enable more people on lower incomes to benefit from any further increases in the value of housing assets. (ODPM, 2005, p 9)

Figure 1.1: Trends in home ownership, 1971–2007

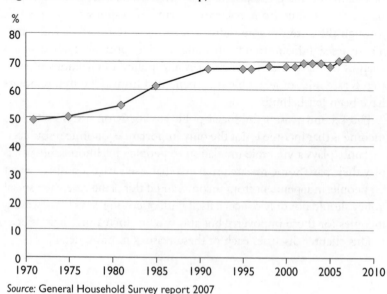

Source: General Household Survey report 2007

The increase in owner-occupation in the 1980s was also accompanied by a massive increase in house prices from the 1970s to the late 1980s and then again from 1995 to 2007 (see Figure 1.2). This increase proved a boon to those in the housing market but made it increasingly difficult for others to get a foot on the housing ladder as house price inflation from 1995 to 2007 far outstripped growth in average earnings (Appleyard and Rowlingson, 2010). The expansion of home ownership has therefore created greater wealth for some but left others further behind:

> In one sense the liberalisation of mortgage finance was socially progressive and helped to widen access to housing finance ... [but] has been undermined by its impact on house prices, which in turn have narrowed access to home-ownership, while housing market instability has sharpened the risks associated with home-ownership by making future price trends uncertain. (Stephens, 2007, p 14)

With the recent 'credit crunch', the great recession and plans for radical public sector cuts, levels of owner-occupation are stagnating. By 2010, house prices had been falling and interest rates were at historic lows, but mortgage lenders were being much less generous than in recent years (particularly in terms of the levels of deposits required) and concerns about financial security seemed to be deterring people from reaching their first rung on the housing ladder (see Chapter Six for a discussion of housing wealth policies).

There have clearly been massive changes in home ownership and housing wealth since 1980. There have also been important changes in other areas of wealth such as private pensions. The year 1980 saw another turning point in this area: the breaking of the link between the state retirement pension and earnings (if earnings were higher than the retail price index [RPI], which they continued to be for at least the next 25 years). This change meant that the value of the state retirement pension fell dramatically over the following decades. While Income Support (or the Minimum Income Guarantee/Pension Credit) provided a means-tested benefit for pensioners, the message was clear and backed up with other policy changes: people should take out their own occupational or personal pensions wherever possible. This was perhaps expressed most clearly in the introduction of personal pensions from 1988 with a generous tax regime and National Insurance rebates.

We might have expected the Labour government that came to power in 1997 to reverse some of these changes to pensions policy

Figure 1.2: Trends in property prices, 1952–2009

Source: Nationwide (2009)

and to restore the role of the state, but New Labour was not 'Old Labour' and, in many respects, continued along a similar road to the previous administration (McKay and Rowlingson, 2008). Indeed, private pensions were encouraged with the introduction of Stakeholder Pensions in 2001 and with the government announcing its wish to reverse the 60/40 per cent ratio of state to private pension provision (DWP, 1998). This was, in fact, very wishful thinking and the ratio was stubbornly hard to change. The target itself was quietly dropped in Annex C, p 174, of the 2006 pensions White Paper, *Security in retirement: Towards a new pensions system* (DWP, 2006). The policy of encouraging private pension provision through 'information and choice' did not prove successful, not least through employers becoming increasingly reluctant to provide good occupational pension schemes. This reflected both increasing longevity and the end of a positive stock market run that plunged many schemes into deficit (McKay and Rowlingson, 2008). But such deficits may not have been quite so large if employers had not taken 'holidays' from making contributions in better years.

Whatever the reason, it became clear by the early 2000s that the market was not providing sufficient security in retirement, and the 2002 pensions Green Paper established a new Pensions Commission to consider the future regime for private pensions. Reports were subsequently published in 2004 and 2005 (with a final comment in 2006 on planned reforms) which proposed increasing the age at which people could receive state pensions, restoring the link between state pensions and earnings growth and introducing a new auto-enrolment pension scheme, the National Employment Savings Trust (NEST).[2] NEST, being introduced nationally in 2012, requires employers to make a minimum contribution (reaching 3 per cent of earnings) to any employee's NEST unless that employee opts out (see Chapter Six for a further discussion of pensions policy). The employee contributes 4 per cent of earnings, and tax relief equates to 1 per cent, making for an overall contribution of 8 per cent of earnings.

Alongside changes relating to housing and pension wealth, the 1980s also saw an increase in the number of people owning shares as the Conservative government privatised many nationalised industries (for example, British Telecom, British Gas and British Rail). They also introduced new forms of tax-privileged savings accounts, now known as ISAs (Individual Savings Accounts). These policies have generally benefited middle and higher income groups who can afford to invest in shares and make savings. Once again, there was a high level of continuity in policy when New Labour came to power in 1997 although it wanted to extend opportunities to save to poorer groups through 'asset-based welfare' policies which drew on much US thinking and research (Sherraden, 1991). Two flagship policies here were the Child Trust Fund and the Saving Gateway.

The Child Trust Fund started an account for all babies born from September 2002. Babies from low-income families received £500 while others received £250. This money was placed into a special account that could not be accessed until the child turned 18. At that point, the young person would be able to spend the money on anything they chose. In 2009, the government gave top-ups of £250/£500 to those children who had reached the age of seven. Parents and other family members or friends could add to the accounts at any point but not access them (Prabhakar, 2008). The other flagship asset-based welfare policy was the Saving Gateway which was due to be introduced in July 2010. This was a scheme designed to encourage people on low incomes (under £16,000 household income) to save by matching £1 of savings with a 50 pence reward (up to a maximum of £25 a month and with the reward only payable after two years). One of the first actions of the Conservative/Liberal Democrat Coalition government was to discontinue the Child Trust Fund policy for any new babies, withdraw further government contributions into these funds, and to scrap the plan to introduce the Saving Gateway. However, the Treasury announced new plans for 'Junior ISAs' for those aged under 18 in October 2010.

This move from collective welfare to a focus on more individual assets reflects a broader move from collective risk and responsibility to more individual risk and responsibility (Clarke and Newman, 1997; Clarke et al, 2001; Taylor-Gooby, 2000; Dwyer, 2002; Gilbert, 2004). It largely began with the 1979 Conservative government, who pursued an approach labelled by Klein and Millar (1995) as 'Do-it-yourself' welfare. Malpass (2008, p 9) has more recently characterised this approach as: 'a freer, more open economy, a greater role for private markets, a reduced role for the state in key areas affecting well-being, more emphasis on individual choice, opportunity and responsibility'.

The approach was then taken up by New Labour with Giddens (1998) becoming a key proponent, calling for a move from what was seen by some as a 'passive' welfare state to a more 'active' one. He argued that:

> ... social democrats have to shift the relationship between
> risk and security involved in the welfare state to develop a
> society of 'responsible risk-takers'.... People need protection
> when things go wrong but also the material and moral

capabilities to move through major periods of transition in their lives. (Giddens, 1998, p 100)

This approach has also been labelled the rather inelegant term 'responsibilisation' (Garland, 1996) and is based on a new model of citizenship with individuals expected to help themselves as far as they can rather than look to the state. As Hewitt (2002, p 189) has argued: 'The good citizen is someone who works for a living (thereby making no claims on social security) saves a portion of their earnings, and uses their savings to contribute substantially to their own and their family's future welfare'. The former Prime Minister Tony Blair clearly advocated such an approach in numerous speeches and papers: 'for too long the demand for rights from the state was separated from the duties of citizenship ... the rights we enjoy should reflect the duties we owe' (Blair, 1998, p 4, quoted in Taylor-Gooby, 2000).

Much of the discussion in this field has revolved around 'activation' and conditionality in relation to benefits for those out of work. Individual 'jobseekers' are now expected to take increasing responsibility for their own welfare by finding work (Dean, 2006). In the field of assets, Dwyer (2002) suggests that pensions are a good example of the shift in responsibility and risk from the state to the individual. When pensions are provided by the state the risks are pooled across the whole of society; personal pensions leave individuals to bear the entire risk. If personal pensions under-perform in the stock market, the individual who invested money in the pension loses out, whereas state pension entitlements are more secure, although governments can change the rules from time to time. The risk involved in occupational pensions depends on the type of pension involved. Defined benefit schemes place the risk on the employer as the employee is entitled to a certain percentage of their (final) salary regardless of how well or how badly the investments perform. But defined benefit schemes are becoming increasingly rare in favour of defined contribution schemes where the risk is much more squarely on the employee. When risks are pooled it is usually those with least resources who are most likely to be sheltered from any adverse effects. When risks are individualised it is this group who are likely to suffer most.

There has also been recent discussion about the role of housing wealth in relation to the welfare state (Regan and Paxton, 2001; Maxwell, 2005; Doling and Ronald, 2010a, 2010b). Policy in this area has certainly promoted home ownership rather than renting but, so far at least, governments have done very little to encourage let alone expect or require people to access their housing wealth as a supplement to (or in place of) Income Support through the state. Long-term care, however, is paid for through housing wealth in many circumstances although this is highly unpopular and has been under review for the last decade or two (see Chapter Six).

The role of assets in people's lives

In the previous section, we saw that there has been a shift from state responsibility and collective risk for financial security to personal responsibility and individual risk. More people own personal assets such as property and pensions, although there are considerable numbers of people who own nothing at all (see Chapter Three), and asset inequality is widening as those at the very top increase their share of wealth still further. It is therefore important to consider the role of assets in people's lives. But whereas there have been many studies focusing on the role of income, there have been few on the role of assets. This is for a number of reasons, not least the wider availability of data on income compared with assets but also, perhaps, because income is seen as providing for people's immediate material needs and so considered more important than assets. However, if we are truly interested in the command of economic resources more broadly, then it is important to consider assets alongside income because assets also play an important role in people's lives. Oliver et al (1993, p 75), for example, have argued that: 'Analyses of income only capture the current state of inequality, while wealth embodies the potential for examining accumulated and historically structured inequality'.

Michael Sherraden has been one of the leading academics in theorising the role of assets as well as carrying out empirical research and promoting discussion of policy in this field. In his book *Assets and the poor* (1991) he argued that income is not a good indicator of consumption/welfare because it varies over the life course, and so a snapshot at any one point in time will not really tell us much about the overall level of resources/welfare that a family has. It might be possible to estimate a family's 'lifetime income' but even this would not be able to capture the fact that one family may have seen its income rise and fall while another's level of income has been stable over time, which may, again, affect levels of welfare. However, stocks of wealth also vary over time as people accumulate more at some points in their life and use up some at other points, and so wealth, on its own, is not a particularly good measure of family welfare. Sherraden (1991) also argued, however, that assets may have important effects beyond consumption, such as:

- improving household stability by providing a cushion against unexpected events;
- giving people hope, and the ability to plan, for the future;
- stimulating the growth of other kinds of assets (for example, human capital);
- enabling people to specialise and focus on a particular life path;
- providing a foundation for risk taking including entrepreneurship;
- increasing personal efficacy by giving people more control over their lives;
- increasing social influence by improving one's status in the community and one's social capital;
- increasing political participation;
- enhancing the welfare of children by providing a stronger intergenerational connection.

To sum up, Sherraden (1991, p 6) claimed that:

> ... income only maintains consumption, but assets change the way people think and interact in the world. With assets, people begin to think in the long-term and pursue long-term goals. In other words, while incomes feed people's stomachs, assets change their heads.

Sherraden (1991, p 294) argued further that assets have greater and more direct effects than income due to the degree of control assets give people. In relation to asset-based welfare policies: 'Asset accumulation and investment, rather than income and consumption, are the keys to leaving poverty'.

This is quite a radical approach and might suggest that, rather than raising the incomes of people in poverty, we should be increasing their assets. Then again, perhaps it is a luxury to try to change people's heads when their stomachs are empty? And one would imagine that if people on the lowest incomes were given a liquid asset they might (and arguably should) cash it in and spend the money quite quickly to meet their immediate needs rather than retain it for some future use. If people on the lowest incomes are given an asset that they cannot cash, it may make them feel differently about the future but it may not be the best thing for their current welfare. Of course, for people whose basic needs are met by their current income, possession of an asset (or encouragement to accumulate an asset) may be beneficial in the ways listed above.

The relative benefits of assets to income, and the relative benefits of different kinds of assets, are not entirely clear. For example, if we consider two people with the same level of income but one has some assets, then it is clear that the one with assets is better off. But how much better off? And in what ways? And how does this vary according to different levels of income and assets and according to different types of assets? What if one person has a higher income but owns fewer assets? Who then is better off than the other? Would we change our opinion depending on the age of the person, perhaps? To consider this point further, let us compare the following two hypothetical people:

- Anna: a 25-year-old single woman with an income of £22,000. She has no private pension or financial savings and is paying £100 per month on debt repayments (which will take another year to pay off). She is renting a flat.
- Andy: a 25-year-old man with an income of £15,000. He has no private pension or financial savings or debts. He has just put a £10,000 deposit down on a £100,000 flat.

Anna is certainly better off in terms of income, earning £7,000 per year more than Andy, nearly a third more in terms of gross income. But in terms of assets, Andy has £10,000 equity in a flat whereas Anna has a debt whose repayment has a cash cost of £1,200. Anna could, in theory, pay off her debt from her annual income and still have greater income in that year than Andy but, in practice, she might find that difficult to do because of other commitments. And it would certainly take her some time to save towards the same level of equity that Andy has. So perhaps Andy is better off overall? But we don't know how much their relative rent and mortgage costs are so their relative disposable incomes after housing costs may not be as great as the difference between their gross incomes. Perhaps Anna is living in a flat with a very low rent whereas interest rates are very high and Andy's mortgage is much higher than Anna's rent? So far, we have only considered this issue in straight financial terms, but how does their situation make them feel? Perhaps Anna feels some degree of burden in terms of her debt and is concerned about whether or not her landlord will allow her to stay in the flat whereas Andy's owner-occupation makes him feel more positive about his status? Perhaps Anna is anxious that house prices are going up fast and it will be difficult for her to become a home owner? But if house prices are going down, renting may be a better financial option and may also give Anna more flexibility to move should she wish to change her job. Andy may be anxious about potential negative equity if prices are going down and may feel trapped where he is.

And what if, rather than having a difference in terms of housing assets, Andy had been paying into a pension for five years? This would make little material difference to his current standard of living but it might make him feel more secure about his long-term future. Having said that, with pension scheme deficits in the news and various changes in pension schemes taking place, the level of security from this asset may not be that great.

If we take another example:

- The Andersons: a couple in their mid-50s with a joint income of £40,000. They own a house outright worth £150,000 and have no savings. They have pension savings that will give them a joint private pension income of £15,000 per year when they retire at 65.
- The Ahmeds: a couple in their mid-50s with a joint income of £30,000. They own a house outright worth £200,000 and have savings of £10,000. They have no private pension savings.

The Andersons are certainly better off in terms of income and so could have a higher immediate standard of living and/or save more for the future. But they have much less housing equity and no savings compared with the Ahmeds, who have £50,000 more in equity and £10,000 of savings. Ownership of liquid savings may make the Ahmeds feel more secure as they have a cushion against unexpected events. But the Ahmeds have no private pension coverage and this could make them feel anxious with their retirement years fast approaching. The Ahmeds could use their savings in retirement and also release equity from their home, but, depending on how long they live, this may not give them as much as the pension pot owned by the Andersons. Having said all this, if the state pension system is means tested then the Andersons may not benefit very much from having saved in a private pension and the Ahmeds may have a similar amount of income in retirement but much greater assets. The extra equity owned by the Ahmeds could signal that they have a bigger or better home to live in but this is not necessarily the case depending on where they live. Their opportunity to downsize and release equity will also depend on this and whether or not they would be prepared to move to a cheaper area and/or smaller home. Once again, the benefits of assets over income and of different types of assets depend on a range of factors.

The impact of assets on people's lives is clearly very complex. They can have an effect not only on someone's financial wellbeing but also on their more general wellbeing. Their value is likely to depend significantly on the nature of state welfare and also on the nature of the market. Much of the literature in this field ignores the fact that assets may have negative effects on people. For example, an owner–occupier on a low income with a house that needs major repairs may see the 'asset' as a burden. And someone who has invested considerable sums in a personal pension may be very anxious if the stock market falls.

Much of the discussion in this field focuses on the economic role of assets, but different kinds of assets may also play a much wider, social role in people's lives. For example, housing provides shelter for people as well as, potentially, a financial investment and source of funds (for example, through re-mortgaging). It may also provide an emotional attachment if someone has lived in the same home for many years or experienced major life changes, such as the birth of children. The home may become a space full of memories and part of one's identity as well as an economic asset. Private pensions and savings are rather different but perhaps can provide people with a feeling of security and greater choice in their lives. For example, if someone in their 50s is unhappy with their job, they will have much greater choice about taking early retirement than someone without such assets.

Is there an asset effect?

As discussed in the previous section, there is a lot of debate and theory about the impact of assets on people's lives but relatively few empirical studies that have tested this kind of theory. The first study in the UK to investigate whether or not there is an 'asset effect' was carried out by Jon Bynner and colleagues (Bynner and Paxton, 2001; Bynner and Despotidou, 2001) using the National Child Development Study (NCDS), which is a birth cohort of all those born in a particular week in 1958 (about 12,000 people are still participating in this study). These people have been followed up at different points (ages 7, 11, 16, 23 and 33 – at the time of this analysis) with data collected on education, income, work, health, relationships and so on. The study by Bynner and Paxton (2001) tested whether or not having assets at age 23 had an effect on:

- labour market outcomes (for example, length of time unemployed);
- health (for example, smoking and mental health);
- citizenship and values (for example, whether voted in the last election);
- parenting (for example, how often people read to their children).

The analysis controlled for number of variables such as family class at birth, family characteristics at age 11, educational outcomes at age 16 and some post-16 variables. 'Assets' in this research were defined as financial savings rather than housing wealth or pension wealth and these were divided into having savings, having investments and having received an inheritance. The majority of the sample (82 per cent) had some savings at age 23 and it is likely that the sums involved were very small in many cases. The research, therefore, failed to distinguish between different levels of savings and between those who were actively saving rather than just having some money in savings accounts (Emmerson and Wakefield, 2001).

A number of different models were run and in a number of these, having savings[3] at age 23 had a positive and statistically significant effect on a number of outcome variables. The size of this 'asset effect' depended on the particular dependent variable being analysed. Assets seemed to have the most significant effect on the labour market variables (particularly for men), on marital breakdown and on some health variables. For example, holding assets at age 23 was associated with a lower rate of smoking at age 37. It was also associated with having more years in full-time employment over that period. There did not, seem, however, to be any significant effects of assets on the parenting variables or the citizenship variables. These findings held true even after adding numerous control variables, including whether the individual owned a house between the ages of 23 and 33 and what the individual earned at age 33.

In a comprehensive review of this research, Emmerson and Wakefield (2001) have pointed out that, as Bynner and Paxton themselves acknowledge, it is always problematic to assume a causal relationship from a statistical correlation in survey data. It is possible, for example, that another factor, not available in the dataset, is responsible for the correlation found. With this particular study, it may be the case that having savings at age 23 is linked to another factor that causes the outcomes at age 33 but that this factor is not in the dataset and so cannot be included in the analysis. One possible factor would be the *process* of saving. Perhaps it is this, rather than the ownership of an asset, which is responsible for the positive outcomes at age 33. The process of saving would be the important factor if it reflected individuals' ability to constrain consumption and to plan ahead (Paxton, 2001). The government certainly seems to think that it is important to 'extend the savings habit to more people' (Labour Party, 2001, p 27).

Emmerson and Wakefield (2001) have suggested that one way of testing whether simply giving people assets rather than encouraging them to develop a savings habit had positive effects on them would be to look at the impact of receiving an inheritance. They point out that Bynner and Despotidou (2001) did indeed look at the effect of inheritances, but this was not particularly related to positive outcomes and so was dropped from the later stages of the analysis.

Even if the correlations found by Bynner are causal, Emmerson and Wakefield (2001) have argued that this does not necessarily imply that giving an asset to people who do not save will improve their outcomes in the same way, since individuals who choose not to hold savings may be affected differently by holding an asset from those who did make that choice. Another limitation of the Bynner and Despotidou study is that it looks at the impact of asset holding for one group of people at one point in time and any relationships found could change over time, due, for example, to the increase in numbers participating in further and higher education.

Emmerson and Wakefield (2001) have pointed out many limitations with Bynner's work but, of course, it is not easy to carry out research in this field and his is one of the few studies on the asset effect. Following on from this study McKay and Kempson (2003) repeated similar analysis on a different sample, the British Household Panel Survey (BHPS). McKay and Kempson (2003) focused on working–age adults (up to the age of 55) in 1995 and investigated any effect on them five years later in 2000. To measure assets, they used three variables: having savings, having investments and people saying that they were putting money away. Using these definitions, McKay and Kempson (2003) began with some bivariate analysis that shows that having assets in one year (1995) was associated with a range of positive outcomes in 2000. For example, those with assets in 1995 were less likely to be out of work between 1995 and 2000, had higher earnings in 2000 and were less likely to be smoking in that year. In most cases, the effect of holding investments was greater than holding savings or regularly saving.

The analysis at this stage, however, did not control for factors that would be linked to having assets and it may be these other factors that are responsible for the associations with positive outcomes. Assets may therefore be acting as a 'proxy' for these other variables. For example, compared to those without assets, those with assets are likely to be older, in paid work and on higher incomes, and it could be these factors that explain the positive outcomes rather than the assets themselves.

Multivariate analysis is therefore crucial to try to disentangle these factors, and McKay and Kempson (2003) then conducted a logistic regression model with the outcome variable being whether or not people held savings. They also included the following control variables:

age, age-squared, housing tenure, highest qualification, region, job status of spouse or single, job status (except in the labour market equations) and marital status (except in the separation/divorce equation). This multivariate analysis largely supported the previous Bynner and Paxton (2000) research as it also showed an effect on smoking and labour market outcomes and a positive effect of assets on voting in the 1997 General Election (for men). But it did not show an effect on marital breakdown.

McKay and Kempson (2003) then took their analysis a step further. They argued that the control variables used in the model should take account of the fact that some outcomes (for example, smoking in 2000) are likely to be highly associated with whether or not someone smoked in the base year (1995 in the BHPS analysis). Similarly, if someone was out of work in the base year then they were more likely than others to be out of work at some future point. Simple bivariate analysis confirmed this. So, for example, if there is an asset effect on smoking we might expect smokers with assets to be more likely to stop smoking compared with those without assets. We might also expect non-smokers without assets to be more likely to start smoking than those with assets. But the research did not produce this finding. In fact, smokers with assets in 1995 were no more likely to give up smoking by 2000 than smokers without assets in 1995. Similarly, among non-smokers in 1995, those without assets were no more likely to start smoking than non-smokers with assets. However, there did seem to be some effects on the labour market outcomes in 2000 compared with labour market status in 1995 but these did not hold when multivariate analysis introduced further control variables.

The research by McKay and Kempson (2003) therefore ultimately called into question the existence of an asset effect on most outcomes. However, further research in this field would be useful to extend the range of controls and outcomes investigated. Also, research might look at different levels and types of asset holding to see if this makes a difference to outcomes. The length of time over which asset holding has an impact could also be varied as perhaps some effects take place quite quickly and some take longer. A larger sample size would also be useful for further research.

There has been considerable research in the US on the impact of income on child development outcomes and much of this has found that 'the long-term economic status of a household is more important than income poverty in one particular year' (Williams, 2004, p 1). Long-term economic status in these studies is used as a proxy for 'permanent income' that is operationalised as average income over five years or more. Williams (2004) also quoted research which suggests that home ownership has positive outcomes for child development, but points out that this may not be due to asset ownership *per se* but largely due to economic stability (which is linked to asset ownership but is distinct and may be provided if tenants were given more security over their housing tenure). But Williams' (2004) own analysis of the Panel Study of Income Dynamics showed that, after controlling for income, parental ownership of assets had an independent effect on child development. She argued that the effect of wealth did not simply hold for housing wealth or net wealth (as some previous studies had suggested) but also for private pension savings, bank accounts and money in stocks. Her research also suggested that the impact of having stocks or private pension savings or some level of assets was greater for African Americans than for other Americans.

Although much is said about an 'asset effect', there is remarkably little strong evidence that such an effect exists. We do not know, for example, whether it might be the *process of saving* or *the ownership of an asset* that might make a difference to people. Nor do we know enough about the role of different types of assets, different levels of asset holding and the relative benefit of different levels of income versus assets. Compared with the huge amount of research on income, research into assets is in its infancy and has been hampered by lack of data although as we shall see in Chapters Four and Five, a new dataset in the UK may eventually help plug some of the data gap.

Conclusions

The rise in policy emphasis on personal assets since 1980 signals a major shift from collective responsibility and risk to individual responsibility and risk for welfare. As we shall see in the next chapter, this has occurred at the same time as, and arguably contributed to, the growing gap between rich and poor. Those on the lowest income have the least capacity to accumulate assets and, if they do, are the most likely to fall victim when the risk taken leads to adverse effects (for example, the risk of taking on a mortgage when on a low income). As we shall see in Chapter Four, the bottom third of the population have virtually no assets at all, or have negative assets, in the form of debts. This group are falling further behind 'mainstream' society. But 'mainstream' society is not homogeneous. Some of those with personal assets have very little and may find it a struggle to keep them (for example, housing with a high level of mortgage repayments or which needs expensive repairs). Others have considerable assets and can draw on these in times of need (for example, to help their children through university or to get a foot on the housing ladder).

Although we have witnessed growth in some forms of personal assets over the last 30 years, the credit crunch and broader economic trends may have brought this expansion to an end, for now at least. Owner-occupation, if anything, appears to be on the decline as lenders become more cautious with their lending, and even though house prices are currently falling, housing is still unaffordable to many. Occupational pensions in the private sector are in retreat as employers seek to reduce their contributions in the face of longevity, stock market changes and attempts to make savings in light of the economic crash. Personal pensions are also affected by stock market falls and/or volatility. Personal savings may, effectively, increase somewhat as people pay off debts and become more cautious with their spending given current economic uncertainty. But, overall, it looks as though we may have reached the limits of the growth of personal assets. The balance between the state, the individual and the employer in providing financial security throughout working life and in old age therefore needs to be reconsidered, and we discuss this further in Chapter Six.

The growth of personal assets may have halted for now but assets clearly play a role in many people's lives. But what kind of role is it? Housing provides shelter for people as well as, potentially, a financial investment and source of funds (for example, through re-mortgaging). It may also provide an emotional attachment, a space full of memories and part of one's identity. Housing is therefore a very complex asset and not just an economic entity. Private pensions are rather different as their liquidity is highly constrained. Their main role is to provide financial security in later life, but various pension scandals and concerns over whether or not pension funds will be adequate may limit the degree of confidence that people have in them. Personal savings seem much more secure, although it was only in 2007 that Northern Rock suffered a run as people feared losing their savings. And interest rates are so low that, over time, some forms of saving are not keeping up with inflation and so constitute a loss in value. Nevertheless, personal savings can provide a cushion in times of need or provide money for special occasions.

So assets play a role but do they have an effect on people, independent of income, for example, on education, employment, family relationships, health and so on? There has been remarkably little research on this given the policy interest. And policy makers have asserted that there is an asset effect when the evidence is actually rather weak. Much of the research focuses on personal savings and fails to distinguish adequately between the ownership of savings and the process of saving. There has been little on housing and pension wealth. There are also difficulties in carrying out this research due to limited data. A new dataset, the Wealth and Assets Survey (WAS), should make it possible to carry out further research in this area although it will take some time for the panel research to provide sufficient waves of data to do this. Until then, the jury is out.

Notes

[1] See Chapter Three for a more detailed discussion of what wealth is, including different forms of capital and more collective forms of wealth. While recognising that these different forms are important, this book focuses on personal assets.

[2] Formerly known as Personal Accounts, and described as a National Pensions and Savings Scheme (NPSS) in the second report of the Pensions Commission (2005).

[3] Investments and inheritance did not have much effect.

TWO

Why the wealthy matter

Introduction

Chapter One focused on why wealth, in the form of personal assets, matters. This chapter explains why the wealthy matter. As argued in the introduction, 'wealth' and 'the wealthy' are related but represent two distinct sets of issues. Most of the wealthy have high levels of personal assets but some might be considered 'wealthy' (or 'rich') due to extremely high levels of income – they may be 'income rich but asset poor'. This raises the issue of who might be considered 'wealthy' and we discuss this, in detail, in the next chapter. In this chapter, however, we argue that there are four key reasons why social policy should focus more attention on the wealthy.

The first is that, partly as a result of some of the trends discussed in Chapter One, the gap between rich and poor has grown since the 1980s, and an increasing body of empirical research suggests that this gap between rich and poor, as distinct from poverty itself, has negative effects on society, for example, in relation to health outcomes. If this is the case, then this provides a reason why social science, and social policy in particular, should not only concern itself with discussing ways of reducing poverty but also ways of reducing the gap between rich and poor.

The second reason for focusing on the wealthy is that the concentration of wealth among a very few people at the top may have contributed to, if not caused, the economic crisis that the world is still struggling to recover from at the time of writing this book.

The third reason for paying attention to the wealthy is that, regardless of the empirical evidence on the social or economic *effects* of inequality, a large gap between rich and poor may be unjust if those who become rich do so through luck of birth rather than merit. It is therefore important to consider the extent of equal opportunity within an unequal society and the role of policy.

And, finally, even if equal opportunities exist there may nevertheless be injustice if the resulting amount of wealth accumulated by some people goes beyond what might be considered a fair reward for differences in effort, skill and so on. It is therefore important to consider what degree of inequality might be just or unjust and how policies might be put in place to secure such an outcome. It is also important to consider what kinds of work receive greater rewards and whether this is fair.

This chapter discusses each of these reasons in more detail but starts by documenting the increasing concentration of income and wealth in recent decades into the hands of the few.

The increasing concentration of income and wealth

In Chapter One, we documented the retreat from the welfare state that has taken place since 1979. This retreat from collective provision in favour of more individual responsibility took place within a context of, and arguably helped to lead to, an increasing concentration of income and wealth. From 1961 to 1979, incomes had actually grown throughout the income distribution with those at the bottom experiencing the fastest income growth. But from 1979 to 1994/95, however, incomes rose fastest for the richest (the richest tenth saw their real incomes rise by 60 per cent while the poorest tenth saw only a 10 per cent rise). Hills (2004, pp 25-6) summarised the trends during this time as 'the poor fell behind the middle; the middle fell behind the top; and the top fell behind the very top'. Due to this, income inequality soared, along with relative poverty.

Since 1994/95, the picture has been quite mixed but most groups shared in fairly rapid income growth until the advent of the recession. Hills (2004, p 26) summarised the trends during this time as: 'the poor catching up on the middle to some extent, but the top moving away from the middle'. The very top therefore 'stretched' away from the rest. For example, research by Income Data Services (IDS) has shown that the average earnings of the chief executives of the country's 100 largest listed companies increased from an average of £2 million in 2004–05 to £2.9 million in 2005–06, a rise of 43 per cent.[1] The typical chief executive of a top 100 company therefore earns 86 times as much as a typical employee in these companies.

Figure 2.1 shows the Gini coefficient[2] for income inequality both before and after housing costs (BHC and AHC). It shows that income inequality was largely stable during the 1960s and 1970s, between 0.25 and 0.30, but from 1979 onwards there was a massive rise to 0.34 (BHC) and 0.37 (AHC). The rate of growth of inequality slowed down during the 1990s and 2000s, but the peak for inequality BHC over this period was 0.36 in 2007/08. And the figure for income inequality AHC peaked in 2008/09 at a figure of 0.41.

Figure 2.1: Income inequality from 1961 to 2008/09, before and after housing costs

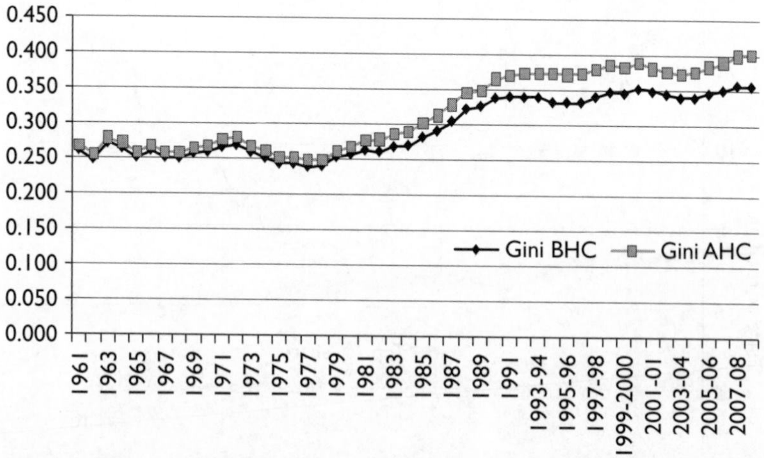

Source: FES/FRS data in IFS online spreadsheet: www.ifs.org.uk/bns/bn19figs.zip

As we can see, income inequality was higher at the very beginning of the 21st century than at any time in the previous 50 years (Hills, 2004), with the top tenth of the population receiving a greater share of total income than the whole of the bottom half in 2002–03. And those at the very top were receiving an increasingly high proportion of income.

A particularly narrow focus on what might be called the 'super-rich' has been the object of study for Atkinson and Salverda (2003), who have used tax records to investigate the changing share of income held by the very top. They show that the share of income of the top 0.05 per cent (sometimes known as the 'top ten thousand') fell between the mid-1920s and mid-1970s but then grew rapidly, so that by 1999 their share of income was higher than it had been in 1937. Atkinson (2007) presented a similar picture, this time concerning the top 0.1 per cent who received more than 10 per cent of total income before the First World War but then saw their income share fall dramatically from then until 1979. Since then, this group has recovered the ground lost since the Second World War. Figure 2.2 shows the share of total income received by the top 1 per cent of incomes. In 1950 the top 1 per cent of earners claimed around 13 per cent of total income. This declined to a low of 6.5 per cent in 1978, but thereafter rose strongly to again approach 13 per cent by the year 2000.

Table 2.1 shows that the growth in incomes between 1996/97 and 2007/08 was higher at each point towards the top of the income distribution. Those on a median income (the 50th percentile) saw their

Figure 2.2: Share of total incomes received by the top 1%, 1950–2000

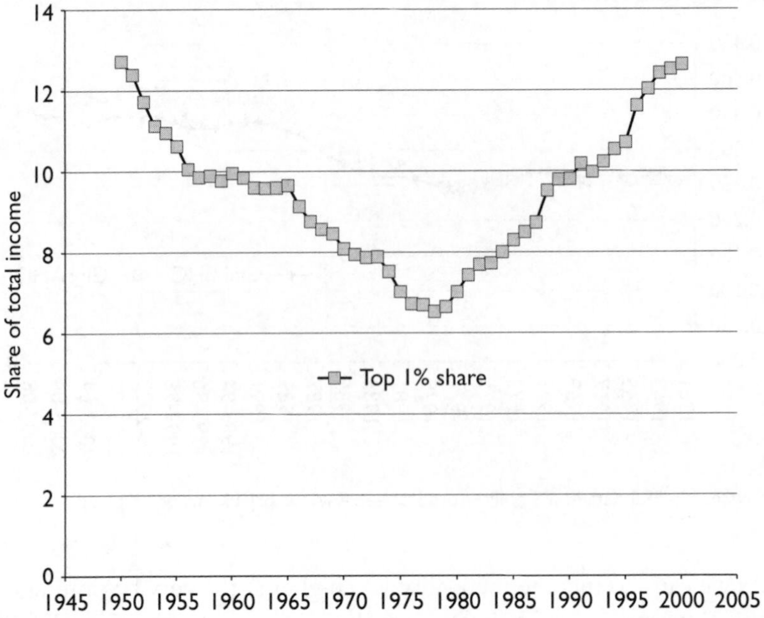

Source: Leigh (2007). UK data are derived from: Atkinson (2007)

Table 2.1: Growth in incomes at different points of the income distribution, 1996/97 to 2007/08

Percentile	Overall income growth 1996/97–2007/08
50	7.2
90	13.1
99	34.3
99.9	64.2

Source: High Pay Commission (2011) calculation using the Survey of Personal Incomes, HMRC data

incomes increase by 7.2 per cent over this period. Those at the 90th percentile (the top 10 per cent) saw their incomes rise by 13.1 per cent. Those at the 99th percentile (the top 1 per cent) saw a 34.3 per cent increase in their incomes, and those at the 99.9 percentile (the top 0.1 per cent) saw their incomes rise by 64.2 per cent.

As with income inequality, asset inequality also decreased during the first three quarters of the 20th century (Atkinson and Harrison, 1978; Atkinson et al, 1986; Hills, 2004). Table 2.2 shows that in 1923, the top 1 per cent of the population in England and Wales owned a staggering 61 per cent of all marketable assets. By 1976, this had fallen

Table 2.2: The changing distribution of personal assets

	Share of marketable assets of the ...			Gini coefficient
	Top 1%	Top 5%	Top 10%	(%)
(a) England and Wales				
1923	61	82	89	–
1930	58	79	87	–
1938	55	77	85	–
(b) Great Britain				
1950	47	74	–	–
1955	44	71	–	–
1961	37	61	72	–
1966	31	56	70	–
1971	29	53	68	–
1976	25	49	65	–
1986	23	46	63	–
(c) United Kingdom				
1976	21	38	50	66
1981	18	36	50	65
1986	18	36	50	64
1991	17	35	47	64
1996	20	40	52	68
2001	22	41	54	68
2005	21	40	54	70

(a) Atkinson and Harrison (1978, Table 6.5)

(b) Atkinson et al (1986, Table 1)

(c) HMRC Personal Wealth statistics

Table panels (a) and (b) are from Hills (2004); panel (c) from HMRC (www.hmrc.gov.uk/ stats/personal_wealth/13-5-table-2005.pdf)

drastically, and the top 1 per cent in the UK owned 21 per cent. This is a dramatic drop of 40 percentage points but still, in 1976, the top 10 per cent owned half of all assets. The 1980s witnessed a stabilisation in the levels of asset inequality but these then began to rise in the late 1990s. The Gini coefficient measure of overall asset inequality rose from 64 per cent in 1991 to 70 per cent in 2005 (www.hmrc.gov.uk/stats/ personal_wealth/13-5-table-2005.pdf). And between 1988 and 1999, the top 1 per cent of the population increased its share of personal assets from 17 to 23 per cent (Paxton and Taylor, 2002). The cause of this rise in asset inequality is unclear but it is probably a result of the increases in income inequality that took place in the 1980s, which then emerged as wealth inequality (Hills, 2004). The stock market boom and rise in property prices in the late 1990s are also likely to have had an effect.

The distribution of assets is far more unequal than the distribution of income. For example, the Gini coefficient for the distribution of assets in 2001 was 68 per cent, twice as high as the comparable figure for income (Hills, 2004).

It is interesting to compare trends over time in Britain with changes in other countries, and Hills (2004, p 37) stated that by the mid-1990s 'Britain's inequality growth was exceptional internationally', with income inequality in Britain becoming second highest (behind the US) when compared with 15 OECD (Organisation for Economic Co-operation and Development) countries. More recently, the National Equality Panel (2010) quoted a major comparison of income inequality across OECD member countries. It showed that by the mid-2000s, the UK had income inequality that was in the top quarter of the 30 OECD countries shown, although significantly below that of the US, Turkey and Mexico. Italy had higher inequality than the UK, but other large European countries such as Germany and France had inequality that was below the OECD average. Nordic countries, particularly Denmark and Sweden, had the least inequality. So Britain's position in the inequality league table had fallen between the mid-1990s and mid-2000s but was still in the top quarter.

This picture is confirmed by further data from the National Equality Panel (2010) showing *changes* in the Gini coefficient for 24 countries from the mid-1980s to the mid-1990s and from then until the mid-2000s. In the first period, the UK was one of the six countries with the most rapid *growth* in inequality; in the second, it was one of the four countries with the largest *fall*. Taking the two decades as a whole, inequality grew in the UK, but by less than the average for these countries. The National Equality Panel report (2010) went on to argue that the UK's high level of income inequality compared to other countries is driven at least in part by its very high level of inequality at the top of the income range, while it is less unusual at the bottom.

The National Equality Panel report (2010) also made comparisons of *wealth* inequality between countries but argued that this was more difficult than comparing income distributions. Data from the Luxembourg Wealth Study (LWS), however, appears to show levels of household *wealth* inequality in the UK are not exceptional in international terms, and indeed much less not only than in the US but also than in Germany and Sweden. So Britain has lower levels of wealth inequality than Sweden, which may come as quite a surprise to many. But it must be remembered that these figures relate to personal assets, and in a country such as Sweden, with high levels of 'public wealth' (in the form of state pensions, for example), people do not have the same level of need to accumulate their own personal assets.

The main conclusion from this review of trends is that those at the top, particularly those at the very top, have increased their shares of income and wealth in recent years. The rest of this chapter goes on to argue that this matters for a range of reasons.

Is the concentration of income and wealth a social problem?

The growing gap between rich and poor in recent decades has sparked a lively debate about the impact this might have on society. In relation to health outcomes several major reviews have found a clear relationship between socioeconomic inequality and health (DHSS, 1980; Townsend et al, 1986; Acheson, 1998; Marmot 2010). The most recent of these, the Marmot Review, found that people living in the poorest English neighbourhoods die, on average, seven years earlier than people living in the richest neighbourhoods (Marmot, 2010). Figure 2.3 shows a

Figure 2.3: Life expectancy at birth for men and women by social class, 2001–03, England

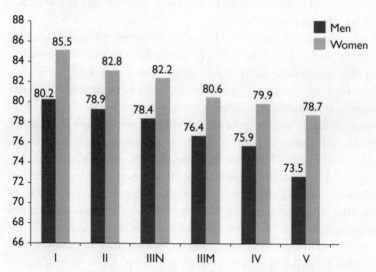

Source: White and Edgar (2010)

Note: Social class here is based on The Registrar General's Social Class. Some examples of occupations within each group are as follows:
I - Professionals: doctors, chartered accountants, professionally-qualified engineers
II - Managerial and managers: journalists, school teachers
IIIN - Skilled non-manual: clerks, cashiers, retail staff
IIIM - Skilled manual: supervisors of manual workers, plumbers, electricians, goods vehicle drivers
IV - Partly skilled: warehousemen/women, security guards, machine tool operators, care assistants, waiters and waitresses
V - Unskilled labourers: cleaners and messengers

similar degree of difference between the life expectancies of people in unskilled jobs and those in professional jobs. The data come from the Office for National Statistics (ONS) (White and Edgar, 2010) and show that, for the period 2001–03, men in professional occupations had a life expectancy at birth of 80.2 years, compared with 73.5 years for those in unskilled manual occupations. Women in professional occupations had a life expectancy at birth of 85.5 years compared with 78.7 years for those in unskilled manual occupations.

The research also shows, very clearly, that there is not a simple threshold below which people have shorter lives. There is, instead, a life expectancy *gradient*, with people in higher socioeconomic positions living longer than those in positions slightly lower than themselves. We can see this in Figure 2.3 in relation to social class but this effect also occurs *within* social classes. In other words, those in the most senior management jobs live longer, on average, than those in slightly less senior management jobs. This latter group, in turn, will live longer, on average, than people in junior management jobs, and so on. Health inequality is not, therefore, an issue just of poverty but of inequality more widely (Marmot, 2004).

We have focused on the relationship between inequality and life expectancy so far, but there is also evidence for a relationship between inequality and mental and physical health (Marmot, 2010).

Research has clearly documented that those lower down the economic distribution in society fare worse than those higher up in the same society on a range of measures (for example, life expectancy, mental health and so on). But some researchers go further to argue that people on similar levels of (absolute) income fare differently depending on the level of income inequality in the country in which they live (Wilkinson and Pickett, 2009a). Those in less equal countries will fare worse than those in more equal countries. In other words, it is not someone's actual or 'absolute' level of income that is responsible for the outcomes in that society but their income relative to others in that society. Wilkinson and Pickett's (2009a) work on this 'relative income hypothesis' has been particularly influential, cited by key people across the political spectrum:

> Research by Richard Wilkinson and Kate Pickett has shown that among the richest countries, it's the more unequal ones that do worse according to almost every quality of life indicator. (David Cameron, Hugo Young Lecture, 10 November 2009)

The gap between rich and poor does matter. It doesn't just harm the poor it harms us all. (Ed Miliband, Speech to the Labour Party conference on becoming Labour leader, 28 September 2010)

Bringing together the findings of many research studies, including his own, Wilkinson has argued that in societies which have exceeded a modest level of economic development, it is the gap between rich and poor rather than the level of poverty which is related to poor health and other social problems. He has argued that this is because:

> ... the extent of material inequality is a major determinant of psychosocial welfare in modern societies and its impact on health is but one of the social costs it carries with it. (Wilkinson, 1996, p 9)

Wilkinson argues that societies that are equal have relatively low levels of poor health and social problems because of the higher degree of social cohesion within such societies. Societies with high levels of social cohesion also have greater involvement in social and voluntary activities outside the home, higher levels of self-esteem, less anti-social aggressiveness, less stress depression, anxiety and insecurity (Wilkinson 1996, 2005; Wilkinson and Pickett, 2009a). Wilkinson and Pickett (2009a) have therefore argued that the explanation for this lies in psychosocial mechanisms such as 'status anxiety' or 'status syndrome' (see also Marmot, 2004; de Botton, 2005; James, 2007). Another argument that is linked to the above is that income inequality is harmful to everyone in society, not just those at the bottom.

Wilkinson and Pickett's (2009a) work has received widespread attention and it is not surprising, therefore, that their work also attracted some strong and equally high profile critiques (not least Saunders, 2010 and Snowdon, 2010). But research in this field is by no means confined to their work, and research suggesting a link between income inequality and health outcomes has been carried out by numerous researchers from a variety of disciplines, dating back at least to Rodgers (1979). Until recently, most of these studies had used only aggregate data (data on average health outcomes), often without controlling for any other factors. Gravelle (1998), however, pointed out that even if there was a correlation between average mortality rates and levels of income inequality, this could be due to individual incomes rather than the role of inequality at a society level. In order to investigate the independent effect of societal level income inequality, it is therefore necessary to control for individual level income. Clarkwest (2008, p 1871) has argued that 'after an initial flurry of supportive cross-sectional findings, the empirical tide turned against the inequality hypothesis in more recent years'. For example, a number of studies started to suggest that the link between income inequality and mortality is sensitive to the time periods examined, the specific causes of mortality examined and the inclusion of controls for other population characteristics (Judge, 1995; Judge et al, 1998a; Mellor and Milyo, 2001, 2002).

More recent reviews of cross-country relationships between inequality and health (Deaton, 2003; Lynch et al, 2004) suggest that studies with better data on inequality and better methods tend to observe a weak or non-existent relationship. For example, Leigh et al (2009, p 394) concluded their review with the following:

> While the currently available evidence suggests to us that the relationship between inequality and health is either small or inconsistent, readers should bear in mind that not everyone agrees, especially social epidemiologists. Achieving more consensus will require more work with better data and better methods than have been usual in the past.

Kondo et al (2009) carried out a major review of nine cohort studies and 19 cross-sectional studies involving over 60 million subjects worldwide. They also pointed out that recent systematic reviews had produced mixed findings about whether or not income inequality has an impact on health. Kondo et al (2009) did indeed conclude that the results suggested a modest adverse effect of income inequality on health, but even though they found only a 'modest' effect, they pointed out that this had important implications given that income inequality involves all members of society. In fact, they estimated that about 1.5 million deaths (9.6 per cent of total adult mortality in the 15–60 age group) could be averted in 30 OECD countries if they reduced the Gini coefficient to a level below 0.3. This is a striking finding, but they also pointed out several limitations to their research and suggested that the findings need to be interpreted with caution. Kondo et al (2009) called for further research to investigate a number of issues further including the time period in which the analysis is carried out, the length of follow-up in the cohort studies and whether or not there is a threshold effect of income inequality on health.

The idea of a 'threshold effect' of income inequality on health is very interesting. In other words, does income inequality cause particular problems after it passes a certain point? Kondo et al (2009) suggested that there might indeed be a threshold effect with Gini coefficient values of 0.3 or more. This might prove a 'tipping point' at which income inequality has adverse effects. This is particularly interesting given Figure 2.3 above which showed the (BHC) Gini coefficient in Britain resting below 0.3 for the 1960s and 1970s but then rising past 0.3 in 1986/87 and then passing 0.35 in 1993/94 to settle close to 0.4 by 1998/99. If the 0.3 threshold is, indeed, significant, it could provide a target for policy (see Chapter Seven).

Research on the impact of inequality on health and other social problems has also hotly debated the role of other factors in affecting poor outcomes. For example, Kondo et al (2009) also pointed out that other contextual characteristics such as social security policy, labour markets and immigration might also be relevant in explaining variation between studies. Other explanations have been put forward such as the neo-materialist approach that focuses on people's material circumstances and the role of welfare institutions in reducing social problems (Lynch et al, 2000; Clarkwest, 2008). Such institutions are usually stronger in more equal societies, but where some unequal societies have strong institutions, any social consequences of inequality are lessened. There has also been considerable discussion about the role of 'race'/ethnicity and culture in relation to both inequality and health outcomes.

Much of the research in this field has looked at average levels of health, but there is some interesting data comparing outcomes for different groups in different societies. Figure 2.4, for example, shows that babies born to men in the highest social class in England and Wales had a higher rate of infant mortality than babies born to similar men in Sweden. Wilkinson and Pickett (2009b) use this evidence to argue that even those in the highest social classes do better in more equal societies. The figure also shows, quite surprisingly perhaps, than babies born to men in the highest social class in England and Wales have about the same rate of infant mortality as babies born to men in the *lowest* social class in Sweden. Once again, Wilkinson and Pickett (2009b) have used this evidence to argue that inequality harms all of us. This is very interesting data although it is very old, taken from a study published in 1992 (Leon et al, 1992).

More recent research by Banks et al (2006, 2007) has provided further evidence here. In their study, people in the US sample were much less healthy than their English counterparts at all points in the socioeconomic distribution. The US–England difference was more pronounced for those in the lowest social groups but higher-status Americans were still at a disadvantage compared with their English

Figure 2.4: Infant mortality by occupational class of father in Sweden compared with England and Wales

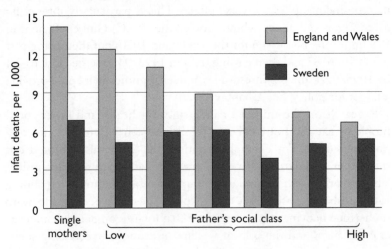

Source: Leon et al (1992), cited by Wilkinson and Pickett (2009b)

counterparts. Table 2.3 shows that 8.1 per cent of 55- to 64-year-olds in the bottom third of the income distribution in England had diabetes compared with 16.8 per cent of their counterparts in the US. Those in the top third of the income distribution in England were also less likely than their US counterparts to have diabetes but the difference was not so great (6.0 per cent compared with 9.2 per cent). And we can see a similar pattern for many of the conditions reported in the table.

These findings were confirmed by Banks et al (2007) when focusing solely on men in the US and England and when using different measures of socioeconomic status. These effects also remained after controlling for various risk factors such as smoking, drinking and

Table 2.3: Self-reported health by income among 55- to 64-year-olds in England and the US (%)

	Income terciles[a] in England			Income terciles in the US		
	Bottom third	**Middle third**	**Top third**	**Bottom third**	**Middle third**	**Top third**
Diabetes	8.1	7.7	6.0	16.8	11.4	9.2
Hypertension	37.9	35.8	31.6	46.1	42.8	38.2
All heart disease	14.3	9.1	6.9	20.2	13.1	12.1
Myocardial infarction	6.7	3.3	2.5	8.6	4.3	3.3
Stroke	3.5	1.9	1.6	5.8	3.7	1.8
Lung disease	7.6	6.3	4.8	12.3	7.0	5.1
Cancer	5.7	5.1	5.5	9.3	9.8	9.5

Note: [a] Terciles divide the population into three equally sized groups

obesity. But whether or not these differences are directly due to levels of inequality (the US is more unequal than England), it is not possible to say using this data.

Another perspective in this field focuses on the increasing insecurity and anxiety caused by the pressures of a particular kind of capitalist–consumer society. This insecurity and anxiety not only affects those at the bottom of the economic distribution but also those in the 'squeezed middle'. Frank (2007, p 13) has argued that: 'we work too many hours, save too little and spend too much of our incomes on goods that confer little additional satisfaction when all have more of them'.

This perspective chimes with other research that suggests that people 'in the middle' feel angry or 'squeezed' about their position. Bamfield and Horton (2009) found, in their focus groups, that people (most of whom considered themselves to be in the middle of the income distribution) were concerned about the negative consequences of inequality, materialism and consumerism. Most were supportive of a social vision focused on improving quality of life for all. Ed Miliband, leader of the Labour Party, has made a particular issue of the anxieties of the 'squeezed middle' although it isn't entirely clear who this group is, leading the BBC's political correspondent, Nick Robinson, to label it 'the squeezed muddle' in November 2010[3] (see Chapters Three and Five for further discussion).

Another related area of research on the impact of inequality relates to happiness and wellbeing. Layard (2005), for example, has studied happiness, arguing that, after a certain threshold, the benefit of extra income on happiness declines with a person's wealth. The implication of this is that if money is transferred from a richer person to a poorer person, the poorer person gains more happiness than the richer person loses. Therefore, 'a country will have a higher level of average happiness the more equally its income is distributed' (Layard, 2005, p 52).

In November 2010, David Cameron announced that, from April 2011, the ONS will ask people to rate their own wellbeing with the first official happiness index due in 2012.[4] Tony Blair had considered something similar and commissioned a review of knowledge (Donovan and Halpern, 2002), but decided it was too complex. Cameron has said that economic growth remains the government's most 'urgent priority' but he also sees gross domestic product (GDP) as a limited way of measuring a country's progress. The index is likely to include a range of variables, not just 'happiness' or life satisfaction or subjective wellbeing, but also some more objective measures of wellbeing such as health and education, but this will be decided following a period of public consultation.

Alongside the research on health and other social outcomes, there is also some research evidence that countries with lower levels of inequality have higher levels of social mobility, suggesting a direct link between equality of outcome and equality of opportunity (Blanden, 2009; see also later in this chapter).

There is, therefore, a great deal of debate about the effect of inequality on health and social problems. This is a complex area in terms of theory and methodology in which there are numerous studies but no general consensus. A recent independent review of the literature in this field found that we can be confident that a correlation exists between income inequality and various health and social problems, but we cannot (yet) be confident about whether or not there is a causal relationship between them, or how large any causal effect might be (Rowlingson, 2011a). Some studies have found that income inequality causes health and social problems but some have not, pointing instead to the role of individual incomes rather than income inequality at a societal level. This echoes Jencks (2002), for example, who concluded that:

> ... the social consequences of economic inequality are sometimes negative, sometimes neutral but seldom – as far as I can discover – positive. (Jencks, 2002, p 64)

The effect of inequality on health and social problems seems to be small relative to other factors but because it affects whole populations, reductions in inequality could save over a million lives across 30 OECD countries. But social and health problems may not be the only negative effect of inequality, as we shall see in the next section.

Is the concentration of income and wealth good or bad for the economy?

Another reason to investigate the concentration of income and wealth in the hands of the wealthy is that it may have effects at the macro-economic level. Indeed, there is increasing discussion about whether inequality caused the financial crash that the world has experienced in the last couple of years (Milanovic, 2009; Moss, 2009). Debate about the link between high levels of inequality and economic crises goes back much further, however. Keynes (1936) argued that wealth inequality increases financial instability and the risk of economic collapse because the wealthy have lower marginal propensity to consume and tend to engage in risky speculation. Galbraith (1961) also blamed inequality's impact on demand as the first of five factors causing the 1929 crash and the Great Depression that followed. And well before the current economic crash, Batra made the general point that:

> ... wealth inequality is a prerequisite for manias and bubbles. The greater the inequality, the bugger the bubble and the more painful its eventual bursting. (Batra, 1987, p 138)

Batra (1987) also suggested that there was a natural economic limit to inequality and that once that limit had been reached, the economy would crash. Robert Reich (2010) attributed the 1930s depression to a form of 'under-consumption' by the middle classes, and also sees this as the cause of the current economic crisis:

> When most of the gains from economic growth go to a small sliver of Americans at the top, the rest don't have enough purchasing power to buy what the economy is capable of producing. (p 1)

Lansley (2009) has pointed out that the 'profits squeeze' of the 1970s has now been replaced with a 'wages squeeze' as the share of national output being taken up by profit reached close to a postwar high in 2007. Real wage increases from 1980 to 2007 rose at 1.6 per cent per annum, thus lagging behind the 1.9 per cent per annum increase in productivity. The gap grew particularly wide after 2000. Lansley (2009) has argued that to maintain their living standards, ordinary people have increasingly borrowed, with the debt/income ratio rising from 45 per cent in 1980 to 157.4 per cent in 2007. Bank assets – loans, financial derivatives and credit advances – have increased from 100 per cent of GDP in the late 1970s to five times that level today (Lansley, 2009). He has also argued that the government, to an extent, encouraged consumption as a way of fuelling growth.

Simon Johnson, former chief economist at the International Monetary Fund (IMF), has argued that a:

> ... financial oligarchy ... played a central role in creating the crisis, making ever-larger gambles ... until the inevitable collapse. (quoted in Lansley, 2009, p 5)

Levels of consumption are then only maintained by borrowing and spending down housing equity. There is also something of a political impact from the wealthy funding of political campaigns and muting opposition to growing inequality. Paul Krugman (2010) has suggested that high consumption by the very wealthy had also encouraged consumption by the middle class, paid for both by borrowing and by less saving, which sowed the seeds of the crisis. He has also linked economic inequality to increased political polarisation, and a decreased ability to put effective regulation in place.

David Moss (2009) has also drawn attention to the correlation between financial regulation and bank failures, and trends in income inequality. His take seems to be that an enriched top income group puts greater power in the hands of those who would deregulate finance. Such deregulation may then have permitted the greater lending to lower-income households that helped precipitate the credit crunch.

Milanovic has drawn attention to the role of deregulation, but has argued that:

> ... deregulation, by helping irresponsible behaviour, just exacerbated the crisis; it did not create it. To go to the origins of the crisis, one needs to go to rising income inequality within practically all countries in the world. (Milanovic, 2009, p 1)

Milanovic has argued that the super-rich had too much wealth to use for consumption only, and so a vast amount of financial capital went in search of profitable investments. The financial sector became increasingly reckless, he argued, and increasingly lent to people 'in the middle', whose incomes were stagnating but still aspired to participate fully in the consumerism displayed all around them. He concluded that:

> ... the root cause of the crisis is not to be found in hedge funds and bankers who simply behaved with the greed to which they are accustomed (and for which economists used to praise them). The real cause of the crisis lies in huge inequalities in income distribution which generated much larger investable funds than could be profitably employed. (Milanovic, 2009, p 3)

There are some common features to these accounts. Concentration of economic power is linked to the concentration of political power and consequences for the running of the financial sector. There are also shades of the theory of 'conspicuous consumption', encouraging many groups to seek a high living standard through borrowing. And there are issues about 'relative deprivation' and people's reference groups as they try to 'keep up with the Joneses' around them (Runciman, 1966).

So far, in this chapter, we have only considered the possible *negative* effects of inequality on the economy, but there is also an argument that it can have positive effect. For example, Conley (2009, p 37) has pointed out that:

> Since the Scottish Enlightenment conservatives have argued that inequality is the engine of progress; differential rewards lead to ingenuity, industriousness, and innovation.

Similarly, Turok (2010) has argued that inequality might be fair if it reflects a meritocratic reward for hard work and skill. He also suggested that it might provide incentives for individuals and firms to take risks which benefit the economy and society has a whole. This raises the issue of the possible trade-off between 'equity' and 'efficiency' or growth. Corry and Glyn (1994) and Glyn and Miliband (1994) used historical and cross-national data to show that more egalitarian countries have higher levels of growth. Alesina and Rodrick (1992) studied 65 countries and also found that more equal countries had higher rates of growth. Atkinson (1997) reviewed the literature here and found as many studies negatively as positively linking inequality and growth. Irvin (2008) has pointed out that there have been periods when the British economy has grown and there has been no increase in inequality (quite the reverse, in fact). But there have also been periods of growth at the same time as increasing inequality. Cross-national studies also show examples of this. For example, the World Economic Forum's *Global competitiveness report 2010–11* (World Economic Forum, 2010) shows that Sweden, a relatively equal country, comes second in its competitiveness league table, two places ahead of the much less equal US.

The argument that inequality is helpful in terms of growth appears to rest on the idea that top earners and wealth creators/entrepreneurs might work less hard if they were paid less. A series of academic journal articles in the 1990s called for more performance-related pay as a mechanism for improving company performance. Jensen and Murphy (1990), for example, argued that executive pay should be increased for those executives able to increase share prices. Since then there has been a dramatic increase in both executive base pay and incentive schemes (Gabaix and Landier, 2008). However, there is no agreement about whether these attempts to use pay to improve company performance have worked or not (Gregg et al, 2005, 2010) and from 2001 to 2011, chief executive remuneration has quadrupled while share prices have actually fallen (High Pay Commission, 2011).

There was certainly concern about damaging incentives to work in the media in March 2009 when the UK government announced a new 50 per cent income tax rate for earnings above £150,000, which would affect only the top 1 per cent of the population (from 2010). It was claimed that that this tax would drive talent from the City and the Premier League, discourage entrepreneurs, actually result in a loss in revenue as efforts would be doubled to avoid tax and represent an unnecessary intervention in the working of the market (Brewer and Browne, 2009; *The Sunday Times*, 31 May 2009). Some newspapers predicted that city bankers would emigrate to Switzerland, but fewer Britons applied for permits to work in the Swiss financial services sector in 2009 than in 2008 (*The Guardian*, 18 February 2010), so the exodus had not begun.

In fact, there seems to be little international movement in the top job market. Isles (2003) found that 86 per cent of FTSE 250 chief executive officers (CEOs) came from the UK, and that most businesses did not recruit from overseas. A survey for the High Pay Commission (2011) also found that 59 per cent of CEOs in the current FTSE 100 companies had been employed by the same company for five or more years before becoming CEO, and 33 per cent had been with the company for more than 10 years. In another survey for the High Pay Commission it was found that 77 per cent of CEOs were UK nationals. The US has some of the highest executive pay in the world so we might expect its companies to attract the best international talent, but only 14 of the top 100 US companies were led by a non-US citizen in 2008 (although this was an increase compared with nine in 1998; Zwaniecki, 2008).

There is little evidence that higher earnings provide incentives to work harder. Ramsay (2005) points out that Japanese CEOs earn less than a fifth of their US peers and have higher marginal tax rates, but there is no evidence that Japanese CEOs work less hard or less profitably than US CEOs. In 2001, a US CEO was paid 31 times an average worker. It was 25 times in the UK, 15 times in France, 13 in Sweden, 11 in Germany and 10 in Japan (Ramsay, 2005; see also 'Un/equal opportunities and un/fair rewards' below).

Rowlingson and Connor (2011) have argued that while monetary rewards certainly play a part in motivating people, there are a variety of other reasons why people work: intrinsic enjoyment, social aspects, status and so on. It seems likely that once a certain threshold has been reached, extra earnings may still play a role but are not going to be as important as other factors. Therefore, for those above this threshold, it might be better to substitute monetary incentives with other incentives such as improved quality of working environments, enhanced terms and conditions, a greater personal sense of being valued and a better work–life balance.

There is also an issue about the nature of 'wealth creation'. To what extent is this the result of individual top earners and entrepreneurs or teams of workers? And the role of the state is also crucial here in providing peace and stability as well as the laws and regulations in relation to business practice. The state also provides (to some extent at least) a healthy and educated workforce. The social aspects of wealth creation therefore need to be at least acknowledged, if not privileged, against the work of individuals (Daunton, 2007).

Once again, the balance of evidence and argument suggests that *extreme levels of inequality*, as many parts of the world have recently experienced, have damaging effects on the economy. How we might tackle such levels of inequality is discussed later in Chapter Seven.

Un/equal opportunities and un/fair rewards

The arguments in this chapter so far have revolved around whether or not the concentration of income and wealth might be a problem in terms of its *outcomes/effects*. A different approach is to consider whether the *processes* by which some people become rich are a problem. If everyone in a particular society has an equal chance to succeed in life, with success depending on hard work, talent and so on, then we might argue that any subsequent inequality is fair. But if those who succeed do so because of the luck of their birth, or because they cheat or bribe their way through life, then we might question the fairness of the outcome.

Equality of opportunity is an idea that unites all political parties. Within the Labour Party, Tony Blair and Gordon Brown were both prominent supporters of equality of opportunity rather than equality of outcome. And more recently, Nick Clegg, the leader of the Liberal Democrats and Deputy Prime Minister, stated in an article in *The Guardian* on 22 November 2010:

> Social mobility is what characterises a fair society, rather than a particular level of income inequality. Inequalities become injustices when they are fixed: passed on, generation to generation.

This section of the chapter considers, first of all, the extent to which people today succeed in life due to their own merit. The weight of evidence and academic argument suggests that Britain is a long way from a meritocracy (Breen and Goldthorpe, 1999). For example, much of the wealth of many rich people is actually due to inheritance and other forms of unearned income (see Chapter Four for a discussion of inheritance). But economic wealth is not the only type of capital that people may inherit from parents. Parents can also transfer human, social and cultural capital to their children to enable them to succeed in life. For example, in the mid-1990s, Johnson and Reed (1996) and Machin et al (1997) reached the conclusion that the best way to become rich was not so much through individual effort and hard work but to choose your parents wisely. The economic standing of parents appeared to be an extremely important determinant of where children ended up in the income distribution. Other studies have also confirmed this, that children from less advantaged backgrounds have poorer outcomes as adults (Hobcraft, 1998; Gregg et al, 1999; CASE and HM Treasury, 1999). Thus 'brute luck' (in terms of whether a child is born to a rich or poor family) plays a major role in determining socioeconomic life chances.

While few people would argue against having 'equal opportunities' and most would no doubt support the idea of society enabling people to climb the socioeconomic ladder if they work hard and deserve to do so, the possibility of *downward* social mobility for some people is not particularly appealing, and yet if the income/occupational structure stays largely the same, then people can only move up if others make way for them by moving down (Crawford et al, 2011).

This section reviews evidence in the related field of social mobility. Studies of social mobility face various challenges. One is whether to focus on mobility in terms of incomes (as economists tend to do) or social class (as sociologists tend to do). Quality of data on parental circumstances is also an issue as the birth cohort studies of 1958 and 1970 collected good quality data on many aspects of parents' lives, but relied on quite coarse, banded measures of incomes, and collected it in ways that differed across the two cohorts. Attrition from the studies, which is substantial, must also be considered (see, for example, Gorard, 2008). The relevance of data from the 1958 and 1970 birth cohort studies for what is happening to today's children and young people is also unclear. But retrospective studies rely on people giving an accurate account of their parents' situation, often many years removed in time and with little guidance about the stability of that parental situation. It is also common for studies to focus on fathers rather than mothers, and sometimes only to be looking at outcomes for male children. Both sets of studies tend to rely on looking at those in paid work, also with parents (or a father) in paid work, which may be increasingly restrictive.

A key issue for any research in this field is whether to examine the relationship between *absolute* outcomes for children and those of their parents, for example, to see if the children better off in real terms than their parents or whether they have 'better jobs' or better qualifications than their parents according to a fixed standard. An alternative approach is to look at the relationship in *relative* terms. With a measure of absolute mobility, everyone in the younger generation can do better than their parents. But with relative mobility, if someone is rising in the ranking, someone else must be falling. The National Equality Panel (2010) have pointed out that the main evidence in the UK relates to absolute and relative mobility in terms of occupational social class, and relative income mobility. The National Equality Panel (2010) have concluded that we can rule out the extreme possibilities: children's life chances are not random nor independent of family background, but nor are they completely pre-determined at birth. The National Equality Panel (2010) also concluded that it is difficult to judge whether social mobility is high or low because such a judgement is similar to the decision to describe whether a glass is half full or half empty. It is possible to say, however, whether social mobility has increased or declined over time and how it compares with other countries.

The evidence on intergenerational income and on occupational mobility tell different stories, which may be because the relationship between occupational social class and income has changed over time (see Cabinet Office, 2009). Blanden et al (2005) have claimed that:

> Intergenerational mobility fell markedly over time in Britain, with there being less mobility for a cohort of people born in 1970 compared to a cohort born in 1958. (Blanden et al, 2005, p 2)

Others looking at social mobility have disagreed on this central finding, and the sociological consensus is closer to the idea of stability over time (Payne and Roberts, 2002). Goldthorpe and Mills (2008), for example, argued, using retrospectively based data from 1972 to 2005, that there is:

> ... an essential constancy over time.... Our results are contrary to the prevailing view in political and media circles that in Britain today the level of social mobility is in decline. (Goldthorpe and Mills, 2008, p 83)

A study using still different data by Nicoletti and Ermisch (2007) also suggested that social mobility had remained relatively stable. And a study only of Scotland, using 2001 data, found 'the association between origin and destination has barely changed for fifty years' (Iannelli and Paterson, 2006, p 540). McKay (2010) has argued that the reason for this difference in findings could be that the stability of occupational mobility – people moving into different levels of jobs – is occurring at the same time as the rewards associated with particular careers are changing. For example, it could be that sons of medics are just as likely to become medics down the ages, but that the pay of medics is moving away from the average. An increasing link between people's incomes and those of their parents may be partly the result of inequality, rather than any closing of barriers (which might be as rigid, or fluid, as ever). Macmillan (2009) found increasing openness for lecturers and professors (and for teachers), but apparently less openness for medics and lawyers, and for accountants and journalists. McKay (2010) pointed out, however, that some of the results were based on rather small samples, such as only 29 doctors in each of the birth cohort studies, and just over 30 lawyers. It is therefore very difficult to generalise from these results with any confidence.

McKay (2010) has also argued that further analysis on this topic should try to include (where possible) those not in paid work, women as well as men, and a focus on particular sub-groups rather than looking at averages across all groups. Following on from this, he has carried out analysis of the General Household Survey 2005, which included a number of questions about the background of people's parents, including parents' occupations and levels of educational qualifications (McKay, 2010). Table 2.4 shows the results separately for men and women, according to how likely they were to be in a 'professional' occupation (based on the National Statistics Socio-Economic Classification, NS-SEC). So, 44 per cent of men born in 1956–65 are in this category, along with 46 per cent of men born in 1966–75, perhaps reflecting a small growth in the service sector across time. The analysis shows that the chances of having professional employment are around 70 per cent greater among children whose parents were graduates, compared to those whose parents lacked any qualifications. There is a similar difference in outcomes comparing sons of professionals with sons of those in more elementary occupations. The chances of becoming a professional are, however, largely unchanged between the two age groups when analysed by the level of parents' qualifications, or the father's occupation. In other words, there is no

Table 2.4: Percentage working in 'professional occupations', General Household Survey 2005 (%)

Sex:	Men		Women	
Age in 2005	**40-49**	**30-39**	**40-49**	**30-39**
Birth cohort	**1956-65**	**1966-75**	**1956-65**	**1966-75**
All	44	46	36	39
Father = graduate	69	68	59	63
Father = no qualifications	38	40	32	33
Mother = graduate	70	62	63	65
Mother = no qualifications	38	40	31	32
Father = professional/technical	61	61	49	53
Father = administration	41	41	41	40
Father = plant, elementary	35	33	26	29
Non-white	37	38	30	33
Disabled	38	38	32	34
Limiting disability	29	26	27	28

Source: McKay (2010): analysis of the 2005 General Household Survey.

sign of any decline in social mobility in these data, across these two groups – nor any increase.

McKay (2010) also found that people's outcomes reflected the mother's level of qualifications as much as that of the father, slightly more so for women. But he also found that being from a minority ethnic background (and 'non-white' includes a diverse group, many with a greater than average disadvantage) or having a limiting disability matter just as much, if not more, than the characteristics of the parents.

The main conclusions from all this research appear to be that social mobility, in terms of occupation, has changed little in 30 years, once we allow for changing occupational structure. But if we look at the earnings of those born in 1970 once they reach their early 30s, these earnings are more closely related to the income level of their parents when they were growing up than was the case for those born in the late 1950s. Social mobility in terms of earnings therefore appears to have declined. Despite the differences between particular studies it is clear that we do not live in a perfectly mobile society: people's occupational and economic destinations depend to an important degree on their origins. And if we compare Britain with other countries, rates of intergenerational mobility in terms of incomes are low and in terms of occupation are below the international average for men and at the bottom of the range for women. Blanden (2009) has shown that social mobility is lower in societies which are more unequal. Britain, the US and Brazil had the lowest levels of social mobility in terms of income.

Furthermore, the decline in social mobility (in terms of income) between those born in 1958 and in 1970 in Britain coincides with the rise in income inequality between the periods when each cohort reached the labour market. It therefore seems to matter more in Britain who your parents are than in many other countries.

In January 2009, the government published its White Paper, *New opportunities: Fair chances for the future* (Cabinet Office, 2009) and in the same year the Milburn panel looking at the professions, *Unleashing aspiration: The final report of the Panel on Fair Access to the Professions*, also reported. The apparent lack of progress in tackling social mobility became an important political cause, particularly associated with Gordon Brown during his premiership, and we return to look at policies in this field in Chapter Seven.

The National Equality Panel (2010) have also pointed out that the impact of the increases in earnings and income inequality that took place across the 1980s has yet to be measured, and it is likely that those who benefited from this inequality will have had greater opportunities than others to support their children. Crawford et al (2011, p 1) conclude their literature review on social mobility for the Department for Business, Innovation and Skills by arguing that: 'it is likely to be very hard to increase social mobility without tackling inequality'. Thus equality of opportunity and equality of outcome seem closely linked. It is difficult to have one without the other.

The research on social mobility measures outcomes in terms of income or occupational structure and how these relate to someone's family background. But the research does not question why some jobs are paid more than others and whether or not this is fair. People generally believe that 'hard work' is a positive social good and therefore deserves a positive reward – 76 per cent of the public in 2009 said that it was essential or very important for hard work to be a factor determining pay levels, according to analysis of the British Social Attitudes Survey (BSAS).[5] However, there are problems with putting this concept into practice, as argued by Rowlingson and Connor (2011). For example, how can we define and measure 'hard work'? Is it the nature of the work or the amount of time spent doing it or the degree of 'effort' put in? What if one person has to put in twice as much effort/time as another to get the same result? Is it therefore the output/productivity or the input/effort that we should be rewarding? How can we measure an individual's productivity if they are part of a team which all contribute to the output?

If we define 'hard work' in terms of hours worked, Rowlingson and Connor (2011) point out that people in management and senior professional occupations certainly work longer hours than most other occupations, but long hours are also common in the skilled trades occupations and among factory workers (Begum, 2004). The difference in wages between these occupations does not seem to fairly reflect the hours worked. There is also an issue about the intensification of the hours worked. Someone on a production line or a call centre generally has to maintain a constant level of work while on that line. Managers and senior professionals, however, will have more flexibility to take breaks and vary the pace of their work. Such workers may have a long-hours culture but there is not necessarily any evidence that this leads to higher productivity (Kodz et al, 2003).

We may also wish to reward 'important' or 'skilled' work. But, as Rowlingson and Connor (2011) point out: what counts as an 'important' or 'skilled' job? Caring for older people, people with disabilities or children is very important and requires particular skills, and yet these are among the lowest-paid occupations. And indeed, many people provide this caring work for no pay at all. The New Economics Foundation (2009) has called for earnings to reflect a social return on investment analysis. This would create a very different distribution of earnings than the one which currently exists. Our current distribution of earnings is based on 'the market' but this is far from perfect and, in a democracy with a strong welfare state, the labour market could better reflect people's views about how different kinds of work should be rewarded.

For example, we may also wish to reward jobs that are more *unpleasant or dangerous/risky*. Evidence suggests that the most physically dangerous jobs are manual jobs, particularly in the construction industry. And while 'executive stress' is a term applied to managers and senior professionals, it is actually those doing health and social care work who suffer most negative occupational stress (HSE, 2009a). It is also well established that it is people lowest down any occupational hierarchy who suffer the most negative stress (Marmot, 2004).

Far from being unpleasant or difficult/dangerous, some jobs may be positively enjoyable, challenging, stimulating and fun. Jobs with a high degree of autonomy and flexibility as well as some creative challenge, linked to personal interest, fit within this category and should perhaps be paid less than other jobs due to the intrinsic rewards which may compensate for lower extrinsic rewards. It is highly likely that many professional jobs provide a higher degree of intrinsic reward than other forms of work.

The concept of 'hard work' is also complex because it is unclear whether it relates to the amount of effort put into a task or the output/achievement. Two people may do the same job with the same amount of effort but achieve very different results. Should we reward the effort or the outcome? Currently, there appears to be very little link between top pay and outcome in terms of output. For example, we might have expected pay at the top to have declined in 2008 given the credit crunch and recession leading to plunging share prices, but in February 2009 non-executive directors in the FTSE 100 companies won an average 6.3 per cent pay *rise* over the previous year (IDS, 2009a, 2009b).

So it seems that we do not have equal opportunity in Britain, and that even if those at the top get there on merit, they may not necessarily be able to claim that their work deserves higher reward than people doing other kinds of work. But even if a society could be engineered such that there was 'deep' or total equality of opportunity and in such a way that the right kind of work or effort were rewarded, would any resulting level of inequality be just? Rawls (1971) argued that it was justifiable for people's natural talents to be rewarded (and to therefore create some inequality) if the consequence of this was to be of benefit to the poorest. In Rawls' (1971) conception of justice as fairness, 'Social and economic inequalities are to be arranged so that they are both: (a) to the greatest benefit of the least advantaged ... and (b) attached to offices and positions open to all under conditions of fair equality of opportunity'.

His argument is that such arrangements would be chosen by people in an 'original position' where they were unaware of their socioeconomic characteristics — such as age, gender, talent — which are, anyway, arbitrary from a moral point of view. Having to select moral principles without knowledge of personal circumstances (the 'veil of ignorance') is designed to ensure impartiality of people's views.

There is very little evidence, however, that in practice wealth at the top does actually 'trickle down' to benefit the poorest. The 1980s saw the accumulation of staggering amounts of wealth in the hands of a minority of US and UK citizens, but the decade also saw an increase in poverty, hardship and 'public squalor'. There is no evidence that those at the bottom benefited from the economic boom of the time.

Various issues remain in relation to previous debates. How do we secure a 'deep' level of equality of opportunity? Is it possible to have equal opportunity for all when some people are born to families that can give them much greater advantages than others from the start? What kinds of work should be rewarded? And should there nevertheless be limits applied to any resulting inequality? Crosland (1956, p 101), believed that inequality of earnings was acceptable even within a socialist framework because people deserved reward if they had superior talent or if it acted as an incentive to do work which was risky and/or burdensome in terms of responsibility. But he also supported equality of outcome to an extent which would 'minimise social resentment, to secure justice between individuals and to equalise opportunities'. Young (1958) pointed out that any 'meritocracy' may not live up to the apparent ideal that many people currently consider it to be. Those at the top might feel more entitled to their higher rewards and more able to condemn those at the bottom for being undeserving. The gap between rich and poor would be likely to widen still further given the apparently more just basis on which resources are distributed.

Attitudes to the gap between rich and poor

It is important to understand the public's attitudes to the gap between rich and poor and how they might change over the coming 'period of austerity' because, in a democracy, policy needs the consent of the people, although politics also exists to persuade the public about the need for different policies. Policy may try to lead as well as follow public opinion (Hills, 2002). But in order to either follow or lead public opinion, politicians and policy makers need, first of all, to understand it. Rowlingson et al (2010) presented data from the BSAS 2009[6] that showed continuing concern for inequality. In 2009:

- 79 per cent said that the 'gap between those with high incomes and those with low incomes' was 'too large'
- 74 per cent agreed that 'differences in income in Britain are too large'
- 60 per cent agreed that 'working people do not get their fair share of the nation's wealth'.

Public concern about inequality peaked in 1995 when 87 per cent of the public said that the income gap was too large. It then fell over the period of the Labour government to 73 per cent in 2004, perhaps because people assumed that the government was reducing inequality. Since 2004, however, there has been a steady increase in concern about income inequality such that 79 per cent of the public in 2009 said that the income gap was too high. This coincides with a period in which poverty did indeed increase. It might seem surprising that a Labour government lost an election at a time when public concern for inequality was increasing, but people may have felt that Labour had failed to tackle the problem. Indeed, they focused their policy energy much more on poverty than inequality. At the same time, the Conservatives were talking in a much more progressive language and the resulting Coalition government that was elected in May 2010 soon stated an intention to tackle issues around inequality, declaring that 'addressing poverty and inequality in Britain is at the heart of our agenda for government' (HM Government, 2010, p 1).

Public concern about inequality seems to be driven slightly more by concern about the outcomes of inequality and beliefs about lack of equal opportunities rather than belief in any inherent unfairness. As Table 2.5 shows, 63 per cent of the public in 2009 believed that inequality contributed to social problems like crime (and were therefore supportive of the arguments put forward by Wilkinson and Pickett, 2009a) whereas 'only' 36 per cent agreed that it was 'morally wrong'. But about half the population believed that inequality was simply unfair (regardless of its outcomes). Some people, however, saw a positive side to inequality, with 61 per cent believing that it gave people an incentive to work hard and 27 per cent believing that it was necessary for Britain's prosperity. While the public have different views about the impact of inequality, the majority (76 per cent) in 2009 believed it was inevitable. Such a view may let politicians and policy makers off the hook if the public do not believe it is their fault or the result of particular policy decisions.

The BSAS 2009 also asked people about their views about equal opportunities and there were clear concerns among the public about a lack of equal opportunities. A large majority, 80 per cent, agreed that 'children from better-off families have many more opportunities than children from less well-off families' (Rowlingson et al, 2010). This might suggest more concern for equal opportunities than equal outcomes, but the public do not necessarily see these as separable: 62 per cent of the public agreed that 'there can never be equal opportunities in a society where some people have higher incomes than others'.

Having said this, when people were asked why some people have higher incomes than others, the most common explanation in 2009

Table 2.5: Attitudes to large differences in people's incomes (%)

% agreeing that large differences in people's incomes ...	All
are inevitable whether we like them or not?	76
contribute to social problems like crime?	63
give people an incentive to work hard?	61
are unfair?	52
are morally wrong?	36
are necessary for Britain's prosperity?	27
Base	2,267

Source: British Social Attitudes Survey 2009

was 'hard work' (given by 47 per cent). A further 27 per cent said the reason was 'inevitability' which may indicate some concern about equal opportunities. Injustice and luck were mentioned by about one in five in total (Rowlingson et al, 2010). These reasons accord with the kinds of explanations that Dorling (2010) analysed that result in the continuation of inequality and the lack of a system of beliefs to challenge entrenched inequality.

In their work for the Fabian Society, Bamfield and Horton (2009) found that attitudes to those on high incomes in their qualitative study changed during their fieldwork period as they experienced the financial crisis of autumn 2008. Up to that point, research participants had tended to argue that those on high incomes deserved them because they worked hard and had particular skills, but after that point, people began increasingly to challenge whether top salaries were really justifiable. People also challenged high salaries on the grounds that they were not needed. In a follow-up survey to the qualitative research, Bamfield and Horton (2009) found that 'only' 28 per cent agreed that 'most people earning £150,000 have special skills: their salary is a fair reflection of their value to the company or organisation'. When asked whether a salary of £150,000 'is too much because it is more than anyone needs to live on', 47 per cent agreed.

The BSAS regularly asks the public what they think about the earnings of different occupations. Heath et al (2010) found that, in 2009, the public were aware that earnings differentials had increased sharply between 1999 and 2009 but they still under-estimated the salaries of top earners. And despite changes in earnings differentials, people's views about the degree of wage inequality that is acceptable have been remarkably stable over time (at 6:1) since the BSAS started asking these questions in 1987. This ratio is far lower than actually exists in practice and even those members of the public who think that people get to the top on their own merit still think that people

Table 2.6: Why do some people have higher incomes than others? (%)

	Have higher incomes
Good luck	9
Hard work	47
Injustice in society	13
Inevitable part of modern life	27
None of these/Don't know	4
Base	2,267

Source: British Social Attitudes Survey 2009

at the top earn far too much. So concern about wage inequality is not driven solely by a perception that the wrong people are getting to the top. It is due to a concern that the top is too far away from the rest of the labour market.

The BSAS 2009 survey also included another question on fair pay as follows:

> Is your pay fair? We are not asking about how much you would like to earn – but what you feel is fair given your skills and effort? Is your pay ...

- Much less than fair
- A little less than fair
- About fair for me
- A little more than fair
- Much more than fair

Table 2.7 shows that nearly half of all wage earners thought that their pay was 'about fair'. Nearly two in five (42 per cent) thought that their pay was (much or a little) *less* than fair. And only five per cent of the public thought that their pay was (a little or much) *more* than fair. So people were much more likely to be dissatisfied with their pay than think they are paid too much. This links in with the fact that people are unaware of the distribution of income. Only 4 per cent of the public in 2009 thought that they were on high incomes. Even among those on household incomes above £44,000 (the top quarter of household incomes), only 9 per cent thought they were on high incomes. Most of this group (78 per cent) considered themselves to be on middle incomes (Rowlingson et al, 2010).

Table 2.7 also shows that 67 per cent of those on high earnings considered their pay 'about fair'. A quarter actually thought that their

Table 2.7: Wage earners' views about the fairness of their own pay by the level of respondents' own earnings (%)

	£10,000 or less	£10,000-14,999	£15,000-19,999	£20,000-28,999	£29,000-37,999	£38,000	All
Much less than fair	18	19	8	7	3	0	9
A little less than fair	23	46	47	35	31	24	33
About fair for me	58	30	41	55	57	67	46
A little more than fair	0	6	4	1	3	9	4
Much more than fair	0	0	0	2	2	0	1
Unweighted bases	62	91	79	130	65	79	964

Source: British Social Attitudes Survey 2009

pay was less than fair, and only 9 per cent of respondents earning £38,000 or more considered their pay to be more than fair. The survey sample is not large enough to analyse people on the very highest salaries to see if they take a similar view, but this analysis suggests there may well be resistance to any attempt to curb pay at high levels as people generally think that what they receive is fair or, if anything, less than fair.

Conclusions

The concentration of income and wealth in the hands of a minority grew dramatically in the 1980s and 1990s, and has continued to push upwards in the last decade or two. One of the main reasons for this is the growing income and wealth of those at the very top (the top 1 per cent or even the top 0.05 per cent – the top ten thousand). There is increasing debate in the academic literature that the resultant gap between rich and poor causes problems for society in relation to health and wellbeing more generally. There is certainly evidence that there is a 'health gradient' with people at each higher level in society enjoying improved health than people below them. So health is not just related to poverty. But the evidence from cross-national studies on the independent impact of inequality on health and social problems is mixed. Some studies show an impact, and given that the impact of inequality affects everyone in a population, even a weak relationship can make a big difference. We need further research on this link and also on what might explain any relationship between inequality and poor outcomes (for example, psychosocial versus more materialist mechanisms).

Research also appears to show that, after a certain point, extra money does not lead to much greater happiness. Thus, redistributing money from the rich to the poor has the potential to increase overall happiness. Policy makers are increasingly interested in 'happiness' and 'subjective wellbeing' and the British government (the ONS, in fact) will soon be measuring this.

But perhaps the opportunity to accumulate large amounts of income and wealth is needed to drive economic growth by providing people with incentives to work hard and innovate and so on. The evidence on this, however, is not strong, and countries with lower levels of inequality appear to have been just as productive and efficient as those with higher levels of inequality. In fact, there is a growing argument that high levels of inequality may have caused the financial crash that the world has just witnessed. And there is also concern that economic growth does not necessarily improve happiness or wellbeing and may put an unsustainable burden on the planet's resources.

There is also evidence that high levels of inequality reduce social mobility. Britain has lower rates of social mobility than countries with lower levels of inequality and mobility is certainly not increasing – if anything, it may be decreasing. It is extremely difficult for children who are born into families with very different levels of economic resources to have equal opportunities to succeed in life. Equal opportunities and equal outcomes are closely linked.

But even if we could engineer society so that everyone had an equal opportunity to succeed, what would be our measure of 'success'? Should society unconditionally allow the 'market' to decide on what kinds of work are rewarded, and to what degree? Or, in a democratic society with a welfare state, should society find a way to reward certain kinds of 'hard work', for example, care work and physically dangerous work, more highly than other kinds of work?

Following on from this, what degree of differential reward might be fair? The pure egalitarian position would be that people in society should have exactly the same resources available to them (or perhaps the same resources except where particular needs such as disability suggest they should have a little more to achieve the same outcomes). At the other extreme there is the total 'free market' approach which would allow any level of inequality to emerge. Between these two approaches it is also possible to argue for a particular limit of inequality. We saw earlier in this chapter, however, that the public consistently support a ratio of 6:1 for wages from top to bottom, and the government recently asked Will Hutton to carry out a review of salaries in the public sector with a view to limiting these to a ratio of 20:1 (see Chapter Seven for further discussion of this). We also saw evidence that there may be a threshold effect in relation to the negative impact of inequality and that the UK crossed this threshold in 1986/87.

Notes

[1] http://news.bbc.co.uk/1/hi/business/6060392.stm

[2] This is a measure of equality. A value of 0 indicates complete equality (everyone has the same) while if just one person had everything the Gini coefficient would be 1. Sometimes this is expressed on a scale from 0 to 100 per cent.

[3] www.bbc.co.uk/blogs/nickrobinson/2010/11/the_squeezed_muddle.html

[4] www.bbc.co.uk/news/uk-11833241

[5] Analysis carried out for this book.

[6] The BSAS is carried out by the National Centre for Social Research (NatCen), Britain's largest independent social research organisation. The survey is funded by a range of charitable and government sources. Further information about NatCen and the British Social Attitudes Survey can be found at www.natcen.ac.uk

THREE

What is wealth and who are the wealthy?

Introduction

In Chapters One and Two we argued that there were strong reasons for focusing our attention on wealth and the wealthy. In the course of those chapters we used the terms 'wealth' and 'wealthy' without too much discussion, but these terms are used in different ways at different times and there has been very little discussion among academics about what these mean, particularly compared with the extensive discussions of 'poverty' and low income. This chapter takes 'wealth' first and discusses how we might conceptualise, define and measure wealth. It then takes the same approach with 'the wealthy'.

Conceptualising and defining wealth

As argued in the previous chapter, wealth has received relatively little attention from researchers. It is a term commonly used but not necessarily used in a consistent manner. So what is it? Our focus in this book is on wealth in the form of personal assets, but it is important to remember that there are other forms of wealth. For example, wealth can also be conceptualised as 'capital', and this term has been the subject of much debate. Various forms of capital have been identified at different times, for example, property and other forms of financial/economic capital as well as human capital (skills and education), social capital (social networks and relationships) and cultural capital (symbolic goods including attitudes, language and habits) (Bourdieu, 1986; Putnam, 2000). All forms of capital play a role in relation to people's life chances and wellbeing, but the relative strength of each and the relationship between them is unclear. For example, economic capital is likely to play a major role in helping people increase their human capital, through paying for education and training. But cultural capital may also play a role if parental attitudes are such as to encourage children to focus on education. It is argued that social capital varies among different socioeconomic groups such that those from more middle-class backgrounds have 'weak social ties' across a large number of contacts which enables them to accumulate more 'bridging capital', and those from working-class backgrounds have 'strong social ties' which enables them to accumulate more 'bonding social capital' (Granovetter, 1973; Putnam, 2000).

While keeping in mind other forms of wealth and capital, this book focuses on *personal* wealth in the form of personal assets. The Royal Commission on the Distribution of Income and Wealth (1975) provided a useful definition of assets as money that is fixed at a point in time (a stock of economic resources) in contrast to income which is money received over a particular time period (a flow of economic resources). This seems a reasonably clear distinction as we can see the difference, for example, between the flow of money from a monthly wage payment and a stock of money held in a savings account. However, there are some complexities here. For example, people can receive income from assets (for example, interest on a savings account or rental income from a buy-to-let property). Furthermore, 'capital gains', for example, from inheriting a house, fall somewhere between income and assets and are treated separately in the tax system. In more theoretical terms, economists often talk of the flow of expected future earnings as representing a stock of human capital and the benefits of owner-occupation may be said to constitute a stream of imputed income or rent. So, both conceptually and in practice, a flow of income can be converted into a stock of assets, and vice versa (McKay, 1992).

So, assets are a stock of economic resources but they do not necessarily remain as a stock permanently. One of the most important classifying criteria for assets is 'liquidity', also referred to as 'marketability'. Assets that provide an income stream but which cannot be 'cashed in' or 'realised' are known as illiquid or non-marketable (for example, occupational pensions and trust funds). Assets that can be realised are known as liquid or marketable assets (for example, savings and property net of mortgages). But levels of marketability vary depending not only on the type of asset but also on factors such as the nature of the market and the divisibility of the asset. For example, a house counts as a marketable asset but a less liquid form than money held in an open-access savings account. And the liquidity of property depends on the nature of the housing market at any particular point in time. It also depends on the availability and nature of financial products such as (re-)mortgages and equity release schemes.

As well as considering different aspects or dimensions of assets it is also common to divide assets into three particular types: financial, housing and pension. Financial assets (usually) represent very or highly liquid forms of money; pension assets are (very largely) non-marketable; and housing assets are somewhere between the two. These different types of assets also play very different roles in people's lives. Housing assets provide a commodity which provides shelter and contributes to someone's current standard of living. Pension assets provide a current or future income stream, and financial assets provide a flexible resource that may be used in diverse ways.

Having the right to remain in a property as a tenant may also be considered as having value – but not the kind of wealth that is easily realised ('fungible' wealth). Leasehold properties also have something of an interesting status as the property ultimately reverts to someone other than the current 'owner'. Future rights to state benefits provide another area of controversy in this field, as these generally entail the right to future income streams analogous to pensions.

Another important dimension of assets is how assets have been accumulated. A broad distinction can be made between assets that have been inherited or given to someone from a family member/generous friend and assets that have been accumulated through one's own personal income. Rowlingson and McKay (2005) found that almost half of the population (46 per cent) had received some kind of inheritance at some point during their lives. One person in 20 (five per cent) had inherited £50,000 or more (see Chapter Four).

Wealth accumulated through one's own personal income can be gained directly from working (earned wealth) or through investing money in housing or savings which then produce a return on investment (unearned wealth).

Another important dimension of wealth is gross versus net. Jenkins (1990) has argued that, as is the case with income, it is important to distinguish between gross and net assets because most analysis of assets focuses on net assets but gross assets may also say something important about the lifestyles and expectations of different groups. For example, there may be two people with £50,000 in net assets. One may own outright a house worth £50,000. The other may have just taken out a mortgage on a house worth £500,000 (using £50,000 as a deposit). If we know both the gross and the net wealth owned by these two people it gives us a different idea about the living standards of the two as the person with gross wealth of £500,000 is likely to be living in a more comfortable property than the person with gross wealth of £50,000.

Alongside *personal* forms of wealth and capital, wealth can also be owned by the state (for example, in the form of property, land and nationalised industries). As discussed in Chapter One, the 1980s saw a transfer of wealth back from the state to individuals with privatisation and other policies such as selling off council housing at a discount under the 'Right to Buy'. Other forms of state wealth, however, can also be held individually. For example, state pension rights accrue to individuals and it is possible to estimate the value of people's state pension assets (see Rowlingson et al, 1999). As we shall see, however, the focus of most recent research on personal assets has been on private pension assets rather than those accrued through state systems.

This chapter focuses on assets in their positive form, but they also have a negative form: debt. Debt is usually divided into 'problem debt' and 'credit'. People have 'problem debt' where they owe money on household bills or are struggling to repay credit commitments. 'Problem debt' is most widespread among people on low incomes. Those on middle or high incomes are more likely than other groups to use credit to spread expenditure over time (for example, a mortgage is a form of credit enabling people to buy property). Debt has been the subject of considerable discussion and research (see Kempson, 2002; Kempson et al, 2004; DTI, 2005) and so we will not focus specifically on it in this book except in so far as it allows us to measure 'net wealth' (that is, assets minus debts).

Measuring wealth

So far in this chapter, we have focused on conceptualising and defining wealth. The next step is to measure it. Until recently, there have been relatively few attempts to do this in the UK despite increasing calls for better data on wealth. These calls date back to at least the Royal Commission on the Distribution of Income and Wealth, which, in 1975, carried out a review existing sources of information on assets. This review concluded that there was a lack of reliable information on wealth. The review led to two feasibility studies in the 1970s by the Office of Population Censuses and Surveys (OPCS). These confirmed that it was difficult to define wealth and also that respondents had difficulty answering some questions about wealth. The conclusion from those studies was that the response rate to a national survey would be unacceptably low. Furthermore, the indications were that non-response would be higher among those groups with higher incomes and substantial investment income. It was therefore decided not to go ahead with further development work (see ONS, 2009 for further discussion of this history).

Since then, however, a number of surveys have included questions on assets. For example, in 1992, the Department of Social Security commissioned the Family Resources Survey (FRS), which included some questions on assets and savings and became an annual survey. The former Department of the Environment (DoE) also asked questions about inheritances on the General Household Survey carried out in 1989/90 and 1990/91. In the 1990s, the Joseph Rowntree Foundation commissioned research on income and wealth that involved analysis of the 'Households Below Average Income' (HBAI) series (using data from the Family and Expenditure Survey [FES] and also the British Household Panel Survey [BHPS]). The English Longitudinal Study of Ageing (ELSA), which went into the field for the first time in March 2002, also included some questions on wealth and assets including pensions. And in 2004, the Joseph Rowntree Foundation funded a survey into inheritance (Rowlingson and McKay, 2005).

There is also data from wills/probate. In the UK Her Majesty's Revenue and Customs (HMRC), formerly the Inland Revenue, regularly produces estimates of wealth using what is known as the 'estate multiplier method'. This involves taking the data on the wealth of those who have died (and collected for the purposes of probate and Inheritance Tax) and using them as a sample for the wealth of the living. Various adjustments are required for the differential chances of death at different ages, and the greater longevity of the wealthy, plus the fact that only around half of deaths generate the necessary information on wealth. Some kinds of wealth are not captured – such as wealth in the form of trusts – and so these need to be added in separately from the main calculations. Other kinds of wealth, and particularly pension wealth which is often extinguished at death, are also not captured. Hence this method may be described as one that looks at marketable wealth. It is perhaps better than most methods at looking at the wealth of the most wealthy at the top of the distribution, although subject to some caveats given the limitations of the methods described in this paragraph.

Despite all this new data being collected, there has still been, until recently, a lack of detailed, valid and reliable data on wealth. This was noted by the Pensions Commission's first report (2004) and ultimately led to the Wealth and Assets Survey (WAS). Development of the survey began in January 2004, funded by a number of government departments. A feasibility study was carried out in June 2005, and following the success of this a pilot study was carried out early in 2006, leading to main fieldwork undertaken in 2006–08.

Given that the WAS is the most thorough attempt to measure wealth so far in the UK, and given that we present a considerable amount of data from the survey in the next two chapters, we focus on it here when discussing ways of measuring wealth (see ONS, 2009 for further details of this). But it is important to bear in mind that the approach taken by the WAS is not the only way that wealth could be measured, nor is it without its limitations.

In terms of operationalising wealth, total wealth in WAS was defined as the sum of four components:

- net property wealth
- physical wealth
- net financial wealth
- private pension wealth.

Ideally, total wealth would also include any business assets held by individuals within the household, but although questions on business assets were included, a high percentage of those who said they held business assets failed to provide an estimate of the value of such assets. The WAS data is therefore restricted to the personal wealth of households and does not include business assets owned by households. In the first wave, WAS also failed to satisfactorily collect data on trusts, and so the value of trusts is also excluded from the main estimates from this source. And there have been some problems with the data on benefit income that limits some of the analysis that can be carried out linking assets and income. Nevertheless, the data is the most detailed information available on personal assets.

We now look in greater detail at the four components of total wealth in the WAS.

Net property wealth

The WAS defined this as the sum of all property values minus the value of all mortgages and value of amounts owed as a result of equity release. First, the survey looked at the gross value of household property assets and the value of mortgages (liabilities). It then reported on net property wealth (gross assets minus liabilities). The survey operationalised property value by asking people to estimate how much they thought their property was worth. The WAS 2009 report rightly advises caution when interpreting the figures on property wealth because people may over-report the value of property that they own in surveys. This may be because people think about the asking prices which they have seen advertised rather than the sold prices (which are arguably the true market values). There may also be a degree of 'wishful thinking' about property prices and at a time when property prices are declining, people may want to think that their property is still worth more than it probably is. On the other hand, if people have not bought their property in recent years, and if prices have risen since the purchase, they may under-estimate the value of their property. Other sources of data on house sale prices can be compared with respondents' own estimates, but data on house sale prices in themselves cannot necessarily provide an accurate estimate of the value of all properties because only certain properties are sold at any particular time.

Physical wealth

In the WAS, physical wealth is made up of the contents of the main residence of a household, the contents of any property which the household owns other than the main residence, collectables, valuables, vehicles and personalised number plates. The physical wealth estimates presented in the WAS 2009 report may be less precise than the estimates of financial, property and private pension wealth because the largest component of physical wealth is contents of the main residence, and people may find it hard to estimate the precise value of contents. Interviewees were asked to give 'the approximate replacement value of the household contents', which 'is the approximate cost of replacing the items now, and may be similar to the insured value'. Respondents were asked to select one of ten bands for the value of household contents, starting with 'less than £5,000' and ending at '£200,000 or more'.

Net financial wealth

In the WAS, *gross* financial wealth is the sum of the value of any formal and informal financial assets such as:

- current accounts
- savings accounts
- ISAs (Individual Savings Accounts) (including both cash ISAs and stocks and shares ISAs)
- National Savings certificates and bonds
- shares (including employee shares and share options)
- insurance products
- PEPs (Personal Equity Plans)
- unit/investment trusts
- bonds/gilts (including fixed-term bonds)
- other formal financial assets.

These are then added to the value of assets held in the names of children, plus the value of endowments purchased to repay mortgages. *Net* financial wealth is gross financial wealth minus financial liabilities (which are current account overdrafts, plus amounts owed on credit cards, store cards, mail order, hire purchase and loans, plus amounts owed in arrears). As mentioned above, money held in trusts – other than Child Trust Funds – was not included in the first wave data due to a technical mistake in the survey process.

Data on financial wealth in the WAS is at household level. This means that all assets held by individuals have been added together to produce household totals. In some cases the household totals represent only one account or holding, whereas in others they represent multiple accounts held by one or more than one individual (see Chapter Four).

Some of the information presented in the WAS report on financial wealth may under-estimate true proportions or values. In particular, analysis by HMRC using its own data and external data sources suggests more widespread ownership of ISAs, PEPs and National Savings certificates and bonds (including Premium Bonds) than that found by the survey. It also estimates higher average values in Child Trust Funds. Informal financial assets may also be under-estimated in the survey, as the questionnaire only asked respondents about informal saving or lending in excess of £250.

Private pension wealth

The WAS collected information about membership of private pension schemes (not state pension schemes), including the types of these pensions and the value of assets held in these schemes, at the time of the survey. In addition, information was collected on private pension schemes from which the respondents expected to receive an income in the future on the basis of contributions made by a former spouse, and also private pensions from which they were receiving an income at the time of the survey (including pension income based on a former spouse's pension membership). Where possible, interviewees were encouraged to consult recent statements from their pension provider to improve the accuracy of their responses. In their study of the within-household distribution of assets, Rowlingson and Joseph (2010) found that some people had little idea about how much money they might have in private pensions. They often mentioned 'frozen' pensions but were not at all sure how much money they might have in them. So asking people to find paperwork on private pensions would be very sensible if they could do so.

Calculating the value of private pensions was more complicated than measuring the other forms of wealth. The Office for National Statistics (ONS) had to apply slightly different valuation methodologies to each of nine categories of private pension wealth. These categories included: defined benefit pensions, defined contribution pensions, personal pensions to which the individual was contributing at the time of the interview, additional voluntary contributions (AVCs) made to current pensions; retained rights in defined benefit and defined contribution schemes, pension funds from which the individual was drawing an income through income drawdown, pensions in payment and pensions expected in future based on the pension contributions of a former spouse. Broadly speaking, the pension wealth figures presented in the WAS represent the amount of money that an individual would have needed to set aside at the date of interview to provide themselves with the same income stream throughout retirement as that which they will receive from their private pensions, given the pension rights accrued at the date of interview.

Operationalising wealth is only one part of measuring wealth. Sampling and fieldwork issues are also crucial. The sample for wave 1 of the WAS was drawn from the Postcode Address File (PAF), which is the Royal Mail's database of all addresses in the UK. The survey sampled all private households in Great Britain. This means that people in residential institutions, such as retirement homes, nursing homes, prisons, barracks or university halls of residence, and also homeless people were excluded from the data and so the survey does not cover all individuals in the country. The WAS was a particularly long survey to administer, taking on average some 90 minutes to be completed for each household, and part of the reason for this long interview was that interviewers encouraged respondents to consult relevant documentation such as bank statements to ensure the information collected was as accurate as possible. Whether or not documents were consulted was recorded for some questions to help assess the accuracy of the results.

Interviewers were also asked to judge how accurate they thought the information was that they had been given, and while this can only be an impression, the proportion of households judged by interviewers to have given 'fairly' or 'very' accurate financial information was consistently high, at between 91 and 97 per cent per month for the first wave of WAS.

The overall response rate for wave 1 was 55 per cent (52 per cent providing full cooperation and 3 per cent partial cooperation) which, given the length and content of the interviews and the general trend towards lower survey response rates, is a respectable level. Some 34 per cent of households refused to take part, with those unable to be contacted forming 7 per cent of the sample of eligible households approached. The degree of non-response bias is the crucial question, however, rather than the overall level of non-response. For instance, the response rate in London was below half (48 per cent), and local response rates were affected by the average wealth of the location – measured using financial ACORN classification. This area-level non-response was incorporated into the weights used for analysis, along with an adjustment to ensure that sample numbers reflected population figures in terms of age group, gender and region. The weighted survey should therefore generate results that are closer to the true population figures than an unweighted survey. Even so, within any of the weighting classes it remains possible that the survey participants are not identical to those refusing to take part, with possible consequences for the estimation of total wealth and its distribution.

The sample size for the WAS is considerable. In developing the survey, ONS produced targets for key changes and from these, it was estimated that an overall achieved sample of approximately 32,000 households, spread evenly over the two years of the first wave, was required. On top of this there was a further target of 4,500 households above the top wealth decile for wave 1. This oversampling of the wealthiest households was carried out to allow for more detailed analysis of this group and to give more precise estimates of the levels of wealth across the whole population. A total of 30,595 interviews were achieved in practice.

One important issue for any analysis of wealth (as it is with income) is whether assets should be measured at the level of the individual, the 'family' or the household. This depends on the degree of sharing within families and households. If we measure assets at the household level we will be assuming that all individuals within the household share these resources (or at least the benefits of these resources) and therefore occupy the same position in the asset distribution. This may or may not be appropriate (see Chapter Four). In the first report on the WAS (ONS, 2009) results were presented for households, with wealth being aggregated across the individuals interviewed in each household. Data was collected from different individuals, but summarised for households.

Another issue that has been considered in relation to income but not really in relation to assets is whether or not, and how, to adjust household incomes for the different needs that different households face, using equivalence scales (see Brewer et al, 2006). In relation to income this is important because a weekly income of £300 will provide a much higher standard of living to an individual living alone than to a family of five. But what about in relation to wealth? For example, a single person in a particular locality with housing wealth of £200,000 is likely to be much better off than a family of five with a similar level of wealth in terms of the size and/or quality of their housing.

Conceptualising and defining the wealthy

The previous two sections of this chapter have focused on 'wealth'. Now we turn to 'the wealthy'. 'The wealthy' have received much less attention from social science and policy makers than 'the poor'. As far as 'poverty' goes, there has been a lively debate in terms of definition (for example, absolute and relative conceptions of poverty) and measurement that has taken place for more than a century (see Rowntree, 1901; Townsend, 1979; Mack and Lansley, 1985; Gordon and Pantazis, 1998; Gordon et al, 2000; Lister, 2004). Debates about poverty often involve the use of other terms such as 'hardship', 'deprivation', 'low income', 'disadvantage', 'social exclusion' and so on. Once again there is a literature on each of these and their definition (also see Lister, 2004). But there is much less of an agreed framework for talking about other groups. Scott (1994) has provided one of the few discussions on riches using the term 'wealthy' to describe people in a state of privilege. He stated that:

> To be wealthy is to enjoy a standard of living that is greater than that normal for members of a particular society. If deprivation is the condition of life of the poor, 'privilege' is the condition of life of the wealthy. (Scott, 1994, p 17)

This, of course, begs the question about what is 'normal' for members of a particular society. This question also concerns discussions of 'poverty' that often revolve around the idea that some people are unable to afford goods or to take part in activities considered 'normal' by most people in a particular society. Coming back to wealth, Scott goes on to say that it is possible to identify a 'wealth line' above which people 'enjoy special benefits and advantages of a private sort' (Scott, 1994, p 152). Furthermore:

> Those who are privileged – the wealthy – are those whose location in the economic system means that the resources available to them are such that they are able to establish 'private' lifestyles and modes of consumption from which others are excluded ... privilege, understood in relative

terms, is a condition in which people are able to enjoy advantaged powers and opportunities, life chances that are superior to those that are normal in their society. (Scott, 1994, p 152)

Scott (1994) and Giddens (1998) both considered those at the 'top' of the distribution to be a particularly privileged group, and they defined them as those who have the ability to exclude themselves from mainstream society or 'the public life of the citizen' or 'normal citizen participation' (Scott, 1994, p 152). This voluntary self-exclusion at the top appears to mirror the 'forced' exclusion experienced by those at the 'bottom' of the economic distribution.

Dean with Melrose (1999) carried out one of the very few empirical studies on the conceptualisation of riches. Their focus groups identified two groups of people beyond poverty: those who lived in 'comfort', and another group that were able to have 'fun' without any economic worries. Other terms used by the public, media, policy makers and politicians for the rich are 'better off' groups, 'affluent' groups, 'the wealthy', 'the super-rich', 'fat cats' and so on. But these terms carry little precise meaning and have received little attention from academics.

Rowlingson (2008) refers to the 'rich' rather than the 'wealthy' because the term 'wealthy' refers to 'wealth as assets' and it is possible, in theory at least, for someone to be rich through extremely high levels of income rather than wealth/assets. In order to locate the 'rich' it is helpful to consider where we might draw the 'riches line' and this draw us into a discussion about the position of groups who are not poor but also not rich. This, in turn, draws us into a discussion about the 'middle'. John Healey, Labour MP, and member of the shadow cabinet, defined what he called the 'squeezed middle' as the 'more than 7 million families with an annual income between £14,500 and £33,800'.[1] In September 2010, during the elections for the next Labour leader, he argued that:

> The squeezed middle seem stuck in no man's land. Too poor to get the best from the market, too well off to claim state benefits. Not wealthy enough to get a mortgage, not sufficiently vulnerable for social housing.
>
> We too easily allow a mobile, metropolitan class to skew our understanding of society. Too many of those in the media, political and public policy world take people earning 40 or 50 thousand pounds or more as typical of 'the middle'.

The real squeezed middle are overlooked by the press, and overlooked by the modern Right.

Ed Miliband, who won the leadership of the Labour Party in September 2010, also began using this term, and made a particular issue of the anxieties of the 'squeezed middle', although it isn't entirely clear who this group is. Miliband did not seem to be using it as narrowly as Healey, but was trying to use it to include some people who might lose Child Benefit under the government's plans to remove it from top-rate taxpayers.

Wakefield (2003) discussed the terms 'middle England', 'middle class' and 'middle income' as they had been used quite widely by politicians and the media in relation to Labour's General Election successes from 1997 to 2005. He pointed out that:

> ... residents of middle Britain are often explicitly or implicitly identified as those on the fringe of being higher-rate tax-payers. (Wakefield, 2003, p 2)

Wakefield (2003) pointed out, however, that higher-rate taxpayers formed only the top 7 per cent of all adults, so even those near this group might still be called the top. However, he also pointed out that it might be possible in theory for a high-rate taxpayer, living with a non-working partner and a large number of children, to have a more modest disposable income, and Wakefield (2003) did indeed find some top-rate taxpayers in 2001/2 who were in the top 30 per cent of the income distribution. Some of these top-rate taxpayers might therefore be *near* the middle, but it is still difficult to count them as *in* the middle.

In the US, Wheary et al (2007) also focused on the 'middle' to see whether the 'middle classes' actually experienced the degree of financial security that is normally seen as guaranteed in that part of the class structure. They defined the middle class in relation to income and wealth rather than occupation. Focusing on working-age people, they argued that the middle classes were those with household incomes at least twice as much as the federal poverty guideline for family size but no more than six times that level. This amounted to an income band of US$40,000 to US$120,000 for a family of four. They also excluded families with substantial personal wealth – those whose net financial wealth placed them in the top 1 per cent of asset holders. This seems a fairly generous definition of middle class, covering those between the 26th and 80th percentiles (that is, 54 per cent of the population, leaving 26 per cent defined as 'poor' and 20 per cent presumably as 'rich'). However, Wheary et al (2007) argued that only 31 per cent of these 'middle-class' families could be classified as 'financially secure', basing this on their 'middle-class security index' which covered five areas: assets sufficient to provide a safety net and nest egg; education to find a good job; quality housing; sufficient income to cover essential living costs; and decent healthcare.

It may not be clear where we draw the line between the 'middle' and the top but it is, perhaps, easier to focus on the 'very top'. Lansley (2006) focused on a group he labelled the 'super-rich', and it may be useful to divide 'the rich' into further sub-groups, depending on their level of riches (see below). Another classification could draw on the wealth management industry's new language that has evolved to define and sub-divide the very rich. Such terms include 'high net worth' and 'ultra-high net worth' (Beaverstock, 2010; see also later in this chapter).

While there has been relatively little discussion of 'the wealthy' or 'riches' in social policy or broader social science, there have been extensive discussions in the social sciences around the concept of social class as a key socioeconomic division. Social class is another contested concept, however, and one which does not link directly to studies of poverty and wealth. Members of the working class may or may not be poor. Similarly, members of the middle classes may or may not be 'rich', depending on our definition of both middle class and 'rich'. But 'middle class' is, again, generally related to labour market position rather than level of income and wealth (although the two are related).

Most discussions of social class in recent decades have concerned the working and middle classes, and there has been very little discussion about an 'upper class' that might relate more closely to 'the wealthy' (Giddens, 1974). Perhaps this is because the first half of the 20th century saw a redistribution of the wealth of those at the top to those in (or nearer) the middle. Changes in the labour market and family forms also led to increasing interest in the working and middle classes, and more general changes in the social class structure rather than those at the very top. And the 'cultural turn' in sociology also led to a more general decline in interest in class 'structures' with greater discussion of issues around culture and identity.

However, there have been writings about the upper class or 'leisure class' going back at least to Veblen (1899) at the end of the 19th century, alongside various socio-historical studies of the upper class (see, for example, Thorndike, 1980; North, 2005) with an emphasis on 'old' money, inheritance, land and the gentry. Scott (1982) has also written about the 'upper classes'. His book was an historical account of change in the upper classes in which he argued that the 20th century saw the emergence of a unified business class, managing the monopoly enterprises of the modern economy. Scott (1982) argued that the upper classes continued to use inter-marriage, the 'old boy network', social codes and social institutions (such as 'the season', public schools, the armed forces, the Church of England and so on) to maintain their solidarity and exercise of power and influence. At the same time, he argued that they:

> ... have projected a view of themselves as part of an extensive 'middle class' ... unequal life chances are, in many respects, invisible; and this invisibility lends plausibility to the image of a continuous and hierarchical middle class. (Scott, 1982, p 175)

Scott's (1982) view still seems highly pertinent today as Kate Middleton was being described in some media on her engagement to Prince William as either middle class[2] or even 'a commoner'[3]. While it is true that she did not have a title (before her marriage) and so is not, perhaps, part of an 'aristocracy', her family own their own business which has enabled them to live in a £1 million house in Berkshire and put their three children through some of the most expensive private schools in the country, which has been estimated to have cost about £250,000 for Kate alone. They also bought her a flat in Chelsea now worth between £750,000 and £1 million.[4] It seems difficult to justify the label 'middle class' in this case.

In many respects, Scott's work on the 'upper classes' links in with a stream of research interest within sociology in 'elites'. Once again, the exact relationship between 'elites', 'classes' and 'wealth' is not entirely clear. Giddens (1974) identified three primary issues in relation to the study of elites: how people are recruited into the elite and the degree of openness or closure in recruitment as well as the kinds of channels used to recruit people; whether the bonds between the elite are based on common ideas and a common moral ethos and/or based on social contacts and ties; and the degree to which the power of the elite is diffused or centralised. One of the key debates is also whether any elite is primarily economic and/or political. Marx argued that the ruling class owed their political power to their economic domination, but Pareto and Mosca saw the source of elite power primarily in relation to their political power (Giddens, 1974).

Mosca (1939) argued that there was a 'ruling class' or 'political class' that had sufficient political power to warrant the title of 'governing elite' (Mosca, 1939). This group may wield political power directly by holding high offices of state or indirectly through their influence. The 'super-rich', however, are more of a socioeconomic elite than a political elite, and Aron (1950), for example, tried to link concepts of social class (which tend to be linked to economic structures and/or socioeconomic status structures than political power) and (political) elites by talking of a 'plurality of elites' which might also include an 'intellectual elite'.

More recently there has been renewed interest within sociology in 'elites' and the 'super-rich'. Once again, however, the exact relationship between 'elites', 'classes' and 'wealth' is not entirely clear. David Beckham may be one of the wealthiest men in Britain but he is not, perhaps, part of any economic, political or intellectual elite. Also, some journalists/newspaper editors may not be particularly wealthy but may wield considerable power that places them within a powerful elite.

Mills (1959) preferred to use the term 'power elite' for the ruling class as he felt that the latter term confused a political term (rule) with an economic one (class). He distinguished three major elites in the US: the economic, the political and the military. These three might be considered part of one upper, ruling class, but Mills was not convinced of this, arguing that the three groups moved in their own circles rather than in a single circle. He argued that they were all part of one upper class but not one ruling elite. Also, elites were not always cohesive. Some of the heads of industry would be competing with each other for market share and so their ability to cooperate and form a powerful united force would be limited. Similarly, political elites would be competing with each other for political power and might have different ideological views. And military leaders from the Navy, Army and Air Force might come into conflict if, for example, they were competing for resources.

Given growing levels of inequality and other changes in the political sphere, there has been increasing interest in elites, and the rich, in the last 10 years. For example, Adonis and Pollard (1997) wrote about the 'super class'. This class, they argued, emerged from the expansion of the City and differed substantially from the previous 'upper class' as they saw their rewards as deriving from hard work and skill whereas the aristocracy were seen as deriving their wealth simply from birth. The 'super class' lived up, it seems, to Young's (1958) warnings about meritocracy providing stronger justification for greater inequality. McElwee (2000) has also argued that there is a 'new class' in Britain, but sees this as more of a political class which has been deliberately cultivated by former Labour Prime Minister Tony Blair through appointments to the House of Lords, various quangos (quasi-autonomous non-governmental organisations), Task Forces and special advisers (see also du Gay, 2008). Andrew Adonis, the author of the book just cited on the 'super class', is a classic example of this 'new class' himself, as he was initially a political adviser to Tony Blair who then turned him into a government minister by virtue of being appointed to the House of Lords, The term 'metropolitan elite' is also often mentioned in Britain today in relation to the centralised networks and power of certain groups in London.

Sampson (2004) reflected on his experience of writing about elites over 40 years and argued that, despite the claims of various prime ministers, including both Margaret Thatcher and Tony Blair, that power would be devolved more to the people, power had in fact become even more centralised and concentrated at the end of the 20th century both in the political and the economic sphere. Sampson (2004, p 360) claimed that as ideological differences have declined, the new elite is 'held together by their desire for personal enrichment, their acceptance of capitalism and the need for the profit-motive'.

He also pointed out that Mrs Thatcher brushed aside the old grandees of Toryism who took a sceptical view of the City (Macmillan apparently called them 'banksters'; Sampson, 2004, p 360) and then Blair and Brown became friends with business and with the City to gain political power. Thus the power of the new financial elite has grown substantially since 1979. However, Moran (2008, p 68) has queried the solidarity of the new business elite, arguing that:

> ... there has been a sharp decline in the institutional solidarity of business as an organised interest but a sharp increase in the extent to which firms, especially big firms, have mobilized to voice their own narrow interests.

Moran (2008, p 76) has also pointed out various contradictions in the political position of business with 'contempt for big business as a system of power but respect, and even affection, for individual big business figures and particular brands'.

Williams (2006) has also written about a new power elite, with a pyramid of power based on political elites, professional elites and financial/business elites. And most recently, Hutton (2010) has talked of a new super elite and a new upper middle class, created from growing wealth in the City and the knowledge economy respectively. He has argued that these groups are increasingly isolated from the rest of society but, echoing Wilkinson and Pickett (2009a), cause anxiety.

While there has certainly been renewed interest in elites recently, there has still been, according to Savage and Williams (2008), a lack of social theory on the contemporary dynamics of social change. Their edited monograph for *Sociological Review* focuses specifically on financialisation as a key concept for understanding recent developments in relation to elites. Such a focus makes sense given that the 1980s undoubtedly saw the City as a place where 'new' money could be made almost overnight and so 'self-made' millionaires were created. Scott (2008), however, argues that elites should not merely be defined by their wealth but through having a 'degree of power'. This begs the question of the relationship between substantial wealth and economic and political power.

Beaverstock (2010) has pointed to the accumulation of wealth through generous executive remuneration packages (share/stock options and salary bonuses), huge returns from financial markets, alternative investments like hedge funds and real estate investment. Alongside this new class of 'self-made' multi-millionaires and billionaires, Britain has become the home of numerous wealthy Russians, Chinese and Indians, sometimes referred to 'oligarchs' according to Beaverstock (2010), who argues that:

> The super-rich are a slippery population to pigeon hole in a generic, let alone distinctive, homogeneous social stratum or 'class' like Sklair's (2001) transnational capitalist class. Collectively, the super-rich have traits of transnationalism, cosmopolitanism and living fast and hyper-mobile lifestyles, which are played out in exclusive circuits of social and capitalist relations.

Beaverstock et al (2004, pp 405-6) noted that the super-rich were, 'perpetually between nation-states, to the extent that they dwell in global space-time ... as key actors in the articulation of the "network society"', and Frank (2007, p 3) has argued that the super-rich have formed their own country, Richi$tan, which he divided into:

- Lower Richi$tan (net worth US$1 million–US$10 million, 7.5 million households);
- Middle Richi$tan (net worth US$10 million–US$100 million, >2 million households);
- Upper Richi$tan (US$100 million–US$1 billion, thousands of households); and
- Billionaireville (over US$1 billion, 400+ households).

The link between economic elites/the wealthy and political elites is documented by Bartels (2008) who carried out an analysis of policy changes to argue that US democracy was in danger from politicians placing the interests of wealthy citizens far higher than those of poorer citizens. Through detailed analysis and argument, he concluded that this explained why income growth has been much lower for middle and poorer groups than for affluent ones.

While studies of elites are important and interesting and certainly overlap with our interest in 'the wealthy', the two groups are conceptually distinct. The very wealthy or super-rich may be able to form part of an elite if they choose to do so as they are likely to have the economic power to either directly or indirectly influence key political and/or economic decisions, but they may choose not to engage in this way. And some of those we might consider only wealthy rather than *very* wealthy may not have sufficient power to be included in an economic 'elite'. So there is an issue about where we draw the 'wealth line' as there is, indeed, about where the boundary around an elite is placed. We therefore return to some of the literature more directly related to 'the wealthy', not least Scott (1994) and Dean with Melrose (1999). But neither of these studies provided a more detailed framework for defining and then measuring 'privilege', 'wealth', 'comfort' or 'fun'. As mentioned above, Scott (1994) argued that the privileged mirrored 'the deprived' in the sense that they could choose to exclude themselves from participation in public life whereas the deprived suffered forced exclusion. Scott's suggestion that privilege mirrors deprivation is useful and we take it further here to consider how wealth mirrors poverty. Poverty has been defined and measured in a number of ways and so we, too, consider various ways of defining and measuring wealth (see also Rowlingson, 2008).

For example, the main official definition of poverty takes a *relative* approach: 60 per cent of median income. As far as the poverty threshold goes, any threshold is bound to be somewhat arbitrary. The figure of 60 per cent of the median superseded emphasis on 50 per cent of the mean. It is also sometimes instructive to look at other thresholds, such as either 50 per cent or 70 per cent of the median, and numbers below such thresholds are routinely reported in the annual HBAI publications. The key figure of 60 per cent of the median is now enshrined in the Child Poverty Act 2010. A similar approach could be taken in relation to riches. For example, we could look at those with twice or three times median income or assets. Or we could use other statistical techniques such as those two standard deviations above the mean. Or we could look at the top decile (10 per cent) of income or assets or the top percentile (top 1 per cent). The choice of threshold would depend on our conceptualisation of wealth.

Another approach commonly used in relation to poverty is the deprivation indicator approach, developed first by Townsend (1979) and then modified by Mack and Lansley (1985), Gordon and Pantazis (1998) and Gordon et al (2000). Since the 1980s, this approach has tended to start with a survey of the general public to identify necessities – the goods or services that people should not have to live without. This could be turned around to help identify relevant sets of luxuries, or items indicating a particularly advantaged position. So, with this approach 'experts' or members of the public could be asked to draw up *indicators* of riches referring to specific possessions (for example, an Apple iPad, an HD television); the quality of goods (for example, type of car owned); activities (for example, number and destination of holidays); or perhaps ability to afford private healthcare, private education, absence of debts or lack of money worries. People would be considered 'rich' if they possessed a certain number of these 'luxuries'. If someone lacked a particular luxury, it would be possible to ask them whether this was because they did not want it or because they could not afford it. Those that could afford a luxury could be included in the measure even if they chose not to have it. This approach is currently being explored in a new Poverty and Social Exclusion Survey. Researchers at the University of Bristol are asking people in focus groups to identify 'necessities', 'desirables' and 'luxuries'. The findings from this research are not yet available.[5]

As well as considering a threshold for measuring 'the rich' or 'wealthy', it does seem that another threshold may be useful to cover the 'super-rich'. We saw in Chapter One that the wealth of the very top has increased dramatically in recent years, and it would be helpful to identify this group for further research. Beaverstock (2010) has quoted the distinction made in the wealth management industry between the following groups:

- high net worth individuals, with at least £1 million in assets excluding primary residences, collectables, consumables and consumer durables. This money is therefore freely available for investment;
- mid-tier millionaires, with £1 million–£30 million available for investment;
- ultra-high net worth individuals, with more than £30 million available for investment.

Another possible method to identify the wealthy would be to ask people who may, indeed, be in this group to discuss this question, and Edwards (2002, p 35) did just this when she carried out interviews and focus groups with 'affluent people' (those with earnings between £34,000 and £60,000 according to her definition) and the 'rich' (those earning over £80,000). Edwards found that many of these did not feel rich themselves and tended to define 'wealthy' as relating to people with more money than themselves:

> "In terms of clients I work with I see a salary of something like £150,000 as where I would notice a marked difference in terms of the car they drive and things like that…."

> "I think there is a huge gap between being wealthy and being comfortable. Wealthy might be earning £1 million a year, owning a house in Chiswick, a couple of properties abroad, having a number of cars … comfortable is people like us who've done all right, own a property, can afford cars and holidays and don't have to worry too much about money…."

> "I'd think I'd need to have something like £4 million in the bank to feel wealthy…."

> "Wealthy? It's £50 million and upwards as far as I'm concerned. £50 million is the point at which you don't have to panic any more."

Rather than consulting people who, themselves, may or may not be or feel wealthy, another approach is to consult those who work with the wealthy. The National Centre for Social Research (NatCen) (2009), for example, approached experts and agents of the very wealthy and asked them how they might define the wealthy. The sample was very small but a key theme mentioned was the ability to make generous lifetime gifts and bequests to future generations. One participant suggested the following categorisation:

• People with less than £5 million total net assets would be considered wealthy but not 'very wealthy', because these people would own a substantial residential property and a stock of capital but would have limited opportunities to transfer money between generations before death.

- Those with £5 million or more would be considered 'very wealthy' as they would have some surplus and so would be able to think about gifts before death.
- Those with £5 million–£30 million would have considerable ability to give away significant gifts in their lifetime.
- Those with £50 million–£100 million would have the ability to consider wealth planning for the following three generations.
- Those with over £100 million would have the ability to have a personal office to manage family finances and pursue dynastic aims.

This focus on future generations brings us back, perhaps, to historical and sociological studies of the upper classes and even the aristocracy. Perhaps these new super wealthy are a new aristocracy?

Measuring the wealthy

As we have just seen, one of the first issues to confront when trying to measure the wealthy is our conceptualisation and definition. As discussed in the previous section, there is no agreement about this and so, for the purposes of the analysis we will be carrying out later in Chapter Five, we suggest the following threefold categorisation:

- rich: those with sufficient financial resources to establish *private* lifestyles and modes of consumption;
- richer: those with sufficient financial resources to establish *highly exclusive* lifestyles and modes of consumption;
- richest: those with the very *highest level* of financial resources in a society.

We use the term 'rich' rather than 'wealthy' to avoid confusion with 'wealth' in the form of assets because people may be rich due to high income rather than wealth. Taking the merely 'rich' first, we argue that this should include the top 10 per cent of the population in terms of income and/or assets. We will see, in Chapter Five, that this group has the resources to establish private lifestyles and modes of consumption that set them apart from more 'mainstream' society. We compare this group with three other groups. First, when looking at income groups, we have people in poverty and then we divide those in the 'middle' of riches and poverty as those above and below median income. This gives us approximately 20 per cent of the population in poverty, 30 per cent who are not poor but are below the median, 40 per cent who are not rich but are above the median and 10 per cent of the population whom we define as rich (see Table 3.1).

When analysing assets we suggest a different categorisation. This involves three groups: those with no, or negative, net wealth (about 50 per cent of the population); those with some wealth but not in the top 10 per cent of wealth holders; and the top 10 per cent (see Table 3.2).

When combining income and assets we suggest that the rich should be considered as those in the top 10 per cent for both income and wealth. This will give us around 8 per cent of the population. At the other end of the spectrum, we focus on people in poverty who are below the poverty line and also have no or negative net wealth. Between these two extremes, we divide the rest of the population into those above and below the median, as in Table 3.3.

These tables relate to the 'rich' but what about the 'richer' and 'richest' groups? We define the 'richer' group as those in the top 1 per cent who

Table 3.1: Operational definition of the rich by income (%)

	People in poverty: 60% median	Below median but not poor (i.e. above 60% median)	Above median but not rich (i.e. below top 10%)	Rich: top 10%
Approximate proportion of the population	20	30	40	10

Table 3.2: Operational definition of the rich by assets (%)

	People with no net wealth or negative wealth	Those with some wealth but not wealthy (i.e. not in top 10% of assets)	Rich (top 10% of net wealth)
Approximate proportion of the population	50	40	10

Table 3.3: Operational definition of the rich by income and assets combined (%)

	People in poverty: 60% median income and no/negative net wealth	Below median but not poor (i.e. above 60% median income) and no/negative wealth	Above median but not rich on income and wealth (i.e. below top 10%)	Rich: top 10% income and wealth
Approximate proportion of the population	20	30	40	8

have seen their incomes (and wealth) concentrate further and further over the past 20-30 years. Finally, the richest people will be those with the very highest level of resources.

Our operational definitions of the rich and the richer groups coincide with the groups identified by Majima and Warde (2008) in their analysis of elite consumption patterns, with the rich defined as the top 10 per cent of the income distribution and the 'very rich' defined as the top 1 per cent. Majima and Warde (2008) admit that income is only a proxy for elite membership and not all those with the highest incomes are part of an elite. They therefore refer to their high income groups as more of a 'pecuniary class', drawing on Veblen's (1899 [1985]) work.

Identifying who the rich and the richer might be is difficult enough, but it only gets us so far in terms of measuring them as we then have to find data on them, and as Rowlingson (2008) has pointed out, there are particular problems with this. General public sample surveys under-report the number of people with very high incomes and also under-state the amount of their incomes. This is likely to be for a number of reasons:

- rich people seem to be less likely than other people to take part in surveys;
- rich people who do take part in surveys may be more likely to refuse to answer particular questions about income and assets;
- rich people who do take part in surveys may, wittingly or unwittingly, underestimate the extent of their income and assets.

If we are interested in the top 10 per cent of the population then a survey such as WAS alongside other national surveys such as the FRS, the BHPS and so on will give us reasonable coverage of this group, but if we are interested in a smaller group – the very wealthy top 1 per cent or super-rich – then general public sample surveys will not be sufficient. Juster et al (1999) have provided further evidence of this in their study of the methodological issues of collecting data on the wealthy. They analysed two surveys in the US and found that the very wealthy are easily missed if standard area samples are used, but that it is also difficult to achieve responses from this group using special samples.

In their feasibility study for research on the very wealthy, Barnard et al (2007) identified a number of potential data sources from which to construct a sample frame, each of which had potential advantages and disadvantages. The first data source they considered was HMRC tax records. These are self-assessment records, which contain information collected for tax purposes. These records produce data on income from investments which could be used to identify very wealthy people and they also produce data on capital gains on investments. Barnard et al (2007) concluded that these data sources would identify a broad range of very wealthy individuals, but that a number of individuals would not be identified using this approach including those who were non-domiciled, those with assets that were held at arm's length, for example, in a business or trust, and those with assets that did not generate a regular income stream, for example, land.

Barnard et al (2007) also suggested, however, that people may have concerns about the legitimacy of using tax record data to draw up a sample frame for a study of the very wealthy. They interviewed a small number of people who gave financial advice to the very wealthy and these people generally voiced concerns around the belief that tax record data should not be used for any purpose other than the assessment of tax liability. This might mean that very wealthy people would potentially react strongly to tax record data being used as a basis for sampling. It was felt this could also lead to unfavourable press coverage that could damage the reputation of the parties involved.

An alternative sampling frame for the very wealthy could be the 'rich lists' put together by journalist-researchers using a range of public sources and interviews with people considered knowledgeable about the very wealthy. These lists include the *Sunday Times* Rich List, the Asian Rich List, the *Australian Business Review* Weekly Rich List and the Forbes 500. However, in their feasibility study, Barnard et al (2007) expressed doubts about the accuracy and coverage of these lists. Furthermore, these lists only include the very wealthiest people, so, depending on the definition of 'very wealthy', they might not reach all of those within the definition. There were also some concerns about inconsistency in the measurement of individual versus familial wealth, and a suggestion that these lists under-estimate the value of individual wealth.

Another potential source of information for a sampling frame could be commercial databases which are developed for organisations such as charities seeking donors, but these are often based on the publicly available rich lists and so suffer from the same disadvantages. Investment information on sales of stocks and shares from Companies House might also be used, but Barnard et al (2007) pointed out that this information was limited to business and investment wealth and so it may favour coverage of individuals with certain wealth/asset mixes.

The conclusion from the Barnard et al (2007) study was that the very wealthy could be considered a 'hidden population' as far as research goes because they do not appear on any existing data sources that clearly and reliably identify them as very wealthy. This means that a sample frame would need to be specifically constructed. But this would not be easy given the limitations of currently existing data sources in terms of their coverage and accuracy. The data held by HMRC in the form of tax records is likely to be significantly more accurate, although people may object to it being used for research purposes, and there are also some potential problems with the accuracy of the data as individual wealth is not recorded directly but instead must be estimated based on the amount of tax paid.

There is also an issue of the quality/accuracy of data that would be gathered in research with very wealthy individuals even if they agreed to take part in such studies. First of all, would very wealthy people themselves know how much money they had in different places given the likely complexity of their arrangements? It might be more appropriate to carry out interviews with their accountants, for example. But even if accurate information was known, would very wealthy people be willing to disclose their financial position to researchers?

There are clearly many challenges involved in studying the wealthy. Barnard et al (2007) argued that the main challenge would be in persuading very wealthy people to agree to be interviewed. The process of recruitment from a sampling frame – the use of an 'opt out' or 'opt in' – raises ethical, legal and reputational difficulties, which would affect the number of people you could recruit and the diversity of the sample. It seems likely that an 'opt in' approach would be the only acceptable method to the study participants and this would significantly reduce the response rate and also introduce bias in response. Even if it were possible to go ahead with an 'opt out' method (which would potentially keep the response rate higher), there may still be great reluctance among the very wealthy to take part and to be open about their wealth. Barnard et al (2007) suggested that offering to make donations to charity and gaining the support of respected stakeholders for the research would help, but may not be sufficient to gain the participation of enough very wealthy people. It is difficult to see how such challenges could be overcome without compelling people to participate, and it seems unlikely that any government would do this.

It therefore looks unlikely that the government (or anyone else) will be able to carry out quantitative research to measure the number of very wealthy people, the distribution of their wealth and their attitudes and behaviour regarding, for example, the tax system. The main problem would be in reaching a sample that is large and representative enough to be statistically significant. Qualitative research would, perhaps, be easier, but there might still be problems in reaching a sample that includes different kinds of wealthy people. Barnard et al (2007) also concluded that any study of the very wealthy would require significant amounts of time and money to fully represent the diversity of the population and therefore to provide the basis for theoretical or representational generalisation. The findings of this study also clearly imply that any attempt at conducting quantitative or qualitative research with this population group would be resource-intensive, both in terms of the amount of time and the extent of financial resources that would be required.

Conclusions

There is much less discussion about what wealth and the wealthy are in theory than there is about income and poverty. This is linked to some of the points made in earlier chapters about wealth and the wealthy not being seen as social problems in the same way as low income and poverty.

We have argued, in this chapter, that personal wealth is a stock of economic resources. The main components of this are: housing wealth, pension wealth and financial savings. Wealth varies in terms of its liquidity and this affects the role it plays in people's lives. Wealth also varies in terms of how it is accumulated. Sometimes wealth is accumulated through earnings and sometimes it is unearned – either through an inheritance/gift or through an existing asset growing in value. This distinction may be important in how wealth is seen – with unearned wealth perhaps seen as more legitimate to tax than wealth which has been accumulated through (hard) work.

Until recently, there has been very little data on personal assets. This has been partly because of a relative lack of interest in assets but also partly because of the difficulties in asking people about their wealth. In the last decade, growing interest in assets has led to a major investment in the WAS. This now provides a goldmine of data on assets for over 30,000 households and we present some analysis from the survey in the next two chapters.

There are many theoretical and empirical challenges in analysing wealth; there are even more so in relation to the wealthy. The study of social class has declined in recent decades, but in any case has seemed to focus more on the working class and middle class. Studies of elites have continued, although slightly removed from discussion of social class. More recently, there has been growing interest in the 'super-rich' but little discussion of the 'merely' rich. We argued in the last chapter that we need to consider different levels of riches from the rich through to those who are richer and then the very richest. Our conceptualisation and operationalisation of these groups is tentative, but we hope it stimulates further thought and discussion.

We see the rich as a group who can afford (should they choose to do so) to establish private lifestyles and modes of consumption. We define this as the top 10 per cent of the population. We see a 'richer' group as those who can afford (should they choose to do so) to establish highly exclusive lifestyles and modes of consumption and we define these as the top 1 per cent. Finally, we draw attention to the richest people in society: those with the very highest level of financial resources, who are the most difficult to research.

Notes

[1] www.labourlist.org/john–healey–britains–squeezed–middle

[2] For example in the *Telegraph*: www.telegraph.co.uk/news/newstopics/theroyalfamily/8137234/Royal-wedding-Kate-Middleton-will-be-first-middle-class-queen-in-waiting.html

[3] As in *The Guardian*: www.guardian.co.uk/uk/2010/nov/16/profile-kate-middleton

[4] www.thisismoney.co.uk/celebrity/article.html?in_article_id=518391&in_page_id=181

[5] See www.poverty.ac.uk/ for further information.

FOUR

The distribution of wealth

Introduction

There is a very high level of wealth inequality in Britain today, far higher even than the level of income inequality. This chapter presents analysis of the distribution of wealth using a range of sources of data, such as the Wealth and Assets Survey (WAS), Family Resources Survey (FRS) and Her Majesty's Revenue and Customs (HMRC) (formerly the Inland Revenue) data from people's estates. It compares the distribution of wealth with the distribution of income and then looks at particular types of wealth: financial savings, private pension wealth, property wealth and physical wealth. The analysis then considers the distribution of wealth by different groups in the population, for example, by age. Age is particularly important because the 'lifecycle model' suggests that some degree of wealth inequality is due to the fact that younger people will inevitably have had less time to accumulate wealth than older age groups. This chapter also looks at the distribution of assets among black and minority ethnic (BME) groups as well as different faith groups and social classes. Gender divisions are also considered, alongside a discussion of the within-household distribution of assets. Finally, the chapter analyses the role of inheritance and lifetime gifts in relation to intergenerational wealth inequality.

The distribution of wealth

The distribution of wealth is even more unequal than the distribution of income. For example, our analysis of the WAS 2006–08 shows that:

- the bottom 30 per cent in 2006–08 owned only 1 per cent of wealth;
- the top 10 per cent owned 44 per cent.

If we turn to income, our analysis of the Households Below Average Income (HBAI) 2007/08 dataset shows that:

- the bottom 10 per cent of the population received only 1 per cent of income;
- the top 10 per cent received 31 per cent.

Figure 4.1 illustrates this point further by dividing the population into deciles (tenths of the population). Shares of both income and wealth increase as we move up the deciles, with the top decile (the richest tenth of the population) having a particularly high share compared with other groups. The figure clearly illustrates that much higher level of wealth inequality compared with income inequality as the bottom three deciles (30 per cent) have virtually no wealth at all, and the top 10 per cent have 44 per cent. The National Equality Panel (2010) pointed out that the top tenth of the population owned 100 times more wealth than the bottom tenth in 2006–08.

Another, perhaps even more powerful, way of visualising the distribution of economic resources is through the idea of a parade of dwarfs and a few giants (Pen, 1971). This was originally applied to income where people's height reflects their income. The population is lined up in height order and paraded past a particular point during the course of one hour. Hills (1995) applied this to the UK in the early 1990s and suggested that average (mean) income could be represented by a height of 5 foot 8 inches. After three minutes a single unemployed mother with two children would go by with a height of 1 foot 10

Figure 4.1: Breakdown of income and wealth in Great Britain, by decile (%)

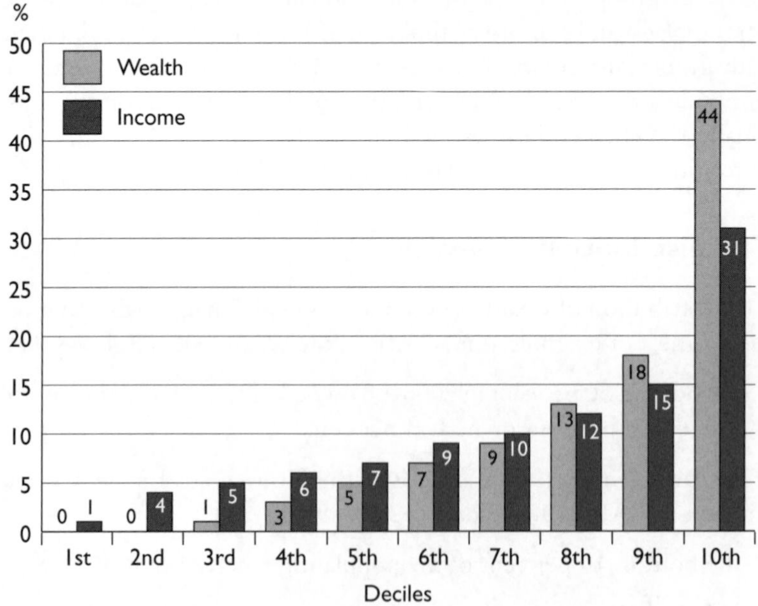

Source: Wealth and Assets Survey 2006-08 [Figure 2.2] for wealth, HBAI for incomes 2008/09 BHC

inches. After 9 minutes a single male pensioner on Income Support would go by at a height of 2 feet 6 inches. People with average (mean) incomes would not arrive until 37 minutes into the parade. After 50 minutes, the heights would begin to rise considerably and we would see the first giants at 8 feet 7 inches tall. After 59 minutes, a chief executive and his wife would walk by: both of them 60 feet tall. In the last seconds, the tallest would go by with their heads lost in the clouds: Britain's highest-income man and his partner would both be four miles high. According to Wakefield (2003), if such a parade had been organised in 2003, then the person of average (mean) height (and income) would be taller than two thirds of the population and so would pass by after 40 minutes had elapsed.

We may also construct a similar parade, but one based on wealth rather than income. For this we use figures on total wealth, including private pension wealth, gathered in the WAS 2006–08, and some of the analysis of the National Equality Panel (2010, Figure 2.19a). For the first six minutes of the hour-long parade, we see those in the bottom 10 per cent of wealth, who have yet to reach a height of *two inches*. By 18 minutes, we have the bottom 30 per cent, and still heights have only just exceeded one foot tall. At the halfway point, 30 minutes, those walking past have reached three feet and two inches – barely more than *half* the 'average' height, and representing the median level of wealth. At this point, only 9 per cent of wealth will have passed, with 91 per cent of wealth still to follow. Half of all wealth will have been accounted for only after 52 minutes – the upper half of wealth being owned by those appearing in the final 8 minutes of the hour. At 54 minutes, the top 10 per cent will start to pass by. They will have more than double the average wealth, at over 13 feet tall. Those in the top 1 per cent will peer down from a height exceeding 40 feet in the final minute when there is still around 17 per cent of wealth to be accounted for, with the final 6 per cent of total wealth appearing only in the last 10 seconds of the hour.

All these figures are derived from a voluntary sample survey (WAS), which has probably missed out on the very greatest/highest wealth holders. If we add in Lakshmi Mittal to the parade – Britain's wealthiest man in *The Sunday Times* Rich List (see Chapter Five) – then he would appear at the end of this wealth parade and have a height of some *64 miles* (retaining this scale based on the WAS level of mean wealth).

The income and wealth parades are a powerful way of visualising inequality but there are other measures of inequality which are, perhaps, more standard. We saw deciles earlier and now turn to the Gini coefficient, which summarises inequality in a single measure with a value between 0 and 1. A perfectly equal distribution would have a Gini coefficient of 0 and a perfect unequal distribution would have a Gini coefficient of 1. The National Equality Panel (2010) analysed the 2006/07 Expenditure and Food Survey to calculate that the Gini coefficient for post-tax income (disposable income less indirect taxes) was 0.38 in 2007/08. They then used WAS for the Gini coefficient for personal assets which they found to be 0.61 for total net wealth. This figure is much lower than had previously been calculated from other sources of data. For example, HMRC analysis of data drawing on the estates of those dying each year gave a figure of 0.67 in 2003. The HMRC data goes back to 1976 and shows that, until the mid-1980s, there was a general trend towards greater wealth equality, but after the early 1990s, inequality fluctuated with stock market cycles but, overall, grew to 71 per cent in 2002. WAS gives a much lower figure which may be a result of the survey method rather than any real reduction in wealth inequality. The difficulties of capturing the very wealthy in surveys may form part of the explanation as the HMRC data on estates is likely to be much more inclusive of the top wealth group.

The Gini coefficient for personal assets, overall, was 0.61 according to WAS in 2006–08. But the level of inequality varied considerably by type of wealth, as follows:

- 0.81 for net financial wealth
- 0.77 for private pension wealth
- 0.62 for net property wealth
- 0.46 for physical wealth.

Thus, net financial wealth (money in financial savings, bonds, stocks and shares) was most unequally distributed, followed by private pension wealth and then net property wealth. The least unequally distributed form of wealth was physical wealth (the contents of the main residence and any other property of a household, collectables and valuables, vehicles and personalised number plates).

The WAS estimated total net wealth in the UK in 2006–08 to be £9 trillion, that is, £9,000,000,000,000. Net wealth is the value of accumulated assets minus the value of accumulated liabilities, such as debts/mortgages. The greatest proportion of this wealth consisted of property (39 per cent, or £3.5 trillion) and private pensions (39 per cent, or £3.5 trillion). Financial wealth and physical wealth each contributed 11 per cent (or £1 trillion each) (see Figure 4.2).

House prices had recently fallen at the time of the WAS and so we might expect housing wealth to have declined as a proportion of all

Figure 4.2: Breakdown of net wealth in Great Britain (%)

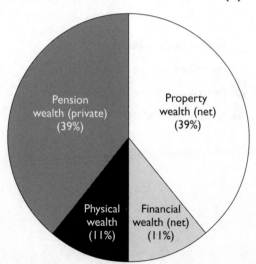

Source: Wealth and Assets Survey 2006-08 [Figure 2.1], Office for National Statistics

wealth. However, share prices had also declined and this will have a knock-on effect on financial and pension wealth. The exact impact of these changes on the relative size of housing and other types of wealth is not clear at present, and it will be interesting to see whether or not the size of the overall pie changes in forthcoming years as well as whether or not the sizes of different slices of the pie will change.

Figure 4.3 illustrates the distribution of different types of wealth by dividing the population into 10 equal groups by size (deciles) and showing the level of wealth of each decile. This clearly highlights huge inequalities between the bottom deciles and the very top decile. The top decile clearly leaps away from the rest in terms of their level of wealth and this is partly why we have decided to concentrate on this group when focusing further on the 'rich' in the next chapter.

We saw, above, that the distribution of different kinds of wealth varies. We also argued, in Chapters One and Three, that different types of wealth play different roles in people's lives so it is worth considering each of the four types of wealth in a little more detail.

Financial wealth is the most unequally distributed of the four types of wealth in the WAS. But it is also a very widely owned type of wealth. In 2006–08, 98 per cent of households had net financial wealth – either positive balances, if assets were greater than liabilities (75 per cent), or negative balances, if liabilities were greater than assets (23 per cent). In 2006–08, half of the households in Britain owned 1 per cent of net

Figure 4.3: Breakdown of wealth in Great Britain, by decile

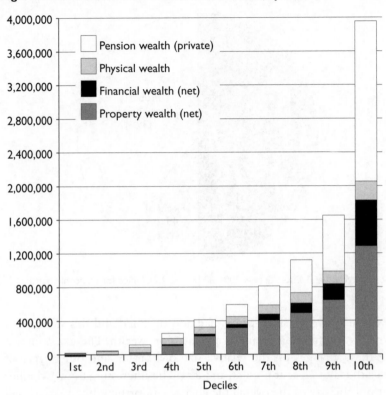

Source: Wealth and Assets Survey 2006–08 [Figure 2.2], Office for National Statistics

financial wealth, while the wealthiest 20 per cent owned 84 per cent of net financial wealth.

Table 4.1 shows the proportion of households with formal financial assets in 2006–08. Current accounts were very widespread although not universal, and people may have very little money in them that could be counted as 'savings'. Apart from this, the most widespread formal financial asset in 2006–08 was a savings account, held by 62 per cent of households with an average (mean) of about £18,000 in each account. Individual Savings Accounts (ISAs) were also fairly widespread – held by 42 per cent of households with an average of nearly £15,000 in each. A quarter of the population had National Savings certificates or bonds (with £6,400 on average in these) and 15 per cent held UK shares (with £24,000 on average in these). Other formal financial assets were much less common but account for a large proportion of assets.

Table 4.1: Proportion of households with formal financial assets and mean amounts in each, 2006–08

Great Britain	% with each product	Mean amount (£)
Current accounts including overdrafts	92.2	2,400
Current accounts excluding overdrafts	84.7	2,900
Savings accounts	61.9	18,300
ISAs[a]	41.7	14,900
Cash ISAs	35.8	13,100
Stocks and shares ISAs	10.1	27,800
National Savings certificates and bonds[b]	23.7	6,400
UK shares	14.9	24,000
Insurance products[c]	10.5	33,000
Fixed term bonds	8.3	40,300
PEPs[d]	7.3	25,200
Employee shares and share options	7.3	30,900
Unit/Investment trusts	5.9	41,900
Overseas shares	1.9	29,700
UK bonds/gilts	1.1	32,800
Overseas bonds/gilts	0.1	17,300
Other formal financial assets	0.4	111,200

[a] Note that households may have both cash ISAs and stocks and shares ISAs, so total is not the sum of cash plus stocks and shares ISAs.

[b] Including Premium Bonds.

[c] Excluding life insurance policies which only pay out in the event of death.

[d] Personal Equity Plans.

Source: Wealth and Assets Survey 2006–08, Office for National Statistics

For example, those who had fixed-term bonds and/or unit/investment trusts had at least £40,000 in them.

As we have seen from Table 4.1, ISAs have proved to be popular. Figure 4.4 shows that by 2009/10 there were around 15 million accounts holding around £45 billion of money in savings and investments. The amount saved grew particularly quickly between 2004/05 and 2008/09.

The WAS (ONS, 2009) also found that 10 per cent of households had informal financial assets (that is, money saved in cash at home, money given to someone to look after or money paid into an informal savings and loan club) worth £250 or more in 2006–08. Some children also held financial assets; half of children had assets in their names, while most children born since 1 September 2002 had Child Trust Funds.

Private pension wealth is the next most unequally distributed form of wealth and it is also a non-liquid form of wealth. The WAS 2006–08

Figure 4.4: Numbers of ISAs and amounts invested, 1999–2009

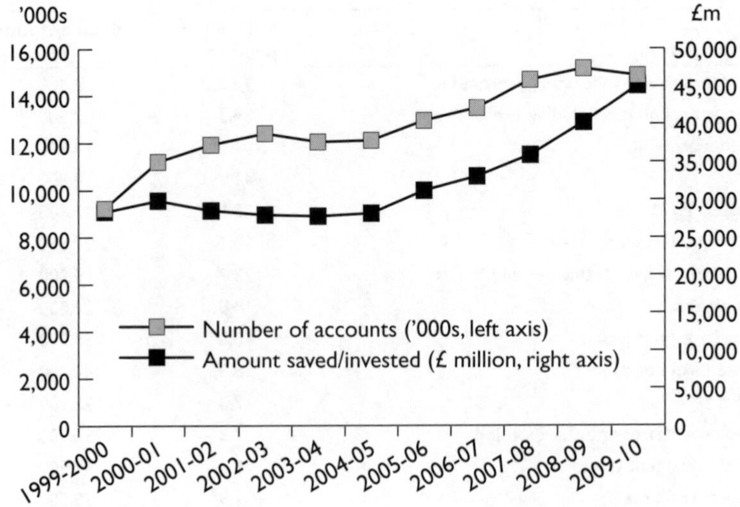

Source: National Statistics, ISAs(www.hmrc.gov.uk/stats/isa/table9-4-all-years.xls)

found that 40 per cent of men and 32 per cent of women were contributing to some type of private (that is, personal or occupational) pension at the time of the survey. As we might expect, rates of current private pension membership were highest for those aged 35–64 with 60 per cent for men in this age group being members and just over 50 per cent of women (ONS, 2009). Once again not surprisingly, mean current pension wealth among those who were contributing was highest in the 55-64 age group. Men in this age group who were contributing to a pension had a mean level of pension wealth in their current pension schemes of £203,600. Women in this age group had much less wealth – with a mean of £130,900. Those aged 16–24 were much less likely to have been contributing to a private pension – only 11 per cent were doing so in 2006–08. However, this is not particularly surprising given that some of this group would still have been in full-time education.

As we can see from Figure 4.5, numbers in *occupational* pensions peaked in the late 1960s, and, despite government exhortation to increase private pensions since 1979 onwards, have been declining subsequently. Moreover most of the decline has been in the private sector, with such pensions remaining strong in the public sector.

There has also been no growth in the numbers of people of working age with personal pensions (see Figure 4.6).

Figure 4.5: Active members of occupational pension schemes, 1953–2008 (millions)

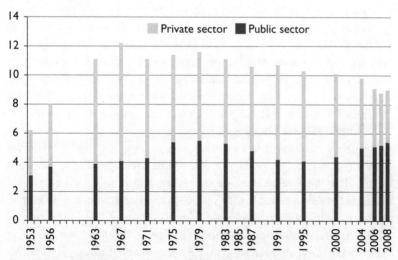

Source: Occupational Pension Schemes Survey, Office for National Statistics

Figure 4.6: Working-age membership of personal pension schemes, by sex, 1996/97–2005/06 (%)

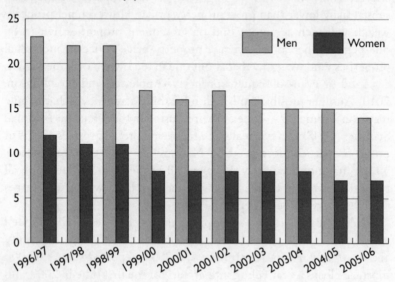

Source: Family Resources Survey

In looking at these figures for personal and occupational pension schemes, we should also remember that many people have entitlements to state pensions. This includes rights to a basic, flat-rate pension, and to an earnings-related component comprising elements of the State Earnings-Related Pension Scheme (SERPS), the State Second Pension and the earlier Graduated Retirement Benefit. Since it is possible to contract out of these state additional pensions, for those without non-state pensions they may well have entitlements to a state additional pension. The value of these pensions has certainly declined over time following legislative changes to reduce their generosity.

While the average level of state pension wealth might be lower than for non-state pensions, the very wide coverage of state pensions means that their value may be quite important and particularly for lower-income households. ONS (2008) calculated that the *median* state pension wealth of men aged 50–54 (in 2002) was £41,000, compared with a median non-state pension wealth of £75,000.

As we have just seen, apart from physical wealth, housing is the most equally distributed type of wealth. According to the ONS (2009), the *mean* net (that is, housing equity after mortgages are taken into account) property wealth for owner-occupiers was £205,500 in 2006–08. The *median* net property wealth was £150,000 or less while a quarter of property-owning households had net property wealth of £85,000 or less (ONS, 2009). These figures seem rather high given that the average (gross) property price was £180,000 in 2007 (Appleyard and Rowlingson, 2010). We might expect *net* property wealth to be substantially lower than gross property prices. However, net property wealth will include any second or subsequent properties owned by one person whereas the average property price concerns individual properties. And we know that about one in ten owner-occupiers owns a second or even subsequent property (Appleyard and Rowlingson, 2010). Another possible explanation for this discrepancy is that people may over-estimate the value of their housing in the Office for National Statistics (ONS) survey. Finally, the figures on property prices are based on all properties mortgaged by Nationwide in a particular period, which may not accurately represent all properties sold, let alone all properties lived in. Limitations with data on both wealth and prices therefore need to be remembered.

While housing wealth is widespread, the recent recession has also led to an increase in negative housing wealth in terms of negative equity and mortgage arrears. MacInnes et al (2009) reported some 200,000 mortgage loans a year falling into arrears for the first time in 2009, and some 400,000 in arrears on the latest statistics. They also reported that there were 24,000 mortgage repossessions in the first half of 2009, a six-fold increase since the first half of 2004. While this is a large increase on 2004, the figure is lower than some had predicted due to record low interest rates that have helped some borrowers to keep up with their mortgage repayments, and a number of government initiatives to help home owners avoid repossession. The government has also introduced a pre-action protocol, under which the courts can grant a repossession order only if all alternative measures to keep people in their homes have failed. And the government has also generally called on lenders to exercise forbearance with those in arrears. While this is clearly to the benefit of struggling home owners, no such measures have been put in place in relation to those struggling to pay their rent to help them avoid eviction. In fact, recent changes to reduce the amount paid out in Housing Benefit are expected to lead to mass evictions from 2011 onwards in parts of London where rents are high. Owner-occupation is, therefore, clearly advantaged over renting.

Mortgages are, of course, only one source of borrowing, and mortgage arrears are only one source of problem debt. The WAS (ONS, 2009) found that nearly half of households (48 per cent) owed money in non-mortgage borrowing, with half of these owing £2,700 or less. In terms of arrears, 10 per cent of households had fallen behind with payments on one or more household commitments, rising to 17 per cent of those with any non-mortgage borrowing commitments. This varied considerably by socioeconomic status, with households comprising lone parents with dependent children, and households in which the head of household was unemployed or looking after the family home, among those most at risk of having done so.

If we compare the UK with the rest of Europe in terms of rates of home ownership, the UK appears mid table with Germany, Sweden and the Czech Republic having the lowest rates and Estonia, Lithuania and Hungary having the highest (Figure 4.7).

The most equally distributed kind of wealth is physical wealth which, according to the WAS, is made up of the contents of the main residence, the contents of any additional property which the household owns, collectables, valuables, vehicles and personalised number plates. Virtually everyone has some physical wealth, with the median value in 2006–08 being £29,900. Much of this comprised the household contents of people's main residence, which had a median value of £25,000. Not everyone, however, owns collectables or valuables, and in 2006–08, only 13 per cent of households said they had any of these, with a mean value – for those who had them – at £12,900. The median value, however, was considerably lower – at £5,000 – suggesting that a few people

Figure 4.7: Home ownership rate (%) in European countries

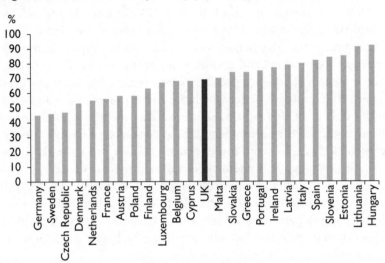

Source: Doling and Ronald (2010a)

have collectables and valuables worth considerably more than most people. As we might expect, vehicle ownership was widespread, with 73 per cent of households owning one or more cars in 2006–08. The mean value of vehicles for households owning cars, vans or motorbikes was £8,000 and the median value was £5,000. A quarter of vehicle owners, however, valued these assets at £2,000 or less.

Combining income and assets

In general, people with high levels of assets also have high incomes, but this relationship is not as close as one might expect because of the role that age plays in relation to both income and wealth (see the next section of this chapter). For example, some young/middle-aged people are on very high levels of income but have not (yet) accumulated large amounts of wealth. Equally, some much older people may be on very low pension incomes but have substantial amounts of wealth. We explore the links between income and assets here, albeit hampered by lack of data due to problems collecting income data on the WAS (see Chapter Three).

The link between income and assets is not merely a matter of academic interest but plays a significant role in relation to who 'the wealthy' are and how policy might treat them. In the debate about Council Tax, for example, the existence of older people living in large houses but on low incomes (and therefore potentially unable to afford Council Tax) has been used to argue that the tax is unfair. But Orton (2006) has analysed data on income and housing assets to argue that low-income households in high value properties are 'exceptional' (2006, p 9). He defined low income as income below the poverty line (less than 60 per cent of median income) and found that households with poverty-level incomes in the three highest Council Tax bands (F, G and H) represented only 0.7 per cent of all households (about 180,000 households). Sodha (2005) used the same income measure but a different measure of housing assets to argue that a small but significant minority of those who were retired were income poor, asset rich. For example, she found that, of those who were retired, 4.2 per cent had an income below 60 per cent of the median and owned housing equity of over £100,000. A further 6 per cent of pensioners had the same level of housing assets and were not in poverty but had an income below Age Concern's 'Modest but Adequate' standard.

Analysis of the FRS (2003/04) in Figure 4.8 shows, in relation to financial savings, that income and assets were closely linked with those on high incomes having higher levels of saving also (for example, nearly a third of those with incomes over £1,000 per week also had savings of over £20,000 in 2003/04), but the analysis also shows that nearly one in ten of these high-income households had no savings at all. At the other end of the income distribution, 8 per cent of those on incomes less than £100 per week had savings of £20,000 or more.

Analysis of the WAS cannot currently include income due to mistakes in collecting data on benefit income, and so we consider the link between *earnings* and wealth and we do, indeed, see a link between annual earnings and level of total wealth – with higher earnings linked to higher wealth, particularly once gross annual earnings exceed a level of £10,000 (see Figure 4.9). However, the link is relatively weak, with a correlation of 0.3 between an individual's gross earnings and their level of household wealth.

The distribution of assets by age, ethnicity and region

The previous section analysed the overall distribution of different types of assets. We now turn to the distribution of assets among different groups of the population. In particular we consider different age groups, ethnic and religious groups and geographical regions. Gender is considered by itself in the next section of the chapter along with issues around the within-household distribution of income.

Figure 4.8: Distribution of savings by total household income

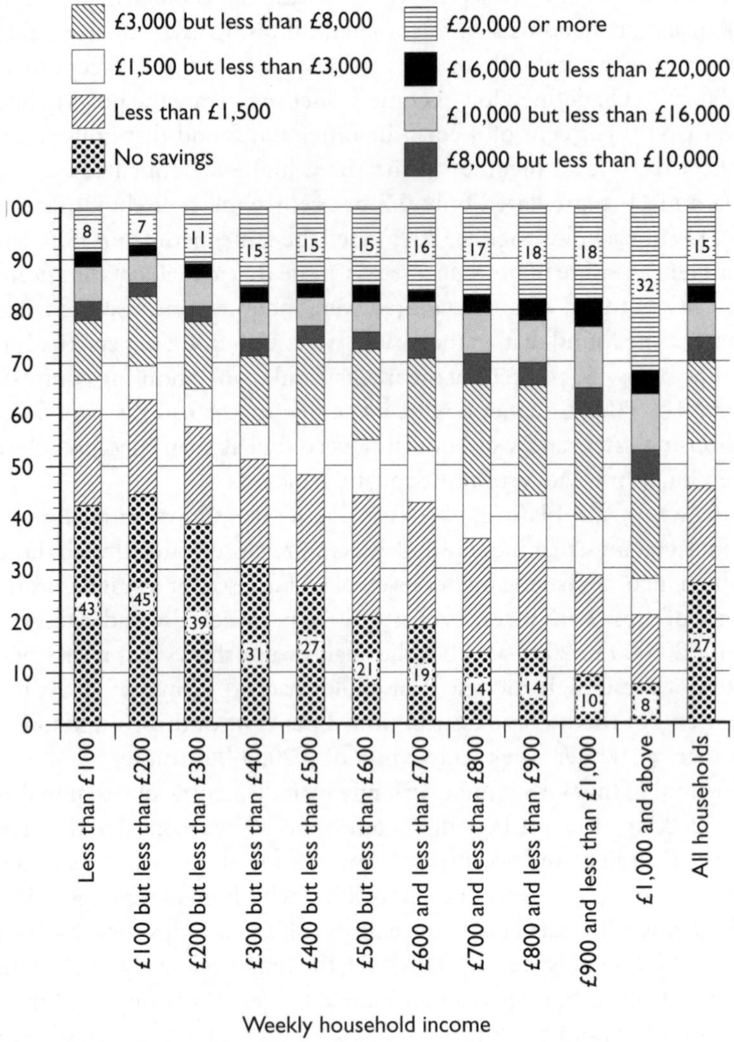
£3,000 but less than £8,000
£1,500 but less than £3,000
Less than £1,500
No savings
£20,000 or more
£16,000 but less than £20,000
£10,000 but less than £16,000
£8,000 but less than £10,000
100
90
80
70
60
50
40
30
20
10
0
8
7
11
15
15
15
16
17
18
18
32
15
43
45
39
31
27
21
19
14
14
10
8
27
Less than £100
£100 but less than £200
£200 but less than £300
£300 but less than £400
£400 but less than £500
£500 but less than £600
£600 and less than £700
£700 and less than £800
£800 and less than £900
£900 and less than £1,000
£1,000 and above
All households
Weekly household income

Source: Family Resources Survey (2003/04)

Age is a key issue in relation to the distribution of wealth because it normally takes people considerable time to accumulate assets. So when considering the distribution of assets it is important to note that asset accumulation is a dynamic process associated with the lifecycle (Modigliani and Brumberg, 1954; Friedman, 1957; Atkinson, 1971). According to general lifecycle theory, young people are typically on low incomes and have not had time to accumulate assets. At this stage

Figure 4.9: Gross annual earnings (individual) and total wealth (household) (log scales)

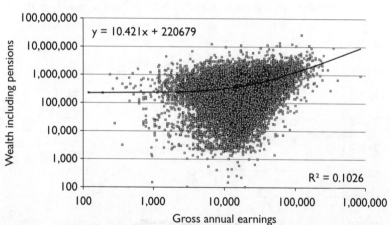

Source: Analysis of the Wealth and Assets Survey

in life, it makes economically rational sense to borrow money, given the likelihood of income increasing in future. Later on, in middle age, incomes are higher and so debts can be repaid and money saved for later life when incomes will fall. In retirement, pension wealth will be used and savings may be drawn on. Lifecycle theory therefore predicts an 'inverted-U' or 'hump' shape to the distribution of assets across someone's life. This means that even if people have the same level of *lifetime* assets, we would expect some inequality in assets, with people in late middle age having higher levels of assets than other groups.

The National Equality Panel (2010) clearly demonstrated a link between age and assets, with median total wealth for those with a 'household reference person' aged 25–34 at £66,000, rising to £416,000 for those aged 55–64, but falling to £172,000 for the oldest group (where pension rights, in particular, are much smaller). This is a difference of £350,000 over an age difference of just 30 years, and reflected lifecycle saving but also other factors such as the timing of house price increases and the relative generosity of private pension schemes, between more and less fortunate cohorts.

Figure 4.10 shows that levels of wealth tended to peak (in 2006–08) among those aged 60–64 (by age of the head of the household). Property wealth reached the highest average levels, followed by private pension wealth, physical wealth (goods and possessions) and net financial wealth (savings minus debts). But financial wealth and physical wealth had much less pronounced relationship with age compared with housing and pension wealth.

Figure 4.10: Median level of assets, by age of household head

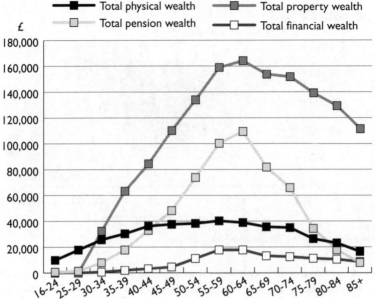

Source: Analysis of the Wealth and Assets Survey

Figure 4.11: Distribution of wealth in Great Britain, by age group

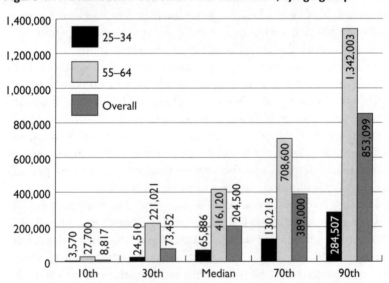

Source: ONS analysis, using Wealth and Assets Survey (2006–08) data for National Equality Panel report

Figure 4.11 also shows differences by age with median wealth among 55- to 64-year-olds at around £416,000 in 2006–08 compared with 'only' around £66,000 for those aged 25–34.

However, the National Equality Panel have also pointed out that there remains considerable inequality *within* every age group. For example, among people aged 55–64, that is, those who are nearing or have reached retirement, a tenth of households still had wealth of less than £28,000, but a tenth had more than £1.3 million (see Figure 4.11). And if we focus on 25- to 34-year-olds, a tenth had wealth of around £3,500, but a tenth had more than £250,000. So the 'lifecycle' explanation for wealth inequality can only explain part of the overall level of wealth inequality.

Banks et al (2005) analysed the English Longitudinal Study of Ageing (ELSA) and also found considerable inequality of wealth among older pre-retired age groups (those between the ages of 50 and 60/65). They found that total assets within this age group were very unequally distributed, with 10 per cent of those in the richest families having at least £1,000,000 of family wealth, whereas the poorest 10 per cent had less than £110,000. They also found that holdings of different assets did not offset each other. For example, older people with low pension assets tended not to have high levels of housing or other assets to compensate; they tended to have lower levels of other assets as well.

Lifecycle/ageing is clearly an issue in relation to assets but so too is generation/cohort. Some generations/cohorts may have benefited from a 'golden age' of wealth accumulation when home and share ownership expanded and house prices and pension pots rose. The baby boom generation (born between 1945 and 1965) has been identified as a cohort that has benefited particularly well (Willetts, 2010) compared with their children and now grandchildren, some of whom will struggle to get a foot on the housing ladder and will have to pay increasing amounts should they wish to go to university. Of course, some of that older generation may make lifetime gifts (see later), and pass on some of their assets to their children to help them, so any intergenerational variations in resources may not be as great as the intragenerational variations.

Age, whether to do with the lifecycle or cohort effects, is not the only source of variation in wealth, of course. Ethnicity and religion are another source although, until the WAS, there was insufficient data to be able to reliably document the extent of inequality between different ethnic and religious groups. And even with the WAS, detailed analysis of ethnicity and religion is slightly hampered by the sample sizes for some sub-groups. Nevertheless, the National Equality Panel

Table 4.2: Median net wealth, by ethnic group of household reference person

Ethnicity of household reference person	Median net wealth (£)
White British	221,000
Indian	204,000
Pakistani	97,000
Other Asian	50,000
Black Caribbean	76,000
Black African	21,000
Bangladeshi	15,000

Source: Wealth and Assets Survey 2006–08

(2010) shows that there are considerable differences in median total wealth between ethnic groups, part although by no means all, of which will reflect differences in age structure. Table 4.2 shows that there was considerable variation in wealth by ethnicity in 2006–08 although the pattern is not a simple White versus BME split. White British households had the greatest level of wealth in 2006–08, on average, at £221,000, but these were followed quite closely by Indian households. Other BME groups were much further behind. The group with the least wealth was Bangladeshi households, with only £15,000 total net wealth on average.

As far as religion goes, sample sizes are, again, relatively small, but the National Equality Panel (2010) showed that the group with the largest median net wealth were Jewish people with £422,000, almost twice as much as the next group, Sikh people (with £229,000). Muslim people were by far the poorest group in terms of wealth, with only £42,000 of net wealth (see Table 4.3).

In the US, Williams (2004) pointed out that there was huge variation in asset holding by ethnicity, with African Americans having much lower levels than Whites. She argued that even when analysis controlled

Table 4.3: Median net wealth, by religion of household reference person

Religion of household reference person	Median net wealth (£)
Jewish	422,000
Sikh	229,000
Christian	223,000
Hindu	206,000
Muslim	42,000
Any religion	161,000
No religion	138,000

Source: Wealth and Assets Survey 2006–08

for income, occupation and education, there were still high levels of asset inequality by ethnicity.

The differences in wealth between ethnic and religious groups were extremely large but so too were the differences by occupational social class. According to the National Equality Panel (2010), while median total wealth for households classed as in routine occupations was £74,000, for those in the top two occupational categories it was more than £450,000 (see Figure 4.12). Mean wealth for the top socioeconomic group was £820,000. Average figures, of course, mask variation within groups and even within socioeconomic groups there are such variations. For example, the wealthiest tenth of the top two groups had total household wealth of more than £1.4 million, although even these groups contain some households with wealth of under £100,000. Part of this variation reflects age differences and lifecycle saving as some of those in the top socioeconomic groups will be relatively young and so have relatively less wealth than others in the same socioeconomic group.

Figure 4.12: Wealth (in £000s), by socioeconomic classification

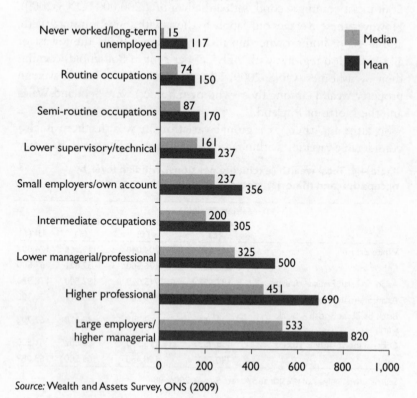

Source: Wealth and Assets Survey, ONS (2009)

Socioeconomic status is linked to ethnicity and so we have controlled for differences in occupational class to consider the particular effect of ethnicity on wealth inequality. Table 4.4 shows that 'White British' people in managerial occupations had greater wealth than other ethnic groups in the same positions, but White British people in intermediate and routine non-manual positions had less wealth than Asian or Asian British/Indian groups in these positions. Black or Black British/Black Caribbean people had considerably lower levels of wealth than other ethnic groups after controlling for occupation.

Finally in this section we consider variations in wealth holding by region. It will come as no surprise that, according to the WAS, the wealthiest part of Great Britain in terms of total wealth (including private pension wealth) in 2006–08 was the South East of England, with median wealth of £287,900 (ONS, 2009). The North West was the English region with the lowest total median wealth, where half of all households had £168,200 or less (including private pension wealth).

As we might expect, the geographical distribution of net *housing* wealth is even more unequal than wealth more generally. London had the highest property wealth (median of £220,000) in 2006–08, with the South East coming second with a median of £200,000 (ONS, 2009). However, these averages only apply to those with some housing wealth, and levels of home ownership in London are actually the lowest of all the English regions, with 'only' 57 per cent of households owning their own homes (ONS, 2009). The regions with the lowest average property wealth (among those who own homes) were Scotland, Wales and the North of England.

So although there is regional variation in wealth, there is also considerable variation within regions and localities. The South East may

Table 4.4: Total wealth (excluding pensions), median level, by occupation and minority status

	Managerial occupations (£)	Intermediate (£)	Routine (£)	All (£)
White British	248,460	204,040	112,966	174,007
Other white	226,320	126,560	32,621	67,500
Asian or Asian British – Indian	187,637	215,520	187,500	178,980
Asian or Asian British – Pakistani	149,280	149,280	90,811	120,300
Black or Black British – Black Caribbean	132,052	62,702	40,070	62,702
Other minority ethnic groups	139,953	115,595	25,802	41,500
Total	240,500	198,460	103,500	163,089

Source: Own analysis of Wealth and Assets Survey 2006–08

Figure 4.13: Breakdown of wealth in Great Britain, by region

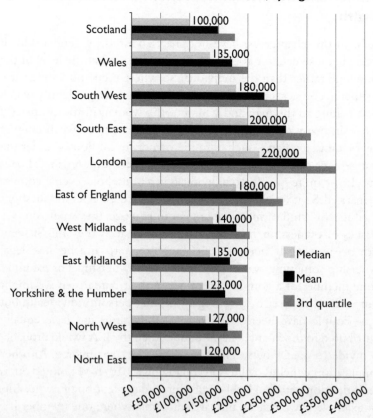

Source: Wealth and Assets Survey 2006–08

be very wealthy overall, but there are pockets of severe deprivation in this region just as there are pockets of 'severe affluence' in the North West. Dorling et al's (2007, p 87) analysis of the geography of poverty and wealth has found that: 'Britain became increasingly segregated and polarised over the past two or three decades of the 20th century', with increasing concentrations of poverty (and wealth) in different local areas, although Levin and Pryce (2011) have argued that there has been no long-term upward trend in spatial housing wealth inequality but that the picture is more cyclical, with rises and falls in spatial inequality. However, they have still argued for more discussion of this and its possible effects on consumption, work incentives and business formation.

Gender and the within-household distribution of wealth

So far in this chapter we have not analysed assets by gender. This is largely because data on assets is normally measured at the level of the household rather than the individual, so where men and women live together in couples it is not always possible to accurately identify which assets belong to the man and which to the woman in the couple. Of course, in many cases the legal ownership of assets between couples may be quite explicit – such as in the ownership of houses under the arrangement of 'tenants in common' rather than 'joint tenants'. Loans may also be quite specific to individuals in a household, even if couples are married. So it would be possible for surveys to ask relevant questions to gather this kind of information, but in practice, they rarely do.

Issues of ownership, however, are not as clear as they might seem both because legal issues are not straightforward and because legal ownership sometimes varies from perceived ownership. For example, if one member of a couple has an ISA in their name then we might assume that this asset belongs, legally, to that person individually, but if the couple have been married for a long time and have equally contributed to the finances in the couple, then the ISA would probably be divided equally between them were they to divorce. Another complication which Rowlingson and Joseph (2010) have pointed out is the distinction between legal ownership and perception of ownership. For example, if we take an unmarried couple where one member has the ISA in their name, the couple may nevertheless consider the asset as a joint asset, whereas in another similar couple they may take a much more individual view of their assets. Once again, surveys could ask relevant questions to tease out both legal ownership and perceptions of ownership, but in practice, they rarely do.

The approach taken by the WAS was to aggregate assets at the level of the household. Presenting results by household includes the implicit assumption that they equally benefit each adult in the household, which, of course, may not be accurate. It is difficult to justify other 'one size fits all' assumptions either – although sensitivity analyses of different assumptions would be interesting to see. In the WAS there were limited questions of relevance to the sharing of assets. One question asked about who had the final say in decision making, and this was asked of the household reference person. The responses were that the 'final say in big financial decisions' was the responsibility of *both* members of the couple in 68 per cent of cases, with either the household reference person or respondent having the final say for 31 per cent of households (there were a few 'other' responses).

Some information was collected about joint current accounts although these do not necessarily contain any assets if people use them purely for ongoing expenditure and empty them every month. Nevertheless, where respondents were part of a couple, and had one or more current accounts, these were declared to be:

- all held jointly – 51 per cent of respondents
- some held jointly – 18 per cent
- none held jointly – 31 per cent.

These figures show a considerable degree of sharing, with half of couples only having joint accounts, but also individuality, with 49 per cent of individuals within couples having at least one current account that was not held jointly with their partner. Last, around three in ten had current accounts that included no sharing with their partner. Incidentally, and reassuringly, there was a very strong degree of congruence between the responses given by respondents and their partners in terms of the number of jointly held currently accounts.

Although it is difficult to analyse the distribution of assets within couples by gender, it is possible to compare the circumstances of men and women each living in single-person households (households without children or any other members), and Table 4.5 shows key results for these kinds of families. The picture is not entirely clear. The *mean* level of single men's wealth exceeded that of single women, but the *median* wealth of single women was greater. While this might suggest that single men's wealth is more concentrated among a relatively few men compared with single women, in fact the top 30 per cent of single women had (slightly) higher wealth than the top 30 per cent of men. Given the gradient within couples – men tending to be of a higher

Table 4.5: Total wealth, by gender and age, for single-person households

	Bottom 30%	Median	Mean	Top 30%
Over SPA[a]				
Single women (£)	58,846	182,000	255,586	304,480
Single men (£)	49,550	157,528	311,074	289,660
Under SPA				
Single women (£)	24,678	100,733	206,032	228,743
Single men (£)	22,020	94,081	226,301	211,188

[a] State pension age

Source: ONS analysis of Wealth and Assets Survey (2006–08) data for National Equality Panel report.

income than their partners – it is also unwise to regard single people as representative of all people. For instance, single women often have higher earnings than women in couples, but the reverse is generally true for men. Bernard (1982) goes so far as to label single women as the 'cream of the crop' and single men as the 'bottom of the barrel'.

Other datasets have also been used to explore the distribution of assets by gender, although they are all limited. Westaway and McKay (2007) analysed data from the BHPS and found that women overall were more likely than men to have savings accounts but their savings were worth less on average. The BHPS could not identify, however, if women in couples had access to their partner's savings and so benefited from them even if they did not legally own them. As far as housing wealth is concerned, most datasets do not tell us whether mortgages are in joint or sole names and whether the equity in the home is considered shared at all.

Unlike housing assets and some financial savings products, private pensions have to be held individually. Couples cannot jointly hold a pension although one member can receive a dependant's or widow/er's benefits, and people may see the asset as a joint one. When married couples divorce, private pension wealth is considered as part of the pot for division and so such wealth is considered joint in many cases even if it is held individually. There has been considerable research into gender and pensions (see Ginn, 2003, for an overview) which has highlighted the fact that men have built up far greater entitlements to state and private pensions than women due to their more prominent role in the labour market. Women have tended to gain access to private pension entitlements through their status as wives. However, women's participation in paid work is increasing, and the 'pension gap' between men and women is correspondingly decreasing, at least as far as the state pension is concerned. The Government Actuary's Department has estimated that by 2025, over 80 per cent of women reaching state pension age will be entitled to a full basic state pension, a slightly *higher* figure than for men (DWP, 2005). However, there are still differences in terms of private pensions, with working-age men more likely to be contributing to a private pension than working-age women (46 per cent compared with 38 per cent), and men's level of contribution is higher. So men are likely to continue to have higher incomes in retirement than women (DWP, 2005).

One of the reasons why gender differences in pension wealth persist appears to be that traditional views of gender roles are still widespread in relation to men being seen as the main (if not the only) breadwinner and women taking the main responsibility for caring for children and other family members (DWP, 2005). This is backed up by Westaway and McKay (2007), who found that women start saving into pensions in the same way as men do, but end up with much smaller pension pots, presumably due to taking time out of the labour market to look after children.

As mentioned above, assets and debts may be held in individual names during marriage but when marriages end divorce law assumes that assets and debts are shared equally unless other factors are relevant (such as the marriage being very short, one partner bringing substantial levels of assets or debts to the marriage and the care of children requiring one partner to have a greater share of any assets). Westaway and McKay (2007) found that women who divorce suffer disproportionately compared with men in terms of savings and debts. However, this study did not analyse housing assets, and Warren et al (2001) found that single women who were separated or divorced had higher levels of housing wealth than single men who were separated or divorced.

Surprisingly, perhaps, Westaway and McKay (2007) also found that women who experience cohabitation breakdown suffer even more than women who go through divorce (and more than men who go through cohabitation breakdown), perhaps suggesting that marriage provides some financial 'protection' for women, compared with cohabitation. But Warren et al (2001) show clearly that women with the highest levels of assets are those who have never been married. Those with the lowest levels are lone parents. So partnerships and children seem detrimental to women's finances. Having said this, there is likely to be a 'selection effect' here: women with the greatest opportunities to accumulate wealth are less likely to partner and/or have children.

The issue of pension sharing on divorce has become increasingly important, with Pension Sharing Orders introduced in 2000 in England and Wales (Price, 2003). However, there appear to have been very few Pension Sharing Orders. Ministry of Justice (2009, p 97) figures show that in 2008 there were 10,417 Pension Sharing Orders made, less than 10 per cent of the 123,000 divorces in the same year. Of course many couples will have no private pension wealth to split, others may have similar amounts and others may trade off housing wealth for pension wealth, as women appeared to do before Pension Sharing Orders were introduced (Arthur and Lewis, 2000). But why this is the case, and whether or not it is in their best interests, is not clear. These provisions only apply, of course, to married couples (or civil partners). Cohabiting couples are not covered in pension sharing legislation, nor indeed do they have the same protection afforded to married couples when dividing other forms of wealth. The Law Commission (2007) had recommended that certain cohabiting couples might be treated the same as married couples in law, but the Labour government at the time did nothing about this, and it seems unlikely that any Conservative (-led) government would introduce a measure which would seem to 'downgrade' marriage.

Debts may also be divided on relationship breakdown, and previous research by Kempson (2002) has shown a correlation between relationship breakdown and being in arrears, a phenomenon sometimes referred to as STDs (sexually transmitted debts). Furthermore, the study showed that debt problems were much greater for women after separation than they were for men. For example, 18 per cent of divorced women and 23 per cent of separated women were in arrears, compared to 12 per cent and 16 per cent of men respectively. Bull (1993) argued that responsibility for joint debts may be left with women following relationship breakdown because they are more likely to stay in the same home while the male partner leaves. This makes it easier for the man to avoid creditors. But women are also more likely to have children to look after and this may place additional strains on their budgets which lead to debt.

Relationship breakdown is common, of course, but so is re-partnering and remarriage. Re-partnered couples may bring assets and/or debts to their new relationship and this may affect how they share and make decisions about finance. It may also affect views about marriage. Burgoyne and Morison (1997) carried out semi-structured interviews with 20 re-partnered couples (15 were married and five cohabiting). The study found that these couples were more likely to keep their money separate than those in first marriages. Partly, this was a response to negative experiences of sharing in first marriages (for example, through having a spendthrift or controlling partner or having difficulties agreeing on a division of assets when the relationship ended). For those with children from previous relationships, the desire to keep finances separate was particularly pronounced in relation to future bequests. Vogler's quantitative analysis (2009) found that there was a difference between re-partnered couples depending on whether or not they were married. Remarried couples were more likely to jointly manage their money than re-partnered couples who were cohabiting.

Another key turning point in financial trajectories is childbirth (Westaway and McKay, 2007), with mothers typically working part time and so reducing their ability to contribute to savings, mortgages and private pensions while fathers become even more likely to do so.

As couples get older and accumulate assets, the question of wills and bequests becomes important. The extent of agreement over wills and bequests may signal the strength of the relationship but may be more difficult in couples with children from previous relationships. At present, the law on intestacy makes a major distinction between married/civil partnered couples and cohabiting couples although a Law Commission (2009) consultation document had suggested reform to give couples, who have cohabited for some time, the same rights as married couples. And this appears to be supported by public attitudes to intestacy, with the majority of the population agreeing that cohabitants should be included on an intestacy depending on the length of commitment and the existence of children from the relationship (Humphrey et al, 2010). The public were divided, however, about whether a second spouse should be favoured if the deceased had left children from a former marriage. And once again, whether the law will be changed to recognise cohabitation more formally in law is not at all certain.

Rowlingson and Joseph (2010) carried out in-depth interviews with 80 members of 40 working-age couples to explore the ownership of, and decision-making issues around assets. They found that 'relative resources' in the couple, and marital status, both seemed important in relation to the distribution of, and decision making about, assets and debts within couples (Rowlingson and Joseph, 2010). Those members of the couple with the higher status job and higher income tended to have a greater share of any assets, particularly in re-partnered cohabiting couples. In couples where the man had the higher income, the couple were more likely to make 'joint' decisions led by him. Where women had jobs in higher socioeconomic positions than their partners, it was the woman who tended to take the lead, or the couple would make more independent decisions. Marital status also appeared to be linked to different models of decision making, with cohabiting couples acting more independently than married couples. Remarried couples seemed particularly likely to employ joint and equal decision-making approaches.

Inheritance and unearned wealth

In Chapter Three we made a distinction between wealth accumulated as a result of saving earnings and wealth accumulated through inheritance and lifetime gifts. A third source of wealth is that which is accumulated through increases in stock market or house price values. This may be due to careful and clever investment decisions or purely due to pure good luck. While it is possible, in theory, to distinguish between these different sources of wealth it is not so easy, in practice, to identify them empirically. The WAS should help us to do this, over time, as we measure rises and falls in wealth and are able to judge the extent to which these are due to different factors. This chapter concentrates on inheritance and lifetime gifts as a source of wealth. As argued in Chapter Two, inheritance and lifetime gifts are important sources of wealth for a small group of people who owe much of their own wealth to 'luck of birth' rather than hard work.

Rowlingson and McKay's (2005) analysis of the Attitudes to Inheritance survey found that 46 per cent of the public had received at least one inheritance at some point in their lives. But some of these were of no or little monetary value. Only one in twenty of the public had inherited £50,000 or more. And a further one in ten had inherited between £10,000 and £50,000. It might seem surprising that the number of people who have received substantial inheritances is still small because the expansion of home ownership led some commentators in the 1980s to argue that 'millions of working people' would start to inherit huge capital sums (Saunders, 1986). However, analysis of Inland Revenue data by Holmans (1997b) suggested that the number of estates including housing assets had not increased but actually declined between 1969-70 (when there were 149,592) and 1992-93 (when there were 142,446). This suggested that there had probably been no or little increase in the scale of housing inheritance over the last 25 years (Hamnett, 1997).

So why has the increase in home ownership not yet turned Britain into a 'nation of inheritors'? One explanation is that the large cohort of people who became home owners in the 1980s are not yet dying in large numbers and passing on their wealth to future generations. At present, owner-occupation is highest among those in their 40s, 50s and early 60s. As these people age it seems probably that housing wealth will become more concentrated among older households (Holmans, 2008). But the life expectancy of this cohort is increasingly being revised upwards, and so it seems that it will take some time before this ends up in inheritance: 'Improving life expectancy ... means that the projected number of deaths among older home-owners ... is now substantially lower than foreseen in studies made more than a decade ago' (p 3). Holmans' conclusion is that: 'the UK is unlikely to become a nation of inheritors in the foreseeable future' (2008, p 3).

Alongside these cohort and ageing effects, another reason why Britain is not yet a 'nation of inheritors' may be related to people's attitudes to inheritance that appear to be changing. Rowlingson and McKay (2005) found broad support for the idea of leaving bequests but also a view that people should not scrimp and scrape to do so. The 'baby boom' generation (those in their 50s and 60s) seemed particularly keen to make use of their assets during their own lifetime although they also wished to pass something on to the next generation when they died. So, rather than feel a duty towards passing on the proceeds of their good fortune, as Willetts (2010) suggests they should, older people may be more inclined to use up their assets during their own lifetime compared with previous generations, and there may therefore be less to pass on when they die.

Rowlingson and McKay (2005) found that owner-occupiers did not see their homes primarily as potential bequests, and a quarter of current or former owner-occupiers had withdrawn equity at some point in one way or another. The most common method was to borrow against the value of the home (for example, through re-mortgaging), followed closely by trading down. The main reasons for withdrawing equity were to carry out property repairs, pay bills/debts and buy essential items. There were relatively few examples of people releasing equity to spend the money on non-essentials (see also Parkinson et al, 2009; Smith et al, 2009).

Of course, as we shall see, some older people give some of their assets away to their children during their lifetime (Overton, 2010), which is why lifetime gifts also need to be considered.

But does inheritance increase wealth inequality more generally? Research on this subject goes back a long way. For example, Wedgwood (1929) estimated that one third of the wealthy owed their position entirely to inheritance. Harbury and Hitchens (1979) found that 67 per cent of the variance in a son's estate was explained by the variance in a father's estate. These studies are quite old now and do not necessarily prove that inherited wealth is a direct source of inequality because wealthy fathers may pass on other advantages in life which account for their sons' later wealth. Nevertheless, theoretical models by Wilhelm (1997) and empirical work by Menchik (1979) support the conclusion that inheritance is a major source of inequality. And other studies (see, for example, Atkinson, 1971) have also found that a pure lifecycle model (that is, with no bequests) is unable to explain the upper tail of the wealth distribution. Hence bequests appear to increase inequality and represent what Lansley (2006) has called a 'cycle of privilege'.

Further evidence of the role of inherited wealth on people's life chances comes from a survey of people's experiences of receiving inheritance(s) (Rowlingson and McKay, 2005). It found strong links between inheritance and social class. Those in middle-class occupations were not only more likely to have received an inheritance, but they also had most experience of the larger-valued inheritances. Among social classes A and B (senior and middle-ranking professionals), around one in ten had received an inheritance worth at least £50,000 (at 2004

Figure 4.14: Receipt of different real amounts in an inheritance, by social class

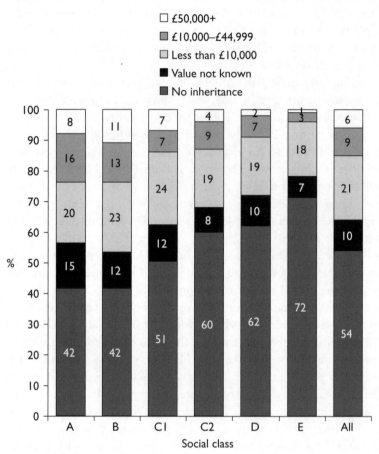

prices). This compares with only 1 or 2 per cent among those in classes D and E. Regression analysis showed that social class was an important factor even after taking into account other factors such as age, tenure and family composition. People from professional occupations were therefore more likely to receive an inheritance, particularly one of great value (see Figure 4.14).

But even a relatively small inheritance may seem a large amount to someone who has no or very little existing wealth. Wolff (2002), for example, has explored this issue using data from the US Survey of Consumer Finances that includes inheritances in the US from 1989 to 1998. He found that richer households did receive greater inheritances and other wealth transfers than poorer households. But, as a proportion of their current asset levels, wealth transfers were actually greater for poorer households than rich ones. Analysis of the 2004 Joseph Rowntree Foundation survey, quoted in Appleyard and Rowlingson (2010), also showed that while those in the professional classes were more likely than other social groups to have received an inheritance, this inherited wealth was more likely, than for other occupational groups, to account for less than 10 per cent of their current wealth stocks (the value of any properties they owned and any financial assets they had, for example, savings, stocks and shares). However, it was unusual for any group to have inherited wealth accounting for more than half of their current stock of wealth, with little real difference between social classes in this respect.

A small inheritance may be a large percentage of someone's current stock of wealth if they have no wealth at all or very little. But it still may make little difference to them because, as Wolff (2002) himself argues, poorer people may be more likely to spend their small inheritances while richer people may be more likely to add them to their current stock of assets. The Attitudes to Inheritance survey data did indeed suggest that those in the higher social classes were more likely to save or invest their inheritances, therefore adding to their stock of wealth (Rowlingson and McKay, 2005).

Inheritance is not the only way that parents can transfer wealth to their children. Lifetime gifts are another mechanism for wealth transfer across generations. And Willetts (2010), for one, has argued that the baby boom generation have a duty to pass on resources to their offspring to compensate them for growing up in a less favourable economic

Table 4.6: Receipt of gifts worth £500 or more (%), by social class

	AB	CI	C2	DE	All
Cash to spend	15	10	6	4	9
Wedding or large social occasion	15	9	6	4	9
Buying a car	11	9	5	3	7
Buying/maintaining property	13	6	4	2	6
Education	9	8	2	1	5
Paying for driving lessons	5	6	3	*	4
Birth of children	6	5	4	3	4
Paying off debts	2	3	3	3	3
Paying for holiday/other luxuries	3	6	2	1	3
General living expenses	3	5	1	3	3
Starting a business	1	1	1	0	1
Other type of gift	3	3	1	1	2
Cannot remember	1	1	*	2	1
Unweighted base	*527*	*537*	*409*	*524*	*2,008*

time. Rowlingson and McKay (2005) collected data on the giving and receiving of lifetime gifts valued at £500 or more. They found that close to one third (31 per cent) of the general public, of all ages, had received gifts worth at least £500 at one point or another (see Table 4.6). Buying or maintaining a property was the fourth most common use of such gifts overall, followed by education. Table 4.6 also shows variation in receipt of gifts by social class, with those in the professional classes (AB) much more likely to receive such gifts than others. For example, 13 per cent of those in social classes AB had received a lifetime gift to help them buy or maintain property compared with only 3 per cent of those in social classes DE (unskilled and semi-skilled manual workers) and C2 (skilled manual workers).

The total *amount* received in lifetime gifts also varied greatly by social class, with more than a quarter of those in the professional classes having received at least £10,000 at some point compared with only 5 per cent of those in social classes DE and 6 per cent of those in social class C2. It seems, then, that some of the baby boom generation may indeed be giving something back to their children to compensate for the less favourable economic climate than that older generation enjoyed (Willetts, 2010). But not all parents have the resources to pass on significant amounts and such gifts mean, effectively, that some people accumulate wealth not on the basis of hard work, skill or merit, but by virtue of being born to wealthy parents.

Wealth is not just accumulated through inheritance or gifts but also when the value of property, land and shares increases. Such increases may occur through no effort on the part of their owners but simply due to national and international shifts in the housing market and the stock market. It is difficult to argue that the resulting increase in wealth is due to hard work, skill or merit when it is due to changes in markets, although some investors may make intelligent decisions about where to put their money and so perhaps deserve some reward for this. There is also a stream of philosophy called 'luck egalitarianism' which supports the idea that those who benefit from pure luck during their lifetimes have as much right to the rewards from this good fortune as those who benefit from hard work, and so on (Cohen, 1989; Arneson, 1989; Dworkin, 2000). Presumably, then, those who suffer misfortune and bad luck deserve no support to cushion them from the effects of this?

Conclusions

The distribution of wealth in 2006–08 was highly unequal, with the top 10 per cent owning 44 per cent of all wealth and the bottom 10 per cent owning only 1 per cent of all wealth. Given that these figures are derived from a voluntary survey in which the wealthiest people are less likely to take part, these figures are probably an under-estimate of the extent of wealth inequality. Even so, the distribution of wealth was far more unequal than the distribution of income.

Financial wealth was the most unequally distributed form of wealth, with the wealthiest 20 per cent owning 84 per cent of net financial wealth. The majority of the population (62 per cent of households) had savings accounts and 42 per cent had ISAs, but the amount that people had in such accounts varied substantially.

Private pension wealth was the next most unequally distributed form of wealth. Only a minority of men and women (40 and 32 per cent respectively) were contributing to a private pension in 2006–08.

Housing wealth is one of the more equally distributed forms of wealth, with the average property wealth among owner-occupiers standing at £205,500 in 2006–08 according to self-valuations. Recent house price falls have led to an increase in negative housing wealth in terms of negative equity and mortgage arrears.

People with high levels of wealth generally have high levels of income also, but some people are 'asset rich, income poor' (particularly some retired people with significant housing, pension and financial wealth but relatively low incomes) and some are 'asset poor, income rich' (particularly young professionals on relatively high incomes but who have not yet accumulated much wealth).

It is sometimes argued that wealth inequality is not a problem because it is due to the fact that it takes time to accumulate wealth, and so there will be wealth inequality between young people who will have little wealth and older people who have had time to accumulate more wealth. There are certainly variations in wealth by age, with older people generally owning more wealth than younger people. But there is also considerable wealth inequality *within* age groups, suggesting that lifecycle factors can explain a limited amount of wealth inequality.

Wealth inequality also varies substantially by ethnicity, religion, social class and region. It is difficult to comment on the distribution of wealth by gender because most datasets do not distinguish, within couples, between *his* wealth and *her* wealth. But it would be possible to ask questions about the legal ownership of assets within couples and the perceptions of ownership within the couple. Marital status seems likely to make some difference to both legal ownership and perceptions of ownership, with married couples more likely to share assets than cohabiting couples. There have been a number of reviews of the treatment of cohabiting couples in relation to assets (on separation and on death of a partner), and these suggest changing the law to recognise long-term cohabitation, but there has been no action on this to date.

In 2004, just under half the population had received one or more inheritances in their lives to date but few (only one in twenty) had received a very substantial amount (£50,000 plus). Professionals were more likely to have received a very substantial inheritance than other occupational groups. They were also much more likely to have received a significant amount in lifetime gifts.

FIVE

The rich, the richer and the richest

Introduction

In recent years there has been growing concern about the concentration of wealth at the top. But, as we saw in Chapter Three, there is no agreement about who is 'rich' or 'wealthy'. Rather than allow this stumbling block to derail any discussion of this group, we use a range of measures in this chapter to investigate three groups. The first group is 'the rich' who we define as the top 10 per cent of the income/asset distribution. The top 10 per cent, however, do not necessarily see themselves as receiving high incomes. let alone as privileged or wealthy or rich, as they are often not aware of how high they are in the wider distribution of income and assets. Indeed, as we saw in Chapter Two, people at the top often place themselves in the middle of the economic distribution (Rowlingson et al, 2010). We define the 'rich' as the top 10 per cent because, as we saw in Chapter Four, this group's income and wealth sets them apart from the rest of society. The distribution of income and assets increases quite considerably at this level, which means that this group has a great deal more economic resources than the rest of society. For example, the top 10 per cent own 100 times more wealth than the bottom 10 per cent, and they own 50 times more than the average (median). And as we shall see in this chapter, it enables them to establish private lifestyles and modes of consumption. This group also has the ability to exclude themselves from some elements of society as they can afford private forms of welfare such as fee-paying schools and private health insurance. This fits in with John Scott's conceptualisation of the privileged (Scott, 1994).

Many of the group we label 'the rich' may not consider themselves wealthy, but the group we label the 'richer' (top 1 per cent) are much more likely to appreciate their economic power and status. This group have pulled away from everyone else in the last decade or so and we therefore consider them on their own as a key 'richer' group. We also consider the top 0.05 per cent, who have also seen their wealth and incomes increase massively in the last 20–30 years – albeit with some limited interruption to this trend during the recession. We therefore look separately at the rich, the richer, and the very richest people living in Britain today.

Table 5.1 shows some of the relevant thresholds to be rich or richer, based on particular definitions of income and of assets. To be in the top 10 per cent by income, a household would need (on average) an income of just under £45,000. To be in the top 1 per cent, a household would need close to £150,000. In terms of assets, households would find themselves in the top 10 per cent if they had more than £250,000 worth of marketable assets (that is, non-pension assets) and the top 1 per cent if they had close to £900,000.

Table 5.1: Thresholds for the rich and the richer, by income and assets

	Income threshold (£)[a]	Asset threshold (£)[b]
Top 10%	44,900	251,611
Top 1%	149,000	895,947

[a] Survey of Personal Incomes 2007–08 (taxable income)
[b] HMRC distribution of personal wealth 2005 (marketable wealth)

The rich

Our analysis of 'the rich' starts with those who are rich in terms of *income*, the top 10 per cent according to our definition. In 2008/09, according to the Family Resources Survey (FRS), entry to the top 10 per cent of incomes required an income of around £750 per week (after housing costs) for a couple. This figure is equivalised – a higher figure would be needed for a larger family to be in the top 10 per cent of incomes (relative to their greater needs), and a smaller figure for a single person. Such an amount, equal to £39,000 per year, would include a number of professional occupational groups such as general practitioners (GPs), dentists, professors, headteachers and so on.

While our main interest is in the 'rich', it is useful to compare them with other income groups in the population which we divide into, and label, the 'upper middle' (those above the median income but not rich, 40 per cent of the population), the 'lower middle' (those below the median income but not poor, 30 per cent of the population) and those in the bottom 20 per cent of the population which equates, approximately, to poverty-level income. Incomes are adjusted for family size, and relate to the income of the family unit – that is, couples and dependent children. Table 5.2 gives some characteristics of these different income groups.

Table 5.2: Characteristics of the rich (higher incomes) (%)

	Bottom half		Top half		
Characteristics	'The poor' bottom 20%	Lower middle 20-50%	Upper middle 50-90%	'The rich' top 10%	All
Female	53	55	49	47	51
Graduates	15	14	31	60	28
Housing tenure					
Outright owner	37	36	30	28	33
Mortgage	21	26	52	62	39
Other (tenants)	42	38	18	10	28
Family type					
Pensioner single	13	20	10	5	13
Pensioner couple	14	18	5	2	10
Couple + children	15	22	30	27	24
Couple no children	12	15	36	53	26
Lone parents	7	6	2	1	4
Single, no kids	40	19	17	13	22
Economic status					
Self-employed	6	7	9	13	8
1-2 adults full time	4	14	41	52	27
1 full time + 1 part time	1	8	18	17	12
Head/spouse aged 60+	29	37	12	4	22
Head/spouse sick or unemployed	26	7	1	*	7
Others	34	27	19	14	24
Has long-standing illness	36	41	23	14	30
White	85	93	94	92	91
Median income (£ per week)	195	370	720	1,565	493
Median age (years)	43	53	45	45	46
Base (unweighted)	8,702	14,030	17,002	3,863	43,597

Source: Own analysis of the 2008/09 Family Resources Survey, using benefit unit income, equivalised.

The analysis is of family units so cannot distinguish between men and women in couples; it is perhaps not surprising that there are only limited differences by gender. Nevertheless, there were slightly fewer women in the rich group (top 10 per cent of incomes) than among the population as a whole in 2008/09 (see Table 5.2).

Table 5.2 also shows that education is strongly linked to income. While just over one quarter (28 per cent) of individuals were qualified to first degree level, this reached as high as 60 per cent among the rich – double the proportion found among the 'upper middle' (the next 40 per cent).

The rich were also the least likely to be tenants and the most likely to be home owners in 2008/09. Only 10 per cent of the rich were renting their accommodation compared with 42 per cent of people on poverty level incomes. The rest of the bottom half of the income distribution had more in common with people in poverty than those above median incomes but not rich. It might seem surprising that outright ownership was more common among those in the bottom income group than among any of the other income groups but this is because income is related to age. Many of those in the lowest income groups will be older people on low incomes. Outright ownership is particularly high among this group and among those with lower than average incomes more generally. The top 10 per cent are more likely to be younger and they are more likely than any other group to have a mortgage (62 per cent compared with 21 per cent of the lowest income group).

This relationship between income and age can be seen, to some extent, in the family types of the different income groups. The rich are much less likely than other groups to include pensioners. Just over half of the top 10 per cent were couples without dependent children. These are likely to be dual-earning couples without children. About a quarter of the rich were couples with children although this particular analysis does not tell us whether such couples are dual-earners.

The rich are much less likely than those in the bottom half of the population to have a long-standing illness. This is likely, again, to be related to age, but is also likely to be related to income. Those on higher incomes are less likely to do work which causes stress and physical injury (such as social care work, construction work and heavy manual work). However, it is probably also the case that those who develop long-standing illness might lose their jobs and so see their income reduce. The relationship between income and health is therefore likely to run in both directions.

People in the bottom 20 per cent were less likely to be White than those above this level, but the rich were no more likely to be White than those on more average incomes.

There was a strong link between being on a high income and employment, and especially full-time employment. Older people tended to be located in the 'lower middle', while the poorest had a relatively higher incidence of the sick and unemployment.

As argued in Chapter Three, higher incomes give access to a different kind of lifestyle than the rest of the population, and in Table 5.3 we show a number of indicators of this, again drawing on the FRS. Almost everyone (92 per cent) in the top tenth has an annual holiday, compared

Table 5.3: Lifestyles of the rich, by income (%) (FRS)

	Bottom half		Top half		
Characteristics	'The poor' bottom 20%	Lower middle 20-50%	Upper middle 50-90%	'The rich' top 10%	All
Have annual holiday	36	48	75	92	63
Money to spend on self	59	66	86	95	78
Live in detached property	17	18	29	44	25

Source: Own analysis of the 2008/09 Family Resources Survey.

with only around one third (36 per cent) of those in the bottom 20 per cent. And virtually all (95 per cent) of the rich have money to spend on themselves compared with 59 per cent in the bottom income quintile. Approaching half (44 per cent) of the top tenth live in a detached property of some kind, compared with one quarter overall and around one sixth (17 per cent) of those in the bottom income quintile.

Of course, this data does not show us how much people spend on their holidays or on themselves or on their homes, and the cost of holidays and homes certainly varies dramatically. Table 5.4 draws on the British Social Attitudes Survey (BSAS) to look at some other examples of 'lifestyle'. The income groups are slightly different than the ones in Table 5.3 because the BSAS measures income in bands. Nevertheless, it shows us that the rich were much more likely to have flown by air in the last year (81 per cent compared with only 28 per cent in the bottom income group). Nearly all of those in the richest group had broadband internet access at home (93 per cent) compared with only 39 per cent in the bottom group. A particularly distinctive

Table 5.4: Lifestyles of the rich, by income (%) (BSAS)

Characteristics	'The poor' bottom 27%	Lower middle 27-54%	Upper middle 54-86%	'The rich' top 14%[a]	All
Flown by air in last year	28	49	66	81	54
Has home access to broadband internet	39	64	85	93	68
Has private health insurance	4	10	25	51	18
Respondent attended a fee-paying school	7	7	10	20	10
Child (if any) attended or attends a fee-paying school	6	9	13	28	12
Unweighted base	*1,037*	*1,030*	*1,219*	*513*	*3,799*

Source: Own analysis of the 2008 British Social Attitudes Survey.

Note: [a] The banded nature of the income question restricts the classifications that are possible.

and important difference between the rich and the rest was their use of private health and private education. Just over half (51 per cent) of the highest income group had private health insurance and, for those with children, over one quarter (28 per cent) were being educated at a private school (or they had older children who received private education in the past). Given the definition of the rich as those who can afford to establish private lifestyles and modes of consumption, this use of private welfare is highly pertinent.

The economic advantages of going to private schools appear to have increased over time, and in particular in terms of success in proportions going on to university. Green et al (2010, Table 1) compare the 1970 and the 1958 birth cohorts and the proportion gaining degrees by the age of 23:

• For the 1958 group, 41 per cent of those from private schools gained a degree, compared with 16 per cent of those from state schools.
• For those born in 1970, 59 per cent of those from private schools gained a degree (+18 percentage points) compared with 19 per cent of those from state schools (+3 points).

To the extent that higher incomes are buying places at fee-paying schools, the prospects of gaining a degree and higher earnings are strong – indeed, in strict financial terms this may be a very good investment (Green et al, 2010).

Having a high income, and using private welfare services, might affect people's wider attitudes, including attitudes towards welfare state provision for those on lower incomes. Besley and Coate (1991) suggested a theoretical model where richer people would tend to opt out of state-provided services, in search of the higher quality they desired in the private sector. This model assumed a uniform level of quality of public services, but a desire for quality based on incomes. The empirical picture is less clear. Costa-Font and Jofre-Bonet (2008) used data from Catalonia in the early 1990s to argue that richer people tended to be more likely to have private health insurance, and that this led to lower levels of support for state provision of health services. However, this study was only in a particular region, in a particular year, and in an area with a long tradition of private healthcare. Using British data from 1991–94, Burchardt and Propper (1999) investigated whether or not there was a separate class – a 'private welfare class' – not using state services and instead only using private welfare. They found that there was indeed a trend towards the rising use of private services but less consistency across different kinds of services in the choice between public and private provision. They found that in 1994, 11 per cent of the sample said that they had been to private school and of those who had ever had children, 12 per cent had sent a child to a private school. These figures are similar to those for 2008. Burchardt and Propper (1999) argued that there was not a private welfare class at that time but it would be interesting to repeat the analysis to see if this picture still held true in data in 2008/09, around 15 years later.

As with holidays, the costs of private education vary considerably as, presumably, do the advantages. Having a child go to Kate Middleton's former school – Marlborough College – cost £29,000 a year for boarders in 2010/11 (£22,000 for day attendance) – far more than many even in our 'rich' group could afford. Other private schools are more affordable to the merely (rather than the super) rich. For example, King Edward's School in Birmingham cost £9,900 for the year 2010/11.

We have seen something of the lifestyles of the rich, but what about their attitudes to state welfare? Table 5.5 shows a number of attitudinal and behavioural differences between different income groups. The data is taken from the BSAS 2008. This has less robust income data than the FRS – respondents select from various categories – but more insightful concepts are measured. The top income group here thought there were far fewer children in poverty than the bottom income group. They estimated that about one in five children were in poverty, whereas the bottom income group estimated the figure was around one in three. The actual figure (using the government's own 60 per cent of median income measure) was about one in four.

The top income group were also much less likely to support redistribution. Only a quarter agreed that the government should spend more on welfare benefits even if taxes had to rise compared with half of those in the bottom income group. And this group also had a much more individualistic approach to welfare, with nearly half saying that responsibility for income in retirement was mainly the individual's rather than the government's (39 per cent) or employers' (12 per cent).

Higher income groups were more likely to state a specific political allegiance than those on lower incomes. They were also more likely to be Conservative supporters – support for the Conservative Party rose from 24 per cent of the 'poor' to reach 42 per cent among the 'rich'.

Table 5.5 also confirms that those in the top income group do not necessarily appreciate how high their income is. Only one in five in this group (22 per cent) thought that they belonged to a high income group, with around one in ten (11 per cent) apparently believing themselves to be on a low income and the majority (67 per cent)

Table 5.5: Personal characteristics of the rich, by income (%)

Characteristics	'The poor' bottom 27%	Lower middle 27-54%	Upper middle 54-86%	'The rich' top 14%[a]	All
Attitudes and views					
Estimated % of children in poverty	33	26	23	18	26
Self-rated income group					
High income	*	2	4	22	5
Middle income	19	45	71	67	52
Low income	80	53	25	11	43
Government should redistribute income from the better off					
Agree	50	42	32	26	39
Disagree	22	30	40	53	34
Government should spend more on welfare benefits, even if taxes have to rise					
Agree	50	39	27	25	36
Disagree	20	32	42	46	34
Responsibility for income in retirement					
Mainly the government	72	61	52	39	58
Mainly employers	8	10	10	12	10
Mainly each person	18	28	36	47	30
Political allegiance					
Conservative	24	29	36	42	32
Labour	33	29	26	27	28
Liberal Democrat	8	8	12	9	9
Others, none, don't know	35	34	26	22	31
Unweighted base	*1,037*	*1,030*	*1,219*	*513*	*3,799*

Source: Own analysis of the 2008 British Social Attitudes Survey.

Note: [a] The banded nature of the income question restricts the classifications that are possible.

thinking they had a middle income (see Chapter Three for a discussion of the 'squeezed middle').

We saw in Chapter Three that Edwards (2002) carried out interviews and focus groups with 'affluent people' (those with earnings between £34,000–£60,000, according to her definition) and the 'rich' (those earning over £80,000), but that few considered themselves to be wealthy:

> "I don't consider myself that well off ... we've got a house worth £850,000 that we bought for £350,000. We've got our eye on a house worth £1.4 million. When I look at the other dads at school I'm probably in the middle."

"I've got a son at boarding school which is astronomically expensive and the responsibility of keeping him there is totally mine because I'm divorced. The pressure is very much on my shoulders to provide and I have to keep a very tight rein on all aspects of the finances."

"We're probably all on pretty good salaries but the more money you have the more you increase your lifestyle so we're living in bigger houses, have bigger mortgages ... everyone's got into that way of life now."

"A million [pounds] is nothing these days. By the time you've bought a couple of cars, been on holiday, treated the relatives ... you're in hock."

"You can't even buy a decent house for one-and-a-half million." (quoted in Edwards, 2002, pp 33-4)

Some of these people appear to be suffering from 'relative deprivation' (Runciman, 1966) whereby they are comparing themselves, unfavourably, with their more affluent peers and so feel less well off than if they compared themselves with the average person or people on lower incomes. Frank (2007, p 43) has also argued that:

> Increased spending at the top of the income distribution has imposed not only psychological costs on families in the middle, but also more tangible costs. In particular, it has raised the cost of achieving goals that most middle-class families regard as basic.

Frank has argued that middle-class families have only managed to keep up with this 'expenditure cascade' or 'consumption arms race' by working longer hours, borrowing more, spending their savings and commuting for longer. This all leads to increased stress for many with relatively high incomes.

We now turn to look at analysis of who is rich, but judged by wealth rather than by income. The Wealth and Assets Survey (WAS) allows us to identify this group and analyse some of their characteristics but it does not, unfortunately, have much data on their lifestyles or attitudes. In Tables 5.6 and 5.7 we examine some of the characteristics of individuals in households with higher and lower levels of wealth. To qualify for the 'rich group' people needed to have wealth of at least £250,000. The average (median) level of wealth of this group was £355,050.

Those in the richest 10 per cent by wealth were much more likely than average to be graduates, and were much more likely to be relatively older than average – with a median age of 58 compared with an overall average of 38. This affirms a strong 'lifecycle' pattern of accumulation of wealth, with those with less wealth tending to be younger than average. By the same token, a high proportion of wealth is represented by property wealth, and so owner-occupiers tended to be found among those with higher levels of wealth.

There were some differences in attitudes between those with higher and lower levels of wealth (see Table 5.7). In particular, close to two thirds (62 per cent) of the wealthiest tenth agreed that they were more savers than spenders. This compared with around one third (33 per cent) of the poorer half.

There were some differences in terms of attitudes towards current living standards compared with choosing to save for retirement. The wealthier groups did lean more towards saving for retirement, rather than having a good standard of living in the present time. Of course the present living standard of the wealthier group may also have been rather more comfortable than average, with enough left over to facilitate saving for retirement.

Table 5.6: Personal characteristics, by wealth (excluding pensions) (%)

Characteristics	Lower half	Upper middle	'Rich' top 10%	All
Wealth	Up to £67,725	£67,726 to £251,355	Over £251,355	All
Median wealth	£34,286	£121,833	£355,050	£67,725
Qualifications (%)				
Graduate	16	23	41	22
Other	58	56	46	56
None	27	20	13	23
Median age (years)	30	45	58	38
Housing tenure (%)				
Outright owner	5	39	62	24
Mortgage	35	58	36	44
Social tenant	35	1	*	18
Private tenant	22	2	2	12
White (%)	84	92	95	88
Live in a detached house (%)	10	39	66	29

Source: Own analysis of Wealth and Assets Survey 2006–08

Table 5.7: Attitudes to money, by wealth (excluding pensions) (%)

Characteristics	Lower half	Upper middle	'Rich' top 10%	All
I am more of a saver than a spender				
Strongly agree	11	21	32	17
Tend to agree	22	30	30	27
Neither/not	26	21	19	21
Tend to disagree	24	19	13	22
Strongly disagree	16	1	1	1
If I had to choose, I would rather have a good standard of living today than save for retirement				
Strongly agree	16	10	6	13
Tend to agree	30	26	17	28
Neither/not	24	28	28	26
Tend to disagree	20	28	36	24
Strongly disagree	6	7	11	7

Source: Own analysis of Wealth and Assets Survey 2006–08

There was a strong association between current wealth, and having received inheritances (see Table 5.8). One in six (17 per cent) of the wealthiest 10 per cent had received an inheritance (of £1,000 or more) in the last five years, and these had a median value of £35,000. By contrast, only five per cent of the least wealthy half had received an inheritance of more than £1,000 and, when they had, the median value was only £5,000.

Going back beyond the last five years, only a quarter (28 per cent) of the wealthiest group had received a significant inheritance – seven times as high a rate as the least wealthy. These figures suggest that inheritance may well have played a role in the accumulation of larger amounts of wealth.

Table 5.8: Inheritance, by current wealth (excluding pensions) (%)

Characteristics	Lower half	Upper middle	'Rich' top 10%	All
Whether has made a will (%)	24	59	81	48
Whether has received an inheritance of £1,000+ in last 5 years (%)	5	10	17	9
Median value of these inheritances (£)	5,000	10,000	35,000	13,500
Before the last 5 years: received a significant inheritance (%)	5	13	28	11

Source: Own analysis of Wealth and Assets Survey 2006–08

Ideally, we would now present data on the top 10 per cent in terms of their combined income and wealth but due to errors in the data collection process, the WAS does not have useable data on income and so we cannot carry out such analysis. Other datasets, which have valid data on income, do not have such valid data on wealth. The second wave of the WAS should provide valid data on income as well as wealth, and so analysis of combined income and wealth portfolios should be possible when the next wave of data is released.

The richer

The top 10 per cent may not necessarily all consider themselves to be on high incomes let alone 'rich', but we have argued that their position in the income and wealth distribution warrants this when we see how this enables them to establish private lifestyles and modes of consumption. But we also accept that there is a smaller group at the top – the top 1 per cent – whose income has pulled even further away from the rest and which enables them to establish highly exclusive lifestyles and modes of consumption. We therefore focus on them here. It is difficult to study the 'top 1 per cent' using sample surveys. There are problems both of under-coverage, and of measurement (see Chapter Three). Many of the richer groups in the population decline to participate in sample surveys, where participation is voluntary. More of the better off may also be self-employed, who have lower rates of cooperation with surveys generally. There are also dangers that the top 1 per cent of any observed responses in any survey may have given inaccurate responses and the data is not reliable. An answer given that appears in the top 1 per cent may be reflecting measurement problems rather than groups with genuinely very high holdings of wealth or very high incomes. High incomes may also be reflecting non-standard sources of earnings, such as bonuses for some employees and business profits for the self-employed, which are probably too specialised to routinely capture well in generalist surveys.

For these reasons, it is common to use top incomes data that are derived from tax records (which are compulsory) rather than voluntary social surveys. In the UK, HMRC produce estimates of the level of top earnings from tax records, which are based on sampling and become known as the Survey of Personal Incomes (see Atkinson, 2007). This may be used to examine those on the highest incomes, including the top 1 per cent. However, a limitation is that the survey only looks at taxable incomes, which covers most but not all incomes (tax-free incomes, such as from National Savings products, are excluded). Any under-reporting (for example, tax evasion) is also not captured by such a system – and would presumably be absent from any other source, too. Income invested in ways that avoid tax is also under-represented in tax records by definition.

The situation of the top 1 per cent is quite distinct from that of those in the next 2–10 per cent, and this group has seen much faster growth in incomes over the late 20th and early 21st centuries. Table 5.9 and Figure 5.1 show that in 1992/93, someone would need an income of just over £60,000 to get into the top 1 per cent, but by 2007/08, this had risen to around £150,000. The incomes of the top 1 per cent grew by some 137 per cent over this time period, compared with growth in median incomes of 61 per cent (see Table 5.9). The growth in the income required to be part of the top 10 per cent was barely faster than the growth of median incomes – at 76 per cent. This indicates that the

Table 5.9: Changes in top and median incomes (%)

Year	Top 1%	Top 10%	Median	Ratio of top 1% to median	Ratio of top 10% to median
1992/93	62,800	25,500	11,500	5.5	2.2
2007/08	149,000	44,900ᵃ	18,500	8.1	2.4
Rate of change	+137%	+76%	+61%		

Source: HMRC analysis of the Survey of Personal Incomes.

Note: ᵃ This is based on taxable income from tax records, and therefore differs from the estimate based on self-reported income in the Family Resources Survey.

Figure 5.1: Incomes at the top from 1992/93 to 2007/08 compared with median incomes

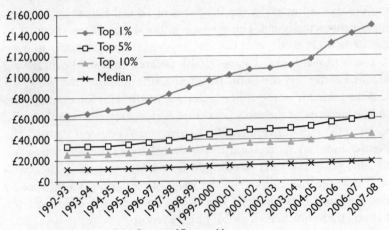

Source: HMRC analysis of the Survey of Personal Incomes

top 1 per cent have moved apart from the remainder of the income distribution. Hence in 1992/93, the top 1 per cent had incomes 5.5 times as great as the median, but this had risen to eight times as much by 2007/08. The ratio of the top 10 per cent to the median increased by a much smaller margin.

This rise in top incomes is a recent phenomenon, reversing earlier trends towards greater equality. Atkinson and Piketty (2007) have carried out research on top income taxpayers during the 20th century, finding that between 1937 and 1949 the shares of each of the top income groups actually declined. Their analysis includes the very highest group – the top 0.05 per cent (the top 10,000). Among this group the drop in incomes was from 2.4 per cent of total after tax income in 1939 to 0.7 per cent. This fall in income at the very top continued until 1969, but by the late 1970s it had reversed and then the momentum increased. By 2000, the share of the top 0.05 per cent had risen to above 2.5 per cent of the total again – higher than it had been in 1937. The share of the income of the top 1 per cent had reached 10 per cent, again its highest since before the Second World War.

Atkinson and Piketty's (2007) analysis also showed an important contrast between the 1980s and 1990s. During the 1980s the top 10 per cent of income taxpayers increased their share of total income by 5 percentage points, with half of this accounted for by the top 1 per cent, and within this the top 0.1 per cent increased their share by 1 percentage point. All of these groups were experiencing an increase in their shares of income, but those at the very top were increasing their shares faster. Hence, inequality was growing *within* those with the highest incomes. By contrast, in the 1990s, the top 1 per cent as a whole increased their share from 8 to 10 per cent of the total (with most of this going to the top 0.1 per cent). But the share of the 'next 9 per cent' actually fell. The increase in the shares of top incomes in the 1990s went to those at the very top, not those quite near to it.

The National Equality Panel (2010) pointed out that the increasing incomes at the very top of the income distribution since the late 1970s also happened in some other countries. In the US, for example, the increasing share of the top 1 per cent was even greater than in the UK, to more than 15 per cent by 2000. However, in France, Germany, the Netherlands and Switzerland, the income shares of the very top fell up to 1980 (as in the UK) but did not then increase again in the 1980s and 1990s: in these countries the share of this group stayed broadly the same during this period. The rise in the incomes of the very top has not, therefore, been a global phenomenon.

Brewer et al (2008) looked at more recent tax–based data in more detail. They compared the four-year period from 1996/97 to 2000/01 with the four-year period from 2000/01 to 2004/05. In the first period, they found that real income growth (after income tax) within the top 10 per cent was faster the nearer the top one looked. However, during the second period, annualised income growth fell to around 1 per cent at most points within the top tenth, and to zero at the cut-off for the top 0.1 per cent. So the increase in the shares of income at the very top seem to have stalled slightly in the most recent years for which we have data. The National Equality Panel (2010) have argued that part of the reason for this is changes in the stock market, and in levels of dividend payments, which will have fallen since 2004. But it also relates to trends in pay for those with the highest incomes. They cite statistics from Income Data Services (IDS) that shows indices of real earnings since 1999 for all full-time employees, and for the chief executive officers (CEOs) of the top 100 and next 250 companies. For all employees, real earnings stayed about the same between 2003 and 2008 (at about 106 per cent of 1999 levels). But between 1999 and 2007 the real earnings of the CEOs of the top 100 companies more than doubled (reaching £2.4 million per year), and those of the next 250 companies almost doubled (reaching £1.1 million). The CEOs did experience a sharp fall in pay in 2008, as one might expect given the financial crash and recession, but it remained higher than in 2004, and substantially higher than in 1999. It is striking that the rapid rise in CEO remuneration came after 2003, just as full-time earnings in general flattened out (National Equality Panel, 2010). Lansley (2009) has also pointed out that remuneration packages for the chief executives of FTSE 100 companies have risen nine times faster than those of the median earner.

So who are these people on such high incomes? The National Equality Panel (2010) also presented data from tax records to show that those with the highest incomes were typically men, aged 45–54, and living in London. To be more precise:

- men comprised five sixths of the top 1 per cent of taxpayers and more than nine tenths of the top 0.1 per cent. in 2004/05;
- those aged 45–54 were a third of the top 1 per cent of taxpayers and half of the top 0.1 per cent;
- those living in London comprised a quarter of the top 1 per cent of all taxpayers and more than a third of the top 0.1 per cent.

Majima and Warde (2008) have analysed the consumption patterns of the top 1 per cent from 1961 to 2004, finding that patterns of consumption had not changed dramatically between 1961 and 1981 but by 2004, some new items of expenditure became prominent. More financial items, including personal pensions and funds for dependants, had appeared by 2004. Spending on private medicine and dentistry also began to mark out the top 1 per cent in 2004. Housing also became a greater priority, partly through the purchase of second homes and through house renovation. Some items of distinct expenditure remained broadly the same, such as travel, but changed in detail (for example, overseas holidays and internal air flights). Spending on leisure services reached unprecedented levels in 2004. So it seems that richer groups are becoming more exclusive than before, with greater spending on private welfare and investments (financial and property-based) that should help to preserve their wealth for future generations.

The top 1 per cent has soared away from the rest in the last 30 or so years and this has happened in some other countries. But this is not part of some inevitable global trend as some countries, including our close neighbours, France, the Netherlands and Germany, have not experienced the same change. In Britain, this select group is disproportionately middle-aged men living in London. We now turn to see whether the same is true for the very richest people in our society.

The richest

We saw in the previous section that the top 1 per cent have pulled away from the rest of the population in terms of their increasing share of income. And within the top 1 per cent, the very top have seen their share of income increase even more so. This section concentrates on the very richest in the UK today, a group we could perhaps call the 'super-rich'. A key source of data on this group comes from *The Sunday Times* Rich List that identifies the top 1,000 richest people living and working in the UK through publicly available information on assets, whether land, property, racehorses, art or significant shares in publicly quoted companies. Bank accounts and small shareholdings in private equity portfolios are excluded because there is no publicly available information on these.[1] The data is therefore likely to under-estimate the actual amounts of wealth owned.

In 1997, the combined assets of the then top 1,000 amounted to £98.99 billion. By 2011, this figure had almost quadrupled, to £395.8 billion. But it had not been a steady increase during those 14 years as the top 1,000 had suffered a sharp loss in fortune between 2008 and 2009 before recovering that loss between 2009 and 2010 and then seeing their wealth increase again by 2011. According to *The Sunday Times* (2010), much of the increase in wealth between 2009 and 2010 was a result of the rebound in stock markets and property values after the government injected hundreds of billions of pounds into the banks and the wider economy to stave off collapse.

Philip Beresford, compiler of the list, said in 2010:[2]

> The rich have come through the recession with flying colours. The stock market is up, the hedge funds are coining it. The rich are doing very nicely....The rest of the country is going to have to face public spending cuts, but it has little effect on the rich because they don't consume public services.

The Sunday Times (2010) reported that city bankers and financiers, for example, had seen their fortunes rise sharply in 2009/10. Louis Bacon, a hedge fund manager, was ranked 49th in 2010 at £1.1 billion, up from £650 million in 2009; Alan Howard, who co-founded Brevan Howard, Europe's biggest hedge fund, was ranked 66th in 2010 with £875 million, up from £375 million. *The Sunday Times* also identified a number of other 'hedgies' who have seen their wealth rise by 50 per cent or more. The City of London has therefore played a key role in generating wealth for some of its employees in the financial services sector (Z/Yen, 2010). When the stock market was at its height in 2007, an estimated 354,000 employees in City-type jobs received bonuses worth £10.241 billion. This then more than halved to 'only' £4.008 billion (to 324,000 employees) in 2008 (see Table 5.10). Between 2008 and 2009, the number of employees decreased but the total value of bonuses actually increased.

The financial services sector is not, however, the main source of people's wealth on the Rich List. Property is a key source, with 246 people on the list having made their fortunes through property, according to *The Sunday Times* (2010). Direct inheritance is also an important source, responsible for 229 people making it to the list. Finance and banking is not too far behind, with at least 170 people on the list who made their fortunes primarily in this way.

Figure 5.2 concentrates on an even more exclusive club: the top 200. It shows the trends in their wealth, with 2003–08 being a particularly good period for them in terms of increasing wealth. While they suffered a massive dip in 2008/09, they recovered from this in the next two years. The linear trend from 2003 to 2008 looks a little suspicious,

Table 5.10: City bonus payouts and employment in City-type jobs, 2001–09

Year	City jobs	City bonus (£ billion)
2001	312,000	3.921
2002	308,000	3.329
2003	317,000	4.893
2004	325,000	5.695
2005	327,000	7.130
2006	343,000	10.059
2007	354,000	10.241
2008	324,000	4.008
2009	305,000	6.012

Source: Centre for Economics and Business Research (2009a, 2009b).

perhaps (and may suggest that the compilers made some assumptions about growth rates and then imputed some of the data), but it is very difficult to gather highly accurate data on this group and this source is probably the best we have.

The most exclusive club of all is the 'billionaire club'. Between 2009 and 2011, the number of people joining this club grew from 43 to 67. In 1997, according to *The Sunday Times* Rich List, there had been a mere handful – 16.

Figure 5.2: Billions owned by top 200 in Britain

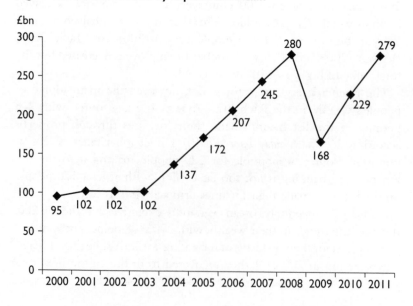

Table 5.11 shows the top 10 in the Rich List, starting with Lakshmi Mittal, who made his fortune in the steel industry and retains his Indian passport but is based in London. His fortune fell from £28 billion to £11 billion from 2008 to 2009 but then recovered some of these losses by 2011 – to £17.5 billion. This was due to the recovery in steel markets. According to *The Sunday Times* (2010), he paid £70 million to Bernie Ecclestone, the Formula One supremo, for a house in Kensington Palace Gardens and spent £30 million on his daughter's wedding. A boom in commodity markets also drove up the fortunes of the mining magnate Alisher Usmanov, up to £12.4 billion, to second place in the list. Third in the list, Roman Abramovich made his fortune from the privatisation of the Russian oil industry, buying the Sibneft oil business in 1995 for about £120 million with his partner, Boris Berezovsky. Ten years later, the company was sold and the stake held by Abramovich and his partners was worth about £7.5 billion. Number four in the list, the Duke of Westminster, owes much of his riches to inheritance. He owns vast estates in Lancashire, Cheshire, Scotland and Canada as well as prime real estate in central London's Mayfair and Belgravia. His assets include substantial art treasures.

The Rich List is not the only source of information on the very richest. Beaverstock (2010) has focused on 'high net worth individuals (HNWIs)': those who have at least £1 million in assets *excluding* primary residences, collectables, consumables and consumer durables. He pointed out that in 2008 there were 8.6 million HNWIs across the world. This figure was down 14.9 per cent from the previous year due to the global financial crisis (Merrill Lynch Capgemini, 2009). But from 1996 to 2007 there had been more than a doubling of the

Table 5.11: Richest 10 people in Britain, 2011

Rank	Name	Total assets (in billions)	Source of wealth
1	Lakshmi Mittal and family	17.5	Steel
2	Alisher Usmanov	12.4	Steel and mines
3	Roman Abramovich	10.3	Oil, industry, football
4	Duke of Westminster	7	Property
5	Ernesto and Kirsty Bertarelli	6.9	Pharmaceuticals
6	Leonard Blavatnik	6.24	Chemicals, oil, aluminium
7	John Friedriksen and family	6.2	Shipping
8	David and Simon Reuben	6.19	Property and internet
9=	Galen and George Westman and family	6	Retailing (Primark)
9=	Gopi and Sri Hinduja	6	Industry and finance

Source: http://business.timesonline.co.uk/section/0,,20590,00.html

number of HNWIs worldwide, from 4.5 million to 10.1 million (+121.7 per cent) and almost a two-and-a-half-fold increase in the value of their private wealth (+145.2 per cent), from US$16.6 trillion to $40.7 trillion (see Table 5.12).

The HNWI group is fairly large worldwide but can be broken down into two groups: the ultra-HNWI category (>US$30 million), mid-tier millionaires (between US$5 million and US$30 million) and the 'millionaire next door' (between US$1million and US$5 million). According to Beaverstock's (2010) analysis of the data from Merrill Lynch Capgemini, the ultra-HNWIs accounted for only about 0.9 to 1.0 per cent of the total number of HNWIs since 1996. In 2008, this amounted to just 78,000 people worldwide, but these people accounted for 34.7 per cent of the total value of private wealth. Beaverstock concluded that although these are a small group, they play a dominant role in relation to global wealth (Table 5.13).

In terms of billionaires, there were 1,011 worldwide in 2010 according to Forbes.com (Forbes, 2010), who compile an annual list in a similar manner to *The Sunday Times* Rich List for the UK. As with the richest people in the UK, the global rich saw a dip in their fortunes from 2008 to 2009, but had largely recovered by 2010. In 2008 there were 1,125 billionaires. This fell to 793 in 2009 but rose again to 1,011 by 2010. This year the world's billionaires have an average net worth of US$3.5 billion, up US$500 million in 12 months.

US billionaires still dominate the world league but this is being increasingly challenged. Forbes (2010) showed that the US accounted

Table 5.12: The growth of HNWIs worldwide and the value of their wealth, 1996–2008

	Number (millions)	Change (%)	Wealth ($ trillions)	Change (%)
1996	4.5	–	16.6	–
1997	5.2	+15.6	19.1	+15.1
1998	5.9	+13.5	21.6	+13.1
1999	7.0	+18.6	25.5	+18.1
2000	7.2	+2.9	27.0	+5.9
2001	7.1	–1.4	26.2	–3.7
2002	7.3	+2.8	26.7	+2.7
2003	7.7	+5.5	28.5	+6.7
2004	8.2	+6.5	30.7	+7.7
2005	8.8	+7.3	33.4	+8.8
2006	9.5	+8.0	37.2	+11.4
2007	10.1	+6.3	40.7	+9.4
2008	8.6	–14.9	32.8	–19.4

Table 5.13: The composition of the HNWI private wealth market, 2002–08

Category	% of the total population of HNWIs						
	2002	2003	2004	2005	2006	2007	2008
Ultra-HNWI	0.8	0.9	0.9	1.0	1.0	1.0	0.9
Mid-tier millionaire and 'millionaire next door'	99.2	99.1	99.1	99.0	99.0	99.0	99.1
Total number of HNWI (millions)	7.3	7.6	8.3	8.7	9.5	10.1	8.6

for 40 per cent of the world's billionaires in 2010, but this was down from 45 per cent a year previously. And the world's richest man in 2010 was not American. He was a Mexican, Carlos Slim Helu, who had benefited from rising prices in his various telecom holdings, including his mobile phone company, America Movil. Slim's fortune was an estimated US$53.5 billion, up US$18.5 billion in 12 months. Shares of America Movil, of which Slim owns a US$23 billion stake, had gone up 35 per cent from 2009 to 2010. Bill Gates had been the world's richest man for 14 of the past 15 years and still owned some US$53 billion in 2010, putting him second in the world. His fortune went up US$13 billion between 2009 and 2010 as shares of Microsoft rose 50 per cent in that time. Warren Buffett's fortune jumped US$10 billion to US$47 billion on rising shares of Berkshire Hathaway. He ranked third.

Although the global economic crisis had stalled the growth in wealth at the very top, this did not last for long as the super-rich recovered in 2010. Beaverstock concluded from his research on the super-rich that:

> ... the booming financial market performance of the last twenty years, coupled with the opening up of emerging markets and high rises in commodity prices, has created unprecedented conditions for significant growth in the ranks of the super-rich across the globe, especially in the self-made, billion and multi-millionaire, from 'new' money sources. (Beaverstock, 2010)

Beaverstock has also argued for more conceptualisation around the wealthy to consider which sub-groups appropriately reflect the different groups and the roles they play. Billionaires, for example, may be considered a separate 'class' from the ultra-HNWIs, who may also be rather different from the 'millionaires next door'. Whereas the billionaires are certainly the global super-rich, with significant economic power (Haseler, 1999; Frank, 2007), Beaverstock argued that the 'millionaires next door' might be better classified as part of the 'new' middle classes (Butler and Savage, 1995). The ultra-HNWIs might also deserve their own grouping as global and super-gentrifiers, and financial elites (Butler and Lees, 2006; Hall, 2009).

The level of wealth of people at the very top is truly staggering. Lansley (2009) has pointed out that the Walton family, who own Wal-Mart, have a combined wealth in excess of US$90 billion, about the same as the poorest third of the entire world population – around 100 million people. What do they do with all this money? One potential use is to give it away – through philanthropy – and we turn to this next.

Philanthropy and charitable giving

The very richest are clearly getting even richer (again), but what do they do with their wealth? *The Sunday Times* Rich List certainly provides numerous examples of conspicuous consumption on yachts, jets, homes and lavish parties. But as people get richer, some elect to give more money to charities and other philanthropic causes. Attitudes to charitable giving may also reflect the extent of state provision – with donations tending to be large in the US, for example, and rather lower in European countries with a long history of state provision of social welfare services. So how much do the rich give and do they give more than the poor (as a proportion of income)?

We start by comparing the 'merely' rich with other members of the public before focusing on the very richest philanthropists. There are relatively few sources of regular reliable statistics on giving to charity. In England the Citizenship Survey asks a large, representative sample of adults if they have donated to charities in the last four weeks. The latest available data cover 2008/09. A range of different means of giving money are included, ranging from buying raffle tickets and shopping at a charity shop, to having a standing order making donations. Some methods were more relevant among richer people – such as giving via a direct debit – while buying at a charity shop was more common among those on lower incomes and can be seen as consumption rather than or as well as giving. Table 5.14 shows that those on higher incomes were, indeed, more likely to give to charity than other groups in 2008/09. The vast majority (86 per cent) of those on £75,000 or more per year said that they had given to charity in the last four weeks compared with 69 per cent of those on incomes under £5,000. However, those on higher incomes clearly have more disposable income than those on

Table 5.14: Giving to charity in last four weeks, by respondent's income (%)

Respondent income	Base (unweighted number)	Overall % giving to charity in last 4 weeks	Main three methods:		
			% buying raffle tickets	% using direct debits	% buying goods at charity shop
Under £5,000	1,450	69	21	14	23
£5,000<£10,000	1,685	70	23	17	24
£10,000<£15,000	1,253	74	28	21	24
£15,000<£20,000	940	77	27	21	23
£20,000<£30,000	1,344	80	30	27	20
£30,000<£50,000	1,061	83	29	35	18
£50,000<£75,000	233	85	32	48	18
£75k+	197	86	31	45	17
Total	8,163	75	26	23	22

Source: Own analysis of the 2008/09 Citizenship Survey, core sample.

the very lowest incomes so it is important to look at the amounts of money donated as well as whether any money is given or not.

Figure 5.3 shows clearly that those on higher incomes certainly give more money than those on lower incomes. The average (mean) amount donated in the last four weeks by people on incomes over £75,000 was over £100. This compared with around £15 donated by those on under £5,000 per year. But these figures are skewed by a few people (in each income group) giving very substantial amounts. If we focus on the medians, there is much less difference between income groups. Half of those on incomes over £75,000 gave £25 to charity in the last four weeks. The same figure for those on incomes under £5,000 was £5. People on higher incomes are certainly giving more money, but they are not necessarily giving as high a proportion of their income: those on incomes some 25 times larger than those at the bottom were giving (in median amounts) 'only' around five times as much.

Put another way, those in the top 21 per cent[3] of incomes gave 39 per cent of the overall total given to charities. However, to put this into context, those in the top 20 per cent of incomes (in the FRS) have some 46 per cent of the total income. So the better off may give more money to charities than those on lower incomes, but not as a proportion of their total resources. Likewise, the bottom 19 per cent of individual incomes were responsible for some 11 per cent of charitable giving, but in FRS data were only able to command around 5 per cent of total incomes. Of course there are important definitional differences in incomes comparing the Citizenship Survey with the FRS, and the Citizenship Survey data is only banded, but the results are suggestive

Figure 5.3: Charitable donations in last four weeks, by income (for those giving anything, non-donors excluded)

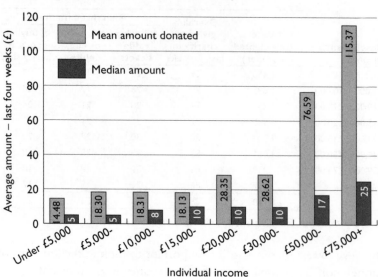

Source: Own analysis of the 2008-09 Citizenship Survey, core sample

of a rising proportion giving as incomes increase, and a rising level of cash donation, but not as a proportion of incomes.

But what about the very richest people? There are some classic examples of philanthropists in the past, not least the great US philanthropist, Andrew Carnegie, who said, in the *Gospel of wealth* 1890, 'he who dies rich, dies disgraced' (Carnegie, 1890, quoted by Lansley, 2006, p 161).

In the UK, other great industrialists including Cadbury, Rowntree, Lever and Salt were inspired by their religious faith to make generous donations to their workers and others more generally. More recently, there has been a debate about the existence of *philanthrocapitalism* (or *venture philanthropy*). The idea here is that there is a new movement of rich entrepreneurs who are using their wealth to help attain innovative goals in terms of entrenched social problems, perhaps particularly those affecting the less developed world. Michael Bishop and Michael Green (2008) have surveyed this group, including interviews with Bill Gates, George Soros and Sir Richard Branson. The analysis looks at ways in which the techniques of business and investment may be applied to achieving the goals of social change, particularly through non–profit organisations. The success of the microfinance movement, and particularly the Grameen Bank led by Yunus, provides an important model. Bishop and Green's main thesis is that: 'Golden ages of wealth creation give rise to golden ages of giving' (Bishop and Green, 2009, p 21).

These philanthropists see their money as having the potential to solve many of the major issues facing the world. For example, Christopher Cooper-Hohn was at the top of *The Sunday Times* Giving List in 2010 with donations of over £500 million to AIDS/HIV, education and humanitarian causes. *The Observer* (2008) has pointed out that Cooper-Hohn supports projects across Africa and the developing world and, alongside his wife, Jamie, has given almost £800 million in four years, making them Britain's most generous philanthropists. According to *The Observer* (2008), the couple search out causes to find those that will produce 'transformational change' on a large scale. Jamie Cooper-Hohn once said:

> I was very eager that, if we did this, we would do it very much in the way Chris invests, making long-term, well-researched investments, bringing business rigour into development. (quoted in *The Observer*, 2008)

Some of the analysis of philanthrocapitalism predates the recession that has brought into question the success of capitalist management approaches. And while private sector techniques can certainly play a role here, the non-profit sector may also be able to provide lessons in dealing with global problems (Edwards, 2010).

The Sunday Times produces an annual Giving List, and in 2009/10, the top 100 leading philanthropists were estimated to have donated £1.7 billion (*The Sunday Times*, 2011). This was £818 million lower than in 2008/09, a massive drop and one that is surprising given the recovery in large fortunes in 2009/10. Only two donors gave more than £100 million in 2009/10 but there were more donors giving larger amounts. The Giving List ranks people by the proportion of total wealth donated or pledged to charity in the past 12 months. Table 5.15 shows the top 10 philanthropists for 2009/10. Top of the list is Anurag Dikshit who gave almost five times the amount of wealth he now has, which was left to his charitable foundation, the Kusuma Trust. This charity is dedicated to educational and social causes, particularly in India where Dikshit was born.

It is sometimes argued that the existence of a welfare state 'crowds' out individual giving. Levels of giving are certainly lower in the UK than in the US, for example, but there are still considerable sums being donated to welfare-related causes. For example, Pharaoh (2009) found that despite the existence of the NHS, people donated £1.1 billion

Table 5.15: *The Sunday Times* Giving List, 2009/10

Number	Name	2011 wealth in £ millions	Recent donations in £ millions	Giving index
1	Anurag Dikshit	35	172	492
2	Bart Brecht	90	80.2	89
3	Christopher Cooper-Hohn	85	75.5	89
4	Richard Ross	58	33	57
5	Dame Viven Duffield	40	19.4	48
6	Diana Ballinger	58	25.6	44
7	Lord Fink	120	33.1	28
8	Lord Sainsbury	960	165	17
9	Sir Elton John	195	26.8	14
10	David Potter	40	4.9	12

Source: The Sunday Times (2011)

to health charities in 2007/08, including £63 million for hospitals. The total amount of voluntary donations to charities in that year was £10.6 billion. The British welfare state was, in fact, built alongside the voluntary sector rather than as a replacement for it. Beveridge certainly supported the voluntary sector and, more recently, John Major introduced Gift Aid and the National Lottery to provide further support for charitable giving. Gordon Brown also extended payroll giving and the Gift Aid scheme in 2000. David Cameron's ideas for a Big Society also suggest a major role for individuals to give money – and time.

Various policies seek to encourage and incentivise charitable donations and the cost of tax relief on various schemes such as Gift Aid, Inheritance Tax relief on charitable donations and so on, amount to a considerable sum. Pharaoh (2009) estimated that this amounted to £1.4 billion of public expenditure in 2007/08.

As we saw earlier, there are small numbers of people who give very significant amounts. Breeze (2010) quoted data from the UK Giving survey that showed that only 8 per cent of donors give more than £100 per month, but they accounted for 51 per cent of the value of all donations.

There are a number of different perspectives on philanthropy. Some take a very critical view, exemplified by Panas (1984, p 49, cited in Breeze, 2010), who argued that philanthropy was: 'people getting credit for giving back what their ancestors should never have taken in the first place'.

Philanthropists are also sometimes criticised for being self-indulgent and self-satisfied. It is therefore seen as a form of self-interest as it may help to legitimise the existence of very high levels of wealth. For example, Toynbee and Walker (2008) take a critical view of the very rich, arguing that their conspicuous consumption far outweighs their conspicuous philanthropy. They go further, indeed, to suggest that where the very rich do engage in philanthropy it is largely an extension of conspicuous consumption and also a way of increasing their status and power. This view of philanthropy goes back at least to Veblen's (1889 [1985]) view of the 'leisure class' whom he saw as using philanthropy as a way of displaying their wealth to win public approval. And indeed, Breeze (2010) found that a large proportion of donations from the wealthy tend to find their way to high profile art and cultural institutions such as the National Gallery's 'Sainsbury' Wing.

On the other hand, supporters of philanthropy argue that all members of society benefit from philanthropic gifts and that many such gifts are given for altruistic rather than self-interested reasons. The discipline of economics may find it difficult to deal with the concept of altruism, since economics tends to emphasise models of self-interest and utility-maximisation, and so economists may try to find ways to theorise acts of generosity and altruism as acts of self-interest. Sociologists and anthropologists may take a different view, but Breeze (2010) has argued that sociologists have generally ignored philanthropy, and although anthropologists have studied gift giving extensively, this has not necessarily extended to a study of modern-day philanthropy in the developed world.

Philanthropy tends to polarise opinion between those who praise it as a generous activity, benefiting those in need, and those who see it as a method used by the rich to gain status and power in a self-interested way. Breeze (2010) has challenged this simplistic polarisation by suggesting eight logics which underpin philanthropic behaviour and motivation. She has argued that the emerging dominant logic is the agenda setters' who are typically younger, more likely to be self-made and seeking to create global change. This ties in with the idea of 'philanthrocapitalism' as mentioned above, and this group tends to receive a great deal of media coverage and are often seen as part of a 'new philanthropy', but Breeze has suggested that they only account for 17 per cent of the most significant philanthropists in the UK in 2006. The others follow different logics from pursuing religious beliefs ('salvation seekers') to empathising with others and sharing their identities ('big fish' or 'kindred spirits') to wishing to support the establishment ('patriots and players') to becoming patrons of the Arts ('culture vultures') to being charitable without a particular cause ('big brands') to those who maintain secrecy about their giving ('secret operators'). Breeze (2010, p 158) has concluded that:

> Philanthropy is primarily a social act, despite it frequently being examined as a purely economic transaction. [Philanthropic] acts are ... undertaken as part of an ongoing process of identity work and the search for a meaningful and 'good' life.

Edwards (2002) identified three types of wealthy donor. The first was an 'ad hoc giver' who gives regularly but without any particular method. These people give in a reactive, spontaneous way when approached to do so. The second type was a 'strategic giver' who has a clear idea about the causes they wish to give to and may give in a more planned way. The final type was a 'social giver' who gives primarily at events such as charity balls and auctions. Edwards (2002) argued that wealthy people have similar motivations to the public more generally when it comes to giving. These motivations include wanting to 'give something back', feeling it is 'important to do my bit', wanting to support deserving causes and those less fortunate than themselves, believing that it is good for society to give, feeling good about giving and feeling bad if they do not give.

One of the questions for major philanthropists to consider is how much to give away to good causes and how much to leave as bequests to family and friends. Warren Buffett decided to give £15 billion of his children's potential inheritance to charity – the biggest donation in history. According to *The Observer* (2008), he once said:

> "I think that a rich person should leave their children enough so they can do anything, but not enough that they can do nothing."

The Observer (2008) also quoted Duncan Bannatyne, one of the so-called 'dragons' from the Dragons' Den, who is a self-made millionaire. He said that he was not planning to pass on his fortune to his six children:

> "I don't think it is in their best interests. Look at the examples of children whose lives have been ruined. There are children who don't have a purpose in life, don't know how to live properly, are on drugs."

The rich also give money to other causes, such as political parties. This may give them influence over policy, or at least be perceived to have influence, but political parties play down such power and influence. Six of the top 10 political donors in 2010 gave money to the Conservative Party, with four donating to Labour and none to the Liberal Democrats (see Table 5.16).

Table 5.16: Top ten political donors in 2010

	Amount (£ millions)	Party
Sir Anthony Bamford and family	1.4	Conservative
Nigel Doughty	1	Labour
Lakshmi Mittal	1	Labour
Michael Farmer	0.75	Conservative
Michael Spencer	0.74	Conservative
Lord Glendonbrook	0.7	Conservative
Lord Edmiston	0.7	Conservative
Lord Sugar	0.4	Labour
Lord David Sainsbury	0.36	Labour
Chris Rokos	0.35	Conservative

Source: Electoral commission quoted in *The Sunday Times* (2011).

Conclusions

We take a relatively broad view of who is 'rich' in this book to include all those in the top 10 per cent by income and by wealth. But we appreciate that many in this group would not consider themselves rich, and for some couples with many children who are just over the threshold perhaps the term is not entirely appropriate. However, the top 10 per cent do have considerably more than other groups and can afford a more exclusive and private lifestyle. Virtually all have an annual holiday, money to spend on themselves and broadband internet access. Half have private health insurance and nearly three in ten parents in this group send their children to a fee-paying school. The rich are much less supportive of spending on welfare benefits, arguing that people should take responsibility for themselves rather than rely on government. We could argue that it is this independent spirit that has helped them to become rich, but given the evidence on inheritance, lifetime gifts and social mobility presented in the previous chapter, it seems more appropriate to argue that this group can only maintain independence from the state because they have been dependent on the support of their families instead.

The rich, as we define them, may not see themselves as such, but the richer group we look at, the top 1 per cent, are an even more exclusive club and one that has moved away from the rest of society in recent years. In 1992, the top 1 per cent had incomes 5.5 times the median income, but this had risen to eight times by 2007/08. By that time, people needed around £150,000 to enter this club. The rise of the top 1 per cent is not part of some inevitable global force as it has not occurred throughout the world. While the US has seen an even greater rise among the top 1 per cent, other countries, such as France, the Netherlands, Germany and so on, have not. There is something particular to Britain and the US which has allowed this rise to occur.

The economic crisis from 2007 onwards saw a dent in the fortunes of the richest people (the top 1,000) in Britain with a sharp fall in wealth between 2008 and 2009. But between 2010 and 2011 the wealth of this group had fully recovered to the levels they were at in 2008. The richest people in Britain may be seen as forming part of a global super-elite, with a new language emerging to distinguish between the 'ultra-HNWIs' and the merely 'mid-tier millionaires'.

Most rich people give to charity but they do not give as high a proportion of their income as less affluent groups. Some of the very richest people give substantial amounts, and proportions, of their fortunes to good causes, and there is discussion about whether the increase in the fortunes of people at the very top has led to a 'new philanthropy' that may also be characterised as 'philanthrocapitalism'. There is also discussion about the motivations of philanthropists and the role philanthropy plays. Some see philanthropy as a wholly positive contribution, stemming from an altruistic spirit, which benefits all members of society. Others are more sceptical, arguing that philanthropy is a form of self-interest which seeks to legitimise large concentrations of wealth. Most recent research suggests that this polarisation of views is simplistic, and both the motivations and role of philanthropy are more varied and complex.

Notes

[1] http://business.timesonline.co.uk/article/0,,20589-2132606,00.html

[2] http://business.timesonline.co.uk/tol/business/specials/rich_list/article7107299.ece

[3] The Citizenship Survey income data is banded, so it is necessary to use the proportions available and not possible to look specifically at the top, say, 10 or 20 per cent.

SIX

Towards a comprehensive policy on assets

Introduction

This chapter is the first of two that critically discuss policy responses to wealth and the wealthy, starting with wealth. Under the Labour government 1997–2010, there was much discussion of asset-based welfare policies but relatively little accompanying policy action. 'Asset-based welfare' was never a holistic policy on assets but focused on financial savings primarily for people on low incomes. Policy has, indeed, rarely joined up the links between pensions, housing and savings, and one goal of a comprehensive policy on assets would be to do this. Such a policy would also need to consider how more affluent groups are affected by policy (for example, through the existence of tax relief on private pensions and the provision of tax-free Individual Savings Accounts, ISAs). Such a policy would also need to consider policies on assets in relation to the other 'pillars' of the welfare state and in particular income-based policies and services.

We begin this chapter with a discussion of the possible goals for a comprehensive policy on assets. We then turn to asset-based welfare and policy on savings before considering policy in housing wealth and pension wealth. The role of the tax system is also vitally important here alongside the various schemes that exist in relation to different forms of wealth. Much of the discussion of assets assumes that they are a household resource, shared equally by members of the same household. But we saw in Chapter Four that this is not necessarily the case, and so we consider the implications of this for policy.

This chapter does not merely document the different policies but also critically assesses their role. For example, should those on very low incomes be encouraged to save rather than spend on their current needs? Should those on very low incomes be encouraged to become home owners and potentially risk mortgage debt and repossession? Should people on low incomes save in private pensions if the state is providing a means-tested benefit in retirement that might make them little, or no, better off in retirement for having saved?

The goals of a comprehensive policy on assets

In Chapter One we documented the shift from collective responsibility and risk through state welfare provision towards more individual responsibility and risk through private welfare provision. Asset-based policies have been central to this shift with policies designed to expand owner-occupation, share ownership, financial savings and private pensions. The goal of policy in the 1980s was clearly to roll back the frontiers of the state by encouraging people to accumulate assets which they could then use in times of need rather than rely on state support. Some of these policies, including the expansion of owner-occupation through Right to Buy, were very popular, and when New Labour came to power in 1997, rather than try to turn back the individualist tide, they embraced it and championed the idea of individual ownership through 'stakeholding' and 'asset-based welfare'.

Prabhakar (2008) has argued that there are two approaches to asset-based welfare: the social policy camp and the citizenship camp. The social policy camp, exemplified by Sherraden (1991), focuses on tackling poverty, whereas the citizenship camp focuses on affirming citizenship rights. Within the social policy camp, Prabhakar (2008) has pointed out that some approaches to asset-based welfare are concerned with 'character development'. The idea here is that asset-based welfare policies can tackle 'welfare dependency' by developing more responsible and independent attitudes and behaviour. It is these changes in character which will then help people out of poverty and also prevent them from falling back into poverty and staying poor. Poverty prevention is therefore central here. A different approach within the social policy camp is the 'incentives' approach: that is the idea that if we give people incentives to act in a certain way (for example, to save) then they will (generally) do so. This approach does not expect or aim to change people's attitudes or characters, and so when the incentives are removed, behaviour may well change (back).

Sherraden (1991) set out 11 basic principles for an asset-based welfare policy, arguing that any such policy should:

1. Complement income-based policies, not replace them.
2. Be universally available to engender a broad base of political support.
3. Provide greater incentives for the poor.
4. Be voluntary.
5. Be long-term, with people participating at some points in the life but not at others.

6. Involve mutual responsibility through joint contributions.
7. Be restricted to use for specific goals (for example, training, higher education).
8. Involve a limited set of investment choices.
9. Promote long-term, lifetime accumulation of wealth.
10. Be accompanied by financial education.
11. Enable people to develop and pursue personal objectives.

Sherraden's 'social policy' approach to asset-based welfare has become very influential and has led to the development of a number of savings schemes (Individual Development Accounts, IDAs, in the US and the two Saving Gateway pilot projects in the UK), but the 'citizenship' approach to asset-based welfare is rather different as it focuses on people's rights to assets. Such a view links to debates in political philosophy about the nature of property rights (dating back to John Locke, 1632-1704 and John Stuart Mill, 1806–73) and the nature of citizenship (Marshall, 1950; Dwyer, 2010). The approach has led to various proposals for capital grants, sometimes described as a 'citizen's inheritance'.

Asset-based welfare policies received strong support from New Labour but have been criticised by others for taking away resources that could be spent on raising the incomes of the poorest or in providing better services. This might occur if the state subsidises an asset-based welfare scheme rather than giving people higher levels of benefit or spending more on services. Asset-based welfare is also sometimes criticised for encouraging people on very low incomes to save when it might be better or essential for them to spend their money on current basic needs. Sherraden (1991) has defended asset-based welfare policies from these criticisms by arguing that people often make huge sacrifices to save, and that this should be recognised and encouraged by rewards/incentives. Sherraden has also argued, strongly, that assets are important, independent of income, and so should be supported by the state alongside income (see Chapter One). Emmerson and Wakefield (2001), however, are still sceptical, and have argued that if the objective of asset-based welfare is to improve welfare outcomes (for example, in relation to employment or health), then it needs to be demonstrated that increasing public spending on asset-based welfare is better than alternative policies aimed at improving work incentives or improving the quality of health or education services.

Ackerman and Alstott (1999) have also defended asset-based welfare against the charge that it diverts money from income-based policies and services. But their defence comes from a different angle as they have argued that this criticism misses the point of their proposals: which see stakeholding as a citizenship programme, not a poverty programme.

Other issues raised by asset-based welfare include the question of whether or not restrictions should be placed on the use of assets accumulated with state support. Would it be acceptable for people to spend their assets on holidays, for example, if the state has helped them accumulate these assets? If we take a social policy approach, we are likely to argue that assets should only be used for welfare purposes (although there is then an issue about what might be included here and, potentially, even a holiday could be good for people's health and welfare). If we believe that people have an absolute right to a capital grant, then it is difficult to argue for any restrictions on use. White (2003), however, has argued that restrictions on use are not important merely because of a concern about stake-blowing and 'irresponsibility' but also because of a concern for 'reciprocity' between those who pay the taxes to fund the grants and those who receive the money. Gamble and Prabhakar (2006) carried out focus groups with young people who generally said that, if they were given a capital grant, they would spend it on things like: education, buying a car, buying a home or starting a business. So they all said that they would behave responsibly with the money, but they did not necessarily trust other young people to do the same, and they felt that the broader public would need reassurance on this matter if they were to support it. They therefore supported placing restrictions on the use of such grants.

Another key issue is whether asset-based welfare policies should be universal or targeted at those who need them most. Once again, the answer will depend on the overall approach taken to these policies, with the social policy camp supporting more targeted policies and the citizenship camp supporting more universal policies. One issue with targeting the very poorest is that, as mentioned above, it may not be appropriate to encourage people to save if they are on very low incomes. A similar issue is relevant in relation to housing wealth. If people are on very low and/or unstable incomes, then it may be a struggle to keep up mortgage payments and may lead to repossession for those unable to sustain payments. Those most in need of asset-based welfare may, therefore, be the very people who are unable to benefit from it. But if policies are universal and available to all, then there may be a problem of 'deadweight', where people who are relatively affluent may be saving already and just switch to state-supported schemes. These schemes will not, therefore, be encouraging new saving but subsidising existing saving. However, this point rarely seems to be raised in the context of ISAs or pensions, which receive generous tax treatment and which may also be subject to large deadweight costs. This issue is routinely raised in discussions about accounts designed for the worst off, more rarely in accounts benefiting the rich and middle class.

As noted above, the idea of asset-based welfare emerged in the UK in association with New Labour, and this signalled a radical change in Labour policy in the late 1980s/early 1990s. Labour had originally opposed the Right to Buy Act in 1980 and also the privatisation of nationalised industries in the 1980s which led to wider share ownership. Many parts of the political left at that time had largely negative views about private property and personal wealth. Under Tony Blair, however, Labour abandoned Sydney Webb's 'Clause Four' of the Party's constitution that had committed them to the 'common ownership of the means of production, distribution and exchange' rather than individual ownership.[1] In 1995, New Labour replaced Clause IV with a commitment to put 'power, wealth and opportunity in the hands of the many not the few'. This change in Labour's approach was part of their new Third Way in politics, and asset-based welfare fitted perfectly here. Giddens (1998) was a key exponent of this approach, arguing for a 'social investment state' to promote individual responsibility rather than a welfare state that might simply hand out money to apparently passive recipients. Kelly and Lissauer (2000, p 25) took a different approach to asset-based welfare, arguing that: 'centre-left strategy on asset-building should be about encouraging social inclusion and a sense of common citizenship across all individuals regardless of income'. They argued that policies to promote private property could go hand-in-hand with progressive aims of equality, opportunity and responsibility.

In 2000, the Treasury published a consultation paper as part of its pre-budget report that emphasised the importance of savings in providing people with independence, security and comfort in old age. This led to further papers emphasising the behavioural benefits of saving in relation to developing self-reliance. These papers also referred to assets as the fourth pillar of the welfare state, alongside jobs, incomes and services (HM Treasury, 2000, 2001). David Blunkett (2001, p 34), a member of the cabinet for most of Blair's premiership, also argued that asset holding offered:

> ... positive behavioural benefits. People who have a material stake in society are more likely to plan ahead for themselves and their children, and to care about what happens in the community around them.

Blunkett (2005) further argued that:

> Assets policies can offer unparalleled opportunity in the fight to prevent future poverty – stopping people falling into poverty when circumstances change and by enabling families to build inter-generational stepping stones out of poverty. Rather than merely being forced to depend on income support and other passive social policies that ameliorate poverty, assets provide a break to poverty in the future. (pp 2-3)

McKay and Rowlingson (2008) have argued that New Labour's support for asset-based welfare was one of the most significant changes in its approach to social security policy compared with the previous government. Many other policies continued along broadly similar lines to Conservative policy, but asset-based welfare was a new approach (along with the focus on reducing/eradicating poverty). But although asset-based welfare was championed by New Labour, it seemed to cut across the left–right divide in politics, appealing to some on the left as a way of reducing wealth inequality and supporting those on low incomes, but also appealing to some on the right as a way of increasing individual freedom and opportunity. For example, Philip Blond, director and founder of the right-wing public policy think tank, ResPublica, and author of *Red Tory* (2010), has argued that:

> Without assets, opportunity seldom knocks.... In a society where economic wealth is concentrated, more and more opportunity accrues to fewer and fewer people. (Blond and Gruescu, 2010, p 1)

Wind-Cowie (2009) and others have also argued for 're-capitalising the poor'. In the foreword to Wind-Cowie's book (2009, p 9) on this subject, David Cameron, then leader of the opposition for the Conservative Party, argued:

> In 1980s Britain, Margaret Thatcher led an ownership revolution that gave millions a new stake in our economy. That was truly popular capitalism.... It's now vital that we put wealth back into the hands of the poorest so they can not only lift themselves out of poverty – but keep themselves out too. (p 9)

We might, therefore, have thought that the Conservative/Liberal Democrat Coalition government would continue supporting a policy that promoted saving for people on low incomes. However, one of the first casualties of the spending axe was the Child Trust Fund in May 2010, and the planned national version of the Saving Gateway did not survive much longer. These policies were very much linked with New Labour philosophy but we might have expected Conservative governments to support such policies given that Margaret Thatcher did so much to extend assets during her time in power through the Right to Buy (see next section), and through widening share ownership through successive privatisations. The deregulation of building societies and financial markets also led to increasing asset ownership. But the views of the current government on this area of policy are not clear, and 'asset-based welfare' appears, surprisingly perhaps, to have been abandoned by them.

The end of asset-based welfare as we know it could prove a useful opportunity to go back to the drawing board and consider, in a more holistic way, the goals of a broader policy on assets and this, in turn, compels us to consider the reasons why people might need or want personal assets, and what the role of the state and other actors might be in relation to this. Assets in the form of pension wealth, for example, are clearly useful to provide an income stream in retirement. Such an income stream could be provided through the state, through employers or through individual savings (or through some combination of all these, as is the case now). The need for individuals to accumulate pension assets themselves will, then, depend crucially on the role of the state and employers, and we consider this issue later in the chapter.

Assets in the form of housing wealth are also useful in a number of ways, albeit rather different ways than pension wealth. First, they can provide people with a home to live in. Once again, the role of the state and the private sector (landlords) in providing people with homes is important here. Where the state withdraws from this role, the need for people, themselves, to become owner-occupiers, will be greater. Owner-occupation can also provide greater control over one's living environment as people have the right to modify their home. For example, in the 1980s, one of the very visible and public signs that someone had bought their own home on a council estate was that they changed or repainted their front door. This sign suggested a change (and rise) in status as well as ownership. Another sign, however, and one that showed the downside of private ownership, was that when the council replaced old windows or roofs, the homes that had been bought were left out of the modernisation process. So private ownership came at a cost.

But housing wealth is not just about *home* ownership. As we saw in Chapter Four, one in ten owner–occupiers owns another property. This may be a second home or it may be a property that is rented out. Housing, therefore, seems to be increasingly seen and used as an investment, and people appear to be increasingly seeing their own home in this way as well. With the great rises in property prices at the end of the 20th century and first years of the 21st, people began to think that 'bricks and mortar' provided at least as good, if not better, investment than the apparently risky stock market and pension funds (Rowlingson and McKay, 2005). The potential use of housing wealth as a 'pension' suggests that the two types of wealth may be playing similar roles in people's lives even though they are very different vehicles for achieving the same aim. And the recent house price falls from 2007 onwards may cause people to reconsider their view of housing as a safe investment. But what role should the state play here? We return to this later in the chapter.

And what about financial savings? Rowlingson et al (1999) drew on Keynes (1936) to identify many reasons to save as follows:

- to provide for predictable periods of low income (such as retirement) or high consumption costs (such as having children);
- as a precaution against unpredictable periods of low income (such as unemployment) or high consumption costs (such as illness);
- to provide positive real returns that might outweigh the costs of forgoing current consumption;
- to enable the future purchase of a particular item;
- to make a bequest;
- for its own sake ('the instinct of pure miserliness', according to Keynes).

As with housing wealth, we will consider what role the state does and should play in relation to financial wealth, given the reasons for saving. For example, if the state provides generous benefits for retirement, children, unemployment and illness through taxation or collective insurance, there is little reason to save for these privately, and it is difficult to see why the state should then help people to save if they will then use the savings merely to make a bequest or purchase a particular item which is not a basic need.

In this chapter we argue for a more holistic asset-based policy that should, at the very least, make current asset-based policies more explicit. The policy should also consider a number of factors, including:

- the respective roles of the state, employers, the private sector, the third sector and individuals/families in providing financial security;
- the interaction between different 'pillars' of welfare, particularly income-based welfare, public services and assets;
- the extent to which individuals should be encouraged to accumulate personal assets rather than spend or borrow;
- the balance and interactions between policies on pensions, housing and financial savings;
- the nature of policies in relation to both accumulation and decumulation;
- specific schemes to promote asset accumulation/decumulation but also tax policy.

Such a policy should also state, explicitly, its goal, which could be one or more of the following:

- to help people achieve financial security through a particular combination of individual and collective wealth;
- to help prevent poverty/disadvantage in the long term;
- to make 'citizenship' a more meaningful concept;
- to reduce wealth inequality/promote social justice.

Government policy currently affects asset accumulation and decumulation in various ways, but this is not explicit or joined up. We argue for a more holistic policy in this chapter.

Asset-based welfare policies, proposals and perspectives

As argued above, asset-based welfare was a major change in policy direction for New Labour in the 1990s (McKay and Rowlingson, 2008). But while there was a considerable amount of discussion about this new policy approach, there was actually very little policy action with the exception of two flagship policies: the Child Trust Fund and the Saving Gateway. This section outlines their key features and the main issues they raised. These two policies came largely from the 'social policy camp' of asset-based welfare (Prabhakar, 2008), focusing on poverty prevention. The citizenship approach has produced various proposals for capital grants but these have had less support from policy makers. However, the Child Trust Fund could be seen as a form of capital grant, albeit a rather different one from the proposals from the citizenship camp.

The Child Trust Fund paid a capital grant to all babies (or, at least, gave vouchers to set up accounts for new children) born from September 2002. Babies from low-income families received £500, while others received £250. This money was placed into a special account that could not be accessed until the child turned 18. At that point, the young person would be able to spend the money on anything they chose. In 2009, the government gave top-ups of £250/£500 to those children who had turned seven. Parents and other family members or friends could add to the accounts at any point up to a limit of £1,200 per year but not access them (Prabhakar, 2008). It was planned that the accounts would be linked to financial education in schools. Three choices of account were possible:

- standard savings account
- share account (greater risk but possibly a greater long-term reward)
- stakeholder account (investment in shares at beginning but then money moved to lower-risk investments).

If the parent/s did not make a choice of account then the government would open a default account for them. Three quarters of parents did open an account although opening rates were lower for families on low incomes. Blond and Gruescu (2010) quote Treasury statistics that show that in 2008/09, families had around £2 billion in Child Trust Fund accounts on behalf of 4.6 million children. The average contribution by friends and family made to Child Trust Fund accounts was £289 per year from 2002 to 2008, with a total value of contributions reaching £278 million (Blond and Gruescu, 2010).

Prabhakar's (2008) focus groups with parents raised a number of issues about the Child Trust Fund: a lack of information about opening an account; unfairness to older siblings who did not have an account because they were born before it was introduced; concerns over whether or not young people would use the money responsibly; a view that policies in this field should be universal rather than targeted; and that asset-based policies should not replace income benefits or public services. One issue with the Child Trust Fund is that parents cannot access the money once they put it in for their children. This may deter them from making a contribution if they feel they may have need of the money at some point and/or if they feel their child will not make best use of the money when they can access it. Kempson et al (2006) found rather patchy levels of parental knowledge about the programme and a concern about the security of savings (that is, a preference among many for the savings rather than share-based account). But, on a more positive note, there was a general expectation among parents that this would encourage savings to be made for children.

About 700,000 babies are born every year and so by the time its demise was announced in July 2010 about 5 million babies and children would have been eligible for the Child Trust Fund (Prabhakar, 2008). Blond and Gruescu (2010) argued that the Child Trust Fund has left an important legacy in encouraging more widespread saving for children. They point out that, prior to the Child Trust Fund, only 18 per cent of children were having regular long-term savings made for them whereas the Child Trust Fund industry average was 31 per cent.

With the demise of the Child Trust Fund a number of alternative policies have started to be discussed. For example, Blond and Gruescu (2010) suggest an ABC (Asset Building for Children) account to: boost savings, increase financial capability and promote responsibility and engaged citizenship around children's savings. The account would be open to all children and young people under 18 with a reward scheme and reward card for those who run an active ABC account. Investment gains and withdrawal at age 18 by the young person would be tax exempt. For those living in poverty (60 per cent below the median income), there would be a Fund available to match every £1 in savings with 50 pence from the Fund up to a maximum of £10 per month and £120 per year. The scheme would, Blond and Gruescu (2010, p 5) argued, 'facilitate the incentivisation of a mass savings culture'.

In October 2010 the government announced a new tax-free children's savings account to replace the Child Trust Fund, dubbed a 'Junior ISA'. The accounts were due to be launched on 1 November 2011 but there will be no government contribution or matched payments under the scheme. Instead, parents will be able to lock away up to £3,000 for each child each year, where they do not already have a Child Trust Fund, available when that child reaches 18.

The other flagship asset-based welfare policy was the Saving Gateway that was due to be introduced nationally in July 2010. This was a scheme designed to encourage people on low incomes (under £16,000 household income) to save by matching £1 of savings with a 50 pence reward (up to a maximum of £25 a month), and with the reward only payable after two years.

The report on the first pilot was very positive. It found that the policy generated both new savers and new savings among existing savers. The average amount saved was £282, with about half of participants saving the maximum of £375. The savers made very positive comments about the scheme, and 40 per cent were still regularly saving after the scheme had finished. The main conclusion from the report was that matched savings were central to the success of the scheme (Kempson et al, 2005). Overall the first pilot indicated that the scheme was being successful in encouraging people to save. Many participants also reported positive psychological and attitudinal changes (Collard and McKay, 2005).

The second pilot of the Saving Gateway looked at alternative levels of matching and ceilings on monthly savings. Harvey et al (2007) conducted an evaluation that found a mixture of some positive effects, and some cautions particularly around the issue of deadweight for (relatively) higher income savers. Again we might note that this saving scheme for lower-income people went through two extensive pilots before being proposed as a national programme, which may be contrasted with the simple introduction of ISAs and the recent increase in the amounts that may be saved into them. The 2010 Budget decision not to implement the Saving Gateway for lower-income families (which would have happened in July 2010) was projected to save £115 million in 2014/15. The decision to index-link ISAs will cost around £50 million in 2014/15.

Asset-based welfare is popular internationally, for example, with the US (with IDAs in a number of states), Canada (the Canada Education Savings Program, Individual Learning Account etc), Australia (Saver Plus) and so on. But such schemes are not limited to the English-speaking world, with Singapore leading the way in this branch of welfare when it set up compulsory saving in the Central Provident Fund in 1955. It now also has a Baby Bonus Scheme and the Edusave Scheme among others (see Blond and Gruescu, 2010, for further details on international schemes).

As mentioned above, the Saving Gateway and Child Trust Fund are largely based on the 'social policy' approach to asset-based welfare although the latter has elements of a citizenship-based capital grant. The citizenship approach has spawned a number of proposals on paper but fewer concrete policies in practice. Arguments for capital grants or citizen's inheritance go back a long way. In *Agrarian justice* Paine (1795–6) wrote:

> In advocating the case of the persons thus dispossessed, it is a right, and not a charity…. [Government must] create a national fund, out of which there shall be paid to every person, when arrived at the age of twenty-one years, the sum of fifteen pounds sterling, as a compensation in part, for the loss of his or her natural inheritance, by the introduction of the system of landed property; And also, the sum of ten pounds per annum, during life, to every person now living,

of the age of fifty years, and to all others as they shall arrive
at that age.

More recently, Ackerman and Alstott (1999) proposed giving every
US adult, on reaching maturity (age 21), US$80,000, funded by a
2 per cent annual tax on all the nation's wealth. Their idea was based
on reaffirming a sense of common, free and equal citizenship drawing
on the classical liberal tradition. They argued that those who receive
the grant, 'stakeholders', would be free to spend the grant on what
they wanted because they should take responsibility, and bear the
consequences, for their choices. Ackerman and Alstott (1999) also
argued that when they died, stakeholders should pay the funds back if
they could, through some kind of estate/inheritance tax, so that others
could gain the same advantage in future.

Nissan and Le Grand (2000) came up with a similar, although more
modest, proposal for a capital grant of £10,000 payable at the age of
18 to be spent only on specified purposes such as education, training
or buying a home. Their proposal thus combined elements of the
citizenship (capital grant) approach with the social policy (restricted
to welfare uses) approach. Like Ackerman and Alstott (1999) they
suggested using Inheritance Tax to pay for this.

Charles Murray (2006) is perhaps a surprising advocate of capital
grants, confirming that asset-based welfare appeals to people on very
different points of the political spectrum. He proposed a universal,
annual capital grant of US$10,000 for all those aged 21 or over,
excluding those in jail. There were two catches: US$5,000 would have
to be spent on pension contributions and health insurance, and the
capital grant would replace all other benefits.

Murray's proposal is interesting not least because it lies somewhere
between a basic income and a one-off capital grant, because people
would receive it every year. Prabhakar (2008) discussed the pros and
cons of basic income versus a capital grant. He argued that we could give
people just a basic income or just a capital grant or a combination of
the two. In fact, the two are perhaps more similar approaches than they
are different. A basic income may give better protection over people
spending their money unwisely ('stake-blowing'), because they are only
given small amounts each time (perhaps every week or fortnight) so
they cannot waste large amounts in one go. But they could still waste
the money each week, so there is no absolute protection against using
the money unwisely. Capital grants may, however, give people more
responsibility, and it is possible to put some restrictions on it to prevent
stake-blowing. Capital grants may also give more capacity to transform

one's life than a basic income because the amount is more substantial. Ackerman and Alstott (1999, p 215) argue that 'basic income cushions failure; stake-holding is a launching pad for success'. But a guaranteed basic income could enable people to borrow money against their future income to provide access to the same opportunities. In practice, however, it may not be so easy to borrow. So perhaps some kind of combination of basic income (or benefits) and capital grant is ideal to get the advantages of each. Prabhakar (2008) did indeed argue that it is possible to do both, and quotes Thomas Paine who argued for both a capital grant to be given to 21-year-olds and an annual income to be given to those aged 50 or over.

This section has focused on asset-based welfare policies and it seems that there are good arguments for supporting people on low incomes to save, not least because other groups receive such support (for example, through the tax system – see later). There is no strong evidence, at the moment, however, of an asset effect, but more research in this area is needed (see Chapter One). And there are other reasons for supporting all groups to save and accumulate assets on citizenship grounds as well as welfare grounds. Progressive universal savings schemes, which support all but those on low incomes more than others, appear to tick both the citizenship and welfare boxes and should be given more consideration.

Asset-based welfare policies in relation to savings for people on low incomes have received most attention when looking at policy on assets, but it is vitally important to also include housing and pension policy and also how the tax system treats assets. We turn to these issues in the next sections of this chapter, but before looking at them in depth, individually, it is important to point out the links between them. For example, there has been a debate about the extent to which people are investing in housing wealth rather than pension wealth. In the UK in 2004 the public were more likely to see housing as a better mechanism for saving for retirement than pensions by a ratio of more than two to one (Rowlingson and McKay, 2005). This might suggest that some people invest more in housing than pensions and so have lower incomes in later life, but are potentially able to draw on some of their housing assets. Doling and Ronald (2010a) have considered the extent to which housing wealth might constitute a potential reserve, supplement or even alternative to pension income across Europe. They concluded that there was considerable diversity across Europe in terms of pension and housing systems as well as diversity in the distribution of housing, pension and savings. But, overall, most of those with the highest levels of housing wealth also had higher incomes, and so the scope for housing wealth to raise the living standards of those on low incomes was very limited.

Doling and Ronald (2011) also draw on examples outside of Europe to highlight how the role of the state in relation to housing wealth can vary quite considerably. For example, governments in a number of East Asian countries have been particularly interventionist in relation to housing wealth as it is seen as central to the 'productivist welfare regime' based on welfare through the family, the company and the community rather than the state directly (Holliday, 2000). In Singapore, for example, people are able to withdraw savings from the Central Provident Fund in order to purchase housing, and so there is a clear and direct trade-off between housing and pension wealth, with home ownership seen as a way for retired people to live rent free and so require a smaller pension (Doling and Ronald, 2011). In Taiwan, government-subsidised home loans help people to become owner-occupiers and similar schemes exist in Japan and South Korea. Such schemes have contributed to a phenomenal growth in owner-occupation in the region. For example, home ownership grew from 29 to 92 per cent of stock between 1970 and 2003 (Chua, 2003).

We discuss this issue in more detail later but it is worth pointing out here that there are also some interesting perspectives on the broader relationship between housing wealth and the welfare state: so-called 'property-based welfare' (Doling and Ford, 2007; Doling and Ronald, 2010b). This perspective became more widely discussed as home ownership expanded internationally and as house prices rose in the mid-2000s. Housing wealth became seen as a potential resource that people might draw on. And although house prices in the UK have fallen in recent years, the recession and government spending cutbacks still mean that housing wealth may provide an important financial resource for people.

As well as considering whether or not those with housing wealth may draw on their wealth in times of need, there has also been considerable debate at a macro level about whether countries with higher levels of owner-occupation have more residual welfare states due to a lack of support from home owners for higher taxes and benefits (Kemeny, 1981; Castles, 1998; Lowe, 2004; Malpass, 2008). An alternative perspective is that countries with higher taxes restrict the amount of money that people have available to buy their own home. As we saw in Chapter Four, the lowest rates of home ownership were in Germany, Sweden and France, countries which have much higher levels of taxation than the UK, with a much higher level of owner-occupation and a much lower level of taxation, but a correlation here does not necessarily imply a causal relationship and, even if there is a causal relationship, the direction of causation and the explanation for such causation is not clear.

The next focuses on the role of housing wealth and related policies.

Policies on housing wealth

Housing wealth is a more equally distributed form of marketable personal wealth than financial savings. It is also a far more substantial source of wealth for most people. It is therefore important to consider the role of policies on housing wealth. Until 1979, however, housing policy in the UK more generally did not focus on housing wealth as such but on supporting people on low incomes to live in decent homes (Doling, 1997). If we go back to the 19th century, housing policy was linked to the public health agenda due to concerns about over-crowding and poor conditions in the new urban slums. The spread of typhoid and cholera led to increasing regulation of housing through the sanitary reform movement. But from the 1880s onwards, the mechanism for enabling those on low incomes to afford decent homes expanded from regulation of housing conditions to further regulation of rent levels and giving tenants more security of tenure (Doling, 1997).

It took the two world wars for governments to start building, or subsidising the building of, homes 'fit for heroes'. So most housing policy until the mid-20th century was focused on renting – either in terms of regulating the private rented sector or building homes for rent through public funding. This is not surprising given that, during the First World War, about 90 per cent of the housing stock was in the private rented sector (Doling, 1997). Up to this point, government policy had been focused more on consumption (physical shelter) than investment (financial shelter), but then in 1953 the government stated its support for home ownership with the Housing White paper, arguing that:

> Of all forms of saving, this is the best. Of all forms of ownership this is one of the most satisfying to the individual and the most beneficial to the nation. (Ministry of Housing and Local Government, 1953, cited in Malpass, 2008)

These were bold claims about housing wealth in relation to savings and pensions and show that issues of wealth were central to housing policy at that time. The key turning point, however, in housing (wealth) policy was the Right to Buy Act 1980. This signalled a sea-change in government policy towards the explicit encouragement and concrete support for home ownership. Other forms of support for home ownership at the time included Mortgage Interest Relief At Source[2] (MIRAS), the exemption of primary residences from Capital Gains Tax and the exemption from tax on imputed rent.

As mentioned above, Labour originally opposed the Right to Buy Act 1980 but subsequently New Labour embraced support for this policy and, more generally, for home ownership. In 2000, the government signalled its awareness of mounting housing pressures with its White Paper, *Quality and choice: A decent home for all: The way forward for housing* (DETR, 2000). The focus of the paper was on sustainable home ownership, the reform of house buying and selling, area-based renewal and home improvement.

In 2004, the Barker Review on housing supply argued that Britain urgently needed to build up to 140,000 extra houses a year if supply was to keep up with demand. Barker argued that between 70,000 and 120,000 of those homes should be provided by the private sector, while around 23,000 should be social housing units (HM Treasury, 2004). In response to the Barker Review, the government committed itself, in 2005, to a target/aspiration of 75 per cent home ownership (cited in Williams, 2007). Only a few years later, when the banking crisis and recession hit, it became clear that the growth of home ownership would stall and this target would be very difficult to achieve in the short or even medium term. Despite this the Conservative/Liberal Democrat Coalition government is:

> ... committed to increasing housing supply and helping those who aspire to own their own home to do so ... we estimate 1.4 million households, renting in the private sector or social sector, aspire to own but cannot, with many excluded from the housing market altogether.[3]

But issues around housing (wealth) are not just about supply. Hills (2007) pointed out that decisions about the current housing stock would affect many more people than building new homes. Nevertheless, housing supply affects prices and the Department for Communities and Local Government (CLG) website points out that, due to a combination of persistently high house prices and reluctance of lenders to offer mortgages, the average age of people able to buy their first home with no financial support from their family or friends has risen to 37. The Coalition government's approach to housing wealth policy is a rather indirect one. They have argued that their key strategy is to achieve economic and financial stability by addressing the public deficit. They argue that this will help to keep interest rates low and improve credit availability.

The government's big idea on housing policy is to shift control over house building from central government to local authorities and the community. Various schemes exist to achieve these aims including the New Homes Bonus – a scheme to provide incentives to increase the supply of new homes. CLG has set aside almost £1 billion government funding over four years from 2011/12 for councils that allow new housing development. The idea is for the government to match the Council Tax raised from new homes for the first six years and then give this to councils who will be expected to work with their local communities to decide how to spend the extra funding. It could be used to give Council Tax discounts for local residents or to pay for frontline services such as rubbish collection or local facilities such as swimming pools and leisure centres:

> Taken together with continuing, but more modest, capital investment in social housing, this will allow the Government to deliver up to 150,000 new affordable homes over the Spending Review period. (HM Treasury, 2010)

The government is also, at the moment, continuing with policies to help social tenants own or part-own their home through the Right to Buy and promoting shared ownership schemes. HomeBuy products provide support for eligible first-time buyers who are unable to purchase a property suitable for their needs without assistance (ODPM, 2005). Social tenants who wish to buy a property through HomeBuy are given top priority. Key workers, such as nurses, teachers, police officers and local authority staff, are also given priority. People can buy a 25, 50 or 75 per cent share in their home. They pay rent on the share they are not buying, normally set at an 'affordable' rate. Obviously, the bigger proportion purchased, the less rent people have to pay. It is also possible to buy increasing shares until the home is owned outright in a process known as 'staircasing'. These policies have not had a massive uptake. Hills (2007) stated that while nearly 1.9 million social homes had been purchased under Right to Buy or related schemes since 1980, the total number of people helped into some kind of shared home ownership was much smaller – about 150,000 since 1991. And the HomeBuy schemes are currently under review given the government's overwhelming priority to cut the public deficit.

The current Coalition government is not only keen to help people become home owners; it is also aiming to keep people in home ownership by preventing a large rise in the numbers of repossessions. Once again, it sees its over-arching policy as addressing the public deficit and making sure that interest rates remain low, but a more specific range of measures are currently in place, largely continued from the previous government, including:

- Financial Services Authority (FSA) regulation of lenders;
- a 'mortgage pre-action protocol' in the courts;
- funding for debt advice services;
- Income Support for Mortgage Interest (ISMI);
- the Mortgage Rescue Scheme;
- the Homeowners Mortgage Support Scheme.

However, the National Audit Office (2011) has suggested that the Mortgage Rescue Scheme went over its £205 million budget but only helped 2,600 households since January 2009, less than half the expected 6,000. Most of the households who qualified for help under the scheme chose to sell their house to a housing association and stay on as a tenant rather than take out an equity loan to reduce their monthly mortgage costs. This choice was a more expensive one than the equity loan choice, and the government had not predicted that so many people would opt for it.

Home ownership is clearly supported by a number of schemes (loans and grants for improvements, means-tested assistance with mortgage costs, Right to Buy discounts and by a series of Low Cost Home Ownership schemes, which allow people to purchase just part of the value of a property). But the value of the resources put into these schemes is far lower than the amount of money spent on subsidising the rented sector through Housing Benefit. The Department for Work and Pensions (DWP) (2010a) has estimated that Housing Benefit cost approximately £20 billion in 2010/11. Housing Benefit is due to be cut significantly in the next few years but it is still by far the largest mechanism for supporting people's housing costs. Hills (2007) estimated that the overall cost of ISMI was £300 million in 2004 (at 2004/05 prices). The cost of Right to Buy was more substantial but has been restricted in recent years and does not, according to Hills (2007), equate to the levels of public support given to those in the rented sector.

There are also some inconsistencies in approach to supporting people's housing costs as Housing Benefit is available to low-paid workers but ISMI is restricted to those out of work.[4] Furthermore, Stephens et al

(2008b) pointed out that most home owners have to wait nine months before they receive ISMI. And while the mortgage industry had initially hoped that more than half of all those with mortgages would take up private mortgage insurance, take-up never reached this figure and has, in fact, fallen; fewer than one in five households now have private mortgage payment protection insurance. With this in mind, Stephens et al (2008b) have proposed a SHOP ('Sustainable Home Ownership Partnership') that would be a compulsory social insurance scheme for those with mortgages. This would be cheaper than current private insurance schemes on the market which are only taken out by 20 per cent of mortgaged households and which have been the subject to criticism about mis-selling.

Gregory (2011) also supported the ideas behind SHOP but raised the concern that this could reinforce tenure distinctions, with owner-occupiers portrayed as responsibly insuring themselves and tenants portrayed as depending on 'handouts'. He has suggested a radical redesign of support for housing finance in the UK by setting up an insurance-based scheme for both renters and owner-occupiers.

But should we give owners more support if this enables some people to accumulate an asset while others are left outside of asset ownership? Should policy aim for everyone to become an owner-occupier at some point in their lives, so that everyone can share in asset ownership? If we do, this would require expanding home ownership to include more households on low and moderate incomes (Forrest et al, 1990; Stephens, 2007; Williams, 2007). These households are often considered sub-prime and are higher-risk borrowers (Forrest, 2008; Stephens et al, 2008b). The cost of home ownership is often prohibitive to many such buyers, and lenders may be increasingly cautious about serving this group. This suggests that many groups are, and will continue to be, excluded from home ownership. Government schemes, mentioned above, may help to some extent, but the sustainability of current levels of owner-occupation look questionable (CLG, 2008; Stephens et al, 2008b; Giles and Pimlott, 2009; Collinson, 2010).

And people themselves appear to be acknowledging that home ownership may be out of their range. For example, young people's attitudes to home ownership have become more negative in recent years in response to housing market recessions. While these attitudes may well improve when the housing market recovers, there appears to be a general trend downwards (Wallace, 2010). Affordability is clearly an issue for young people here and is likely to continue, particularly as the cost of university education increases substantially following the review of tuition fees (see Paton, 2009). It therefore looks unlikely that home ownership will continue to expand, leaving some people without any housing wealth.

Nevertheless, most people are currently owner-occupiers and many of these experienced significant increases in house prices over the last couple of decades. Holmans et al (2007) have argued that the growth in home ownership combined with rising house prices helped to slow the general growth in wealth inequality as more people in the 'middle' expanded their asset base. But those at the bottom are being left further behind and there is an increasing divide between those with and those without wealth.

The growth of housing wealth has led to increasing discussion about the role it might play in relation to welfare, especially if the state has helped to subsidise housing wealth accumulation. If housing wealth is expected to play a role in relation to welfare, then people need to be able to draw on it. There is increasing discussion about this (Maxwell, 2005), with some hope that housing wealth might be used to substitute for low income, particularly in retirement. As mentioned earlier, people themselves appear to be recognising this, with 61 per cent of the public in 2004 believing that housing was a better way of making financial provision for retirement than pensions. Only 26 per cent opted for pensions (Rowlingson and McKay, 2005). There is some debate, however, about whether those on low incomes have sufficient levels of housing wealth for it to make a difference to them (Doling and Ronald, 2010a, 2010b).

Hancock (2000) found that 12 per cent of those aged 65–79 had incomes in the lowest fifth of the income distribution but lived in properties which placed them in the second (from top) fifth of the housing wealth distribution. This suggests a small group who might benefit from withdrawing equity from their homes. The Pensions Commission (2005) also considered this and came to the conclusion that those with low pension wealth also had low housing wealth, and so housing wealth cannot be seen as a way of plugging the pension gap. But Sodha (2005) was more positive about the existence of a 'housing rich, income poor' group. She used £100,000 for her housing wealth threshold and found that one in five pensioners in poverty owned housing wealth above this threshold. Furthermore, she argued that the number of people who might be considered 'income poor, asset rich' was likely to rise in the next few decades.

So there may be a small group of people with low incomes but significant housing wealth in later life. Can, will this group withdraw equity from their homes to improve their living standards?

Some already are doing so and, in fact, some are not waiting till retirement but are withdrawing equity through re-mortgaging during their working lives, for example, to pay for property maintenance, property extensions, children's university fees and so on (Smith, 2005; Smith and Searle, 2008). The planned increase in student fees may make this phenomenon more widespread. Of course, the money borrowed would need to be repaid at some point, and this phenomenon might explain why people appear to be approaching retirement with increasing amounts of outstanding mortgage debt (Ford, 2006; McKay et al, 2008).

There are also other ways in which people can access the equity in their homes without re-mortgaging. For example, people can move to a cheaper house. But this might mean moving to a cheaper neighbourhood which may not be where they want to live. Or it might mean moving to a smaller home and, depending on the size of the initial home, there might not be much scope for 'downsizing'. Moving house is also quite expensive with legal, estate agent and stamp duty fees to pay. The Pensions Policy Institute (2009) suggested that downsizing from a property worth £350,000 to one worth £230,000 in order to release £120,000 would cost about £13,100, taking into account the cost of stamp duty, surveys, legal fees and so forth. Trading down may also have social and psychological costs if it means leaving friends, family and a family home (Davey, 1996; Aleroff and Knights, 2008). People do, however, sometimes 'trade down' when their children leave home or on retirement, and so the capacity to do this again at a later stage in life may be limited. People may also move from home ownership to renting although this seems to be relatively rare.

Another way of accessing housing equity is through an equity release product (lifetime mortgage or home reversion plan). But these are not available to all owner-occupiers as they are currently restricted to those with homes worth over £100,000. Also, those in receipt of means-tested benefits may lose entitlement to some of their income from this source (Overton, 2010). Sodha (2005) estimated that about one million older people have housing wealth of more than £100,000 but incomes small enough to entitle them to means-tested benefits. Furthermore, equity release is a complex financial product that the FSA advise people take independent advice about prior to taking out a plan, but those on low incomes may not feel they can afford to do this (Ring, 2003).

In a survey of the general public carried out in 2004, the majority of people said they liked the idea of equity release in theory but only one in twenty owner-occupiers said they would consider taking out such a scheme (Rowlingson and McKay, 2005). Equity release schemes were most popular among 60-year-olds and those from the professional classes. Owner-occupiers thought that equity release schemes as they currently stood were complex, risky and difficult to understand. They had little trust in the current providers. But they did like the idea in theory. This suggests that there is scope for developing policies that enable people to release some equity in their home while retaining some for bequests.

It has sometimes been thought that the desire to leave wealth to future generations may be an additional barrier to drawing on housing equity. Rowlingson and McKay (2005) found that most members of the general public strongly supported the principle of making bequests. But attitudes seemed to be changing, with 50- and 60-year-olds in 2004 generally taking a more pragmatic view that it was a good idea to use up some assets in later life if needed. Rowlingson (2006) also found that older people seemed more pragmatic about their wealth than previous cohorts. While they wanted to leave some of their wealth as a bequest, they also expected to use some themselves. They expected their future incomes to be quite low and they no longer expected the state to provide a decent income in retirement and so expected to have to release equity for themselves.

Equity release might seem like a good option for these pragmatists and the government has played a quiet, although increasing, role here, regulating lifetime mortgages in 2004 and home reversion plans in 2007. However, at the moment, equity release plays a very small role in relation to improving pensioners' living standards because so few use such schemes. Overton (2010) carried out research with those who had used equity release and found that people who used equity release plans were 72 years, on average, when they took out their plans. Three quarters had children and they were neither the very richest nor poorest pensioners. Most customers had income from a private pension, so money from equity release was a supplement rather than a substitute for private pensions. Indeed, equity release was used more to provide capital than regular income. Customers seemed to divide into one of three groups: those who were withdrawing equity to make 'early bequests' to children and large one-off purchases. This group were typically better off than the other groups. The second group were using the money to increase their financial security and have a more comfortable lifestyle than they would otherwise have had. And the third group were drawing on their housing equity to relieve financial difficulty. This group were more likely to have been in debt than the other groups.

Most equity release customers thought that home owners should not be forced to use the value of their homes to supplement their pension incomes, but in qualitative interviews the customers said that they, themselves, were quite happy about using the value of their homes to improve their living standards (Overton, 2010). As one customer said:

> "What's the point of having savings and all this sort of thing and you haven't done anything with it and then you die?" (male, aged 66, married, quoted in Overton, 2010, p 17)

Until now, we have talked about people making a choice about whether or not to access the equity in their homes but there is, of course, one policy area in which people have no choice about doing so. This is the very unpopular policy of means testing the primary home when it comes to paying for continuing social care. As of December 2010, people living in England who had over £23,000 in capital were assessed as being able to meet the full cost of care, which typically cost around £500 per week. Over the last decade or so, there have been a number of reviews of policies to pay for continuing care, given the ageing population (Royal Commission on Long-Term Care for the Elderly, 1997; Wittenberg et al, 2004; Johnstone, 2005; Hirsch, 2006; Wanless, 2006; DH, 2009).

Wanless (2006, p xxi) pointed out that there was 'widespread dissatisfaction with the current funding system' of long-term care. In the same year, the Joseph Rowntree Foundation (Hirsch, 2006) suggested various reforms that could be introduced in the short term, including two that directly involved housing assets:

- plot a voluntary equity release scheme for home-based care that would enable home owners to access their housing wealth. Costs would depend on take-up and would be low in the long term because the loans would be repaid;
- double the capital threshold for home support to prevent home owners from using up too much of their own housing assets before they could access state support.

For the long-term, however, the Joseph Rowntree Foundation report suggested a similar partnership approach to Wanless (2006). The Foundation suggested that those receiving care should be charged 20 per cent of the costs, with the remaining costs being paid by the state through general taxation. The report suggests that this would cost around £2 billion.

This policy issue became hotly debated during the 2010 General Election with the Labour government proposing £20,000 so-called 'death tax' to pay for care. Details of the proposal were never released, and so it was not clear which estates would have had to pay the tax. But the proposal was not popular and Labour withdrew it. By contrast, the Conservatives suggested that people should make an optional, one-off payment of £8,000 at 65, to effectively insure themselves against the future costs of care.

But despite all this debate, governments have preferred to do very little, no doubt nervous about the potential consequences of raising general taxation or introducing new social insurance schemes to pay for care. Current policy therefore remains unpopular and controversial but there are no signs that major reform is on the horizon. Another Commission, this time 'on the Funding of Care and Support', headed by Andrew Dilnot, published its report in July 2011, highlighting that funding is hard to understand, often unfair and unsustainable. People can be faced with catastrophic care costs with no way to protect themselves. The Commission therefore argued that the current funding system is in urgent need of reform and they suggested that there should be a cap on individuals' lifetime contributions towards their social care costs – at around £35,000. They also proposed that the means-tested threshold, above which people are liable for their full care costs, should be increased from £23,250 to £100,000. These reforms would cost around £1.7 billion (Commission on Funding of Care and Support, 2011). Qualitative research carried out for the Commission confirmed that people were not keen to pay for care through housing wealth, preferring to pay for it through pensions or insurance instead (Hewitson et al, 2011).

Housing wealth policy is a crucial component of a comprehensive policy on assets. It is fairly widespread and is more equally distributed than other forms of wealth but there is still a significant and increasing minority who have no housing wealth at all. Government supports people to accumulate housing wealth in various ways and, at a time of major public sector cuts, there is a question about how far people should then access the equity in their homes to improve their economic wellbeing. People already do this in various ways and they do recognise that housing is part of their investment for retirement as well as a potential source of finance during working life (through mortgage equity withdrawal). But people on the lowest incomes have least housing equity and, even among those who do have some equity to access, use of equity release schemes is, in practice, very limited. There is a great deal of interest in these schemes among the public but a concern that they are poor value for money and that they may not be trustworthy.

Government could, in theory, play a more active role here in encouraging people to consider such schemes, in providing schemes itself (or supporting the third sector to do so) and even in subsidising such schemes to make them better value for money. This would mean extra resources being put in place to support owner-occupiers but the advantages in terms of equity released to maintain living standards may make it worthwhile. As we shall see later in this chapter, private pensions are effectively subsidised in a massive way by tax relief and some of this could, in theory, be cut back to support equity release instead.

Governments in some countries are already supporting equity release schemes in different ways (Doling and Ronald, 2011). For example, in Japan, the government in 2006 introduced a scheme to help older people downsize by renting their houses out to larger families, enabling the older people to pay for housing in more suitable (smaller) accommodation. Some local governments and housing corporations in Japan have developed reverse mortgages. In South Korea, the state-owned Korea Housing Finance Corporation introduced a reverse mortgage in 2007 and provides protection against the risk of living longer, lower housing prices and higher interest rates. Those taking out reverse mortgages are also given a number of tax concessions including exemption from registration, education and special rural taxes. They also receive a 25 per cent income tax liability. The governments in these countries are variously providing schemes, providing guarantees and providing financial incentives to withdraw equity in later life.

Cross-national research such as this (see also Izuhara, 2009) provide interesting examples of how the state can play various roles in relation to housing assets and welfare. Such studies also highlight the role of demographic change, public attitudes, cultural beliefs and legal frameworks in relation to housing assets. Drawing on such studies, it is time to take a fundamental look at the tenure balance in the UK and the way that government policy affects this. Owner-occupation has been heavily subsidised and favoured, not least with mortgage interest relief in the past and still today with subsidies for Right to Buy, exemptions from capital gains tax on primary residences, tax-free imputed rent and support for people who fall behind with their mortgages (Hills, 2007). A review is needed to consider the primary objective of housing policy and then how to achieve it. For example, rather than focusing on the promotion of a particular tenure type, policy might be better focused on goals such as providing housing security and quality. This might lead to more investment in social housing and improved rights for tenants. A review of housing taxation would also be helpful here (Lloyd, 2009; Shelter, 2009). This is a complex issue, however, not least because of the considerable regional variations in housing wealth and the potential use of housing wealth as a retirement fund.

Pensions policy

The third major asset type that we focus on in this book is pension wealth. The policy trends here are not dissimilar to those on housing wealth, with increasing collective provision during much of the 20th century until 1979, when the role of the state was then diminished and private provision encouraged. But while housing wealth has significantly expanded in the last 30 or so years, private pension wealth has not grown so dramatically, and we consider why this is the case.

The first step made towards the *modern* social security system[5] in Britain was not made by Beveridge but by Lloyd George, with his 1908 Old Age Pensions Act.[6] The pension was non-contributory and aimed at those aged 70 plus on low incomes. A simple means test was used to check eligibility and the scheme was administered through the Post Office. This signalled a move away from the more arbitrary discretion and stigma of the Poor Law towards a more rational approach (Fraser, 1973; Thane, 1982; McKay and Rowlingson, 1998). It was also Lloyd George who first introduced National Insurance into the welfare state in 1911 although this was only for unemployment and sickness at first, and it was not until 1925 that this was extended to pensions. But if the 1908 Act was the first step, then it was the National Insurance Act 1946 that was the great leap forward in pensions, establishing a comprehensive National Insurance scheme for all workers. Married women were covered through their husband's contributions and so, if married women were also workers, they could (until 1978) take the 'married women's option' to opt out of paying contributions. The assumptions about the relationships between men and women, and between women and the labour market, have been a major issue for pension policy (as with other elements of social security policy). Changing views about gender relationships, along with women's increasing engagement with the labour market, have led to substantial changes in pension policy in this area.

From the start, state pension policy in Britain has always sought to maintain incentives for individuals to save for themselves on top of their state pension. In the 19th century, Britain had developed a strong sector of friendly societies and Beveridge certainly did not want to discourage these (Beveridge, 1942; Gladstone, 1999). Thus, the level of state pension payments had always been relatively low. And these payments have never been paid out of a funded insurance scheme. Such a scheme would have taken time to mature and the government wished to start paying pensions straight away so the payments made into the scheme (current workers) were immediately paid out to those benefiting from the scheme (current pensioners). The idea that individual contributions were saved or invested and then paid out to those contributors later on was a myth. It was an important and popular myth, however, because people felt they had a right to their pension on the basis of their contributions.

The Beveridge social security system, alongside changes in health and education policy, was a dramatic change in welfare provision, but the cracks in the system soon become clear, and in the 1960s there was a 'rediscovery of poverty' (Abel-Smith and Townsend, 1965; Coates and Silburn, 1970). Much of the concern about poverty at this time was related to families with children and the unemployed but the debate at the time raised the issue of whether benefit contributions and payments, including pensions, should be flat-rate (as they were) or earnings-related. This debate led, in time, to the introduction of the State Earnings-Related Pension Scheme (SERPS) in 1978, which actually built on a small Graduated Pension Scheme that had existed from 1961. Earnings-related benefits are more common in some countries than others. For example, France and Germany have generally taken this approach as their welfare states are not just about alleviating poverty but about enabling people to save different amounts depending on their capacity to save (Palier, 2009). Those who can save more, will later receive more. The British system has focused on enabling people to save just enough (and sometimes not even enough) to avoid poverty in later life.

Whatever the merits of an earnings-related pension, support for SERPS was short-lived once the Conservative government came into power in 1979. While they baulked at abolishing SERPS altogether, they did reduce it (by about half) and increased incentives for people to take out occupational and personal pensions (McKay and Rowlingson, 1998; Pemberton, 2006).

The last two decades have seen several important changes in pensions policy, affecting both the private sector and state pensions. It would be consistent with Pemberton (2006) to note that reviews are conducted about once every decade. These reviews tend to note the complexity of the system and then propose the introduction of a new pensions product to fill some of the gaps identified. Nevertheless, the addition of a new product then inevitably complicates the range of choices on offer still further.

As mentioned above, there was a general appetite for reducing the role of the state and increasing the share of the private sector in the 1980s. This went beyond pensions into different areas of public policy, including the housing stock (as we have discussed) and the ownership of nationalised industries. There was also a concern to ensure that the costs of welfare provision were held in check, although underlying trends and higher unemployment meant that levels of spending on social security benefits actually continued to increase.

One of the most important changes for the future of pensions was the decision in 1980 to link increases in state pensions to changes in prices (retail price index, RPI) rather than to changes in either earnings or prices, whichever was higher, as had happened before. As earnings generally increased more rapidly than prices in the 1980s and 1990s, this inevitably meant that the level of the basic pension fell further behind the level of earnings. In 1979, the basic state pension represented 26 per cent of average earnings (DWP, 2010b). By 2009 this had fallen to 16 per cent of the earnings of the average worker. So pensioners were becoming much worse off than workers, when they had to rely on state pensions.

The Conservative government's answer to this issue was to encourage people to take out private pensions rather than rely on the state. For example, 'personal pensions' with favourable tax treatment for employees were introduced in the 1980s alongside existing occupational pensions. And in the late 1980s, it became possible for people to contract out of SERPS into a personal pension – with encouragement through generous tax treatment. It was also ensured that employers could not require employees to join or remain in their occupational schemes. This was aimed at providing greater choice, but to some extent opened the door to aggressive sales tactics during 1988–94 encouraging people to quit occupational schemes (often with a generous employer contribution) and to move into personal pensions. This would ultimately lead to lower pensions income for many people, and government intervention subsequently forced the payment of compensation in what became a large mis-selling scandal (McKay, 2009).

Pension scandals also affected occupational pensions most notably in 1991 when some 20,000 people lost £480 million they believed to be safe in pension funds but which had instead been used by Robert Maxwell to (temporarily) prop up ailing companies in his group. Most of the lost money was replaced by £100 million from the government and a settlement for £276 million from financial institutions.

When Labour came to power in 1997 we might have expected a reversal of policy and reviving of the role of the state in relation to pensions, but this was not the case and there was to be no return, for example, to faster uprating of state pensions in the New Labour governments like the Conservatives before them. New Labour also wished to encourage more private pension provision but had begun to realise that there was a significant problem of pensioner poverty. They hoped to address this problem through the introduction of the means-tested benefit, Pension Credit, to support poorer pensioners. Like most means-tested benefits, however, it failed to achieve a high level of take-up. But it was an increasingly generous benefit and pensioner poverty did decline quite dramatically following its introduction (McKay and Rowlingson, 2008).

It soon became obvious that reliance on the private sector was problematic. The Maxwell scandal may have been something of a one-off, but under New Labour several companies ceased trading and exposed gaps in their pension funds. For instance, the company Allied Steel and Wire became bankrupt in 2002 leaving non-retired members with substantially reduced pension pots – some claiming losses of over 80 per cent (McKay, 2009). This was a risk whenever the parent company of an underfunded defined benefit pension scheme ceased trading. These issues led to the introduction of a Financial Assistance Scheme, which was to be backdated, and then to the Pension Protection Fund.

Dissatisfaction with the suitability of personal pensions, and the high level of fees, prompted the introduction in 2001 of Stakeholder Pensions. However the main sets of reforms were to accompany a wide-ranging review by a Pensions Commission led by Adair Turner. In the first of three reports it famously concluded that the UK had 'the most complex pension system in the world' (Pensions Commission, 2004, p 210). It later made recommendations in a range of areas, with the clearest elements of reform comprising in particular:

- reforms to bolster the system of state pensions, particularly through easing the extent of contributions needed to qualify for a full state pension;
- the introduction of a new savings programme, the National Pensions and Savings Scheme (NPSS), into which individuals would *automatically* be entered on starting work.

A new low-cost savings scheme, originally labelled 'personal accounts' and now recast as the National Employment Savings Trust (NEST), followed most of the NPSS reforms suggested by the Pensions Commission. This is the key element of the proposed reforms and it is expected that 10 million people without access to occupational pensions will have a personal account in due course.

While many areas of social security have been proposed for cuts under the Coalition government, older people have, so far, generally been spared from the changes being made. The Coalition have also pledged to improve the uprating of the state pension, applying a 'triple lock' of uprating by the highest of earnings change, price changes or 2.5 per cent. This is a major departure from the past, and a return to uprating by earnings (at least) that has been absent for the past 30 years – albeit the value of the state pension is now much lower, relative to earnings, as a result.

To save money, however, the Coalition have speeded up plans for the equalisation of pension ages (reaching 65 for women by 2018, and 66 for both men and women by 2020, with further increases to follow). There have also been some changes to the maximum amounts of tax relief available within pensions, and John Hutton (former minister under Labour) has been appointed to review the future of public sector pensions, through an independent Public Service Pensions Commission. An interim report played down the idea that all civil servants were entitled to 'gold-plated' pensions (J. Hutton, 2010). However, it also found that public service schemes paid out £32 billion in 2008/09 (two thirds of the amount paid through the basic State Pension), and is investigating reforms that move away from a final salary basis of entitlement towards more career-average schemes.

Like many developed countries, the UK has an ageing population and hence a particular need to ensure that we have a pensions policy that will provide financial security for people in later life. After 30 years of encouraging people to take out, and contribute more, to private pensions by both Conservative and Labour governments, this policy approach seems to have run out of steam. While there will always be scope for 'the rich' to make significant private provision, most people rely mostly on the state and it is therefore time for the state to improve its provision. The new NEST may help, but contributions are set at a relatively low level, 8 per cent of earnings in total. Changes in state pension uprating may also help, but more is needed. In October 2010, Steve Webb MP, the Liberal Democrat Minister for Pensions, was reported as considering proposals for a universal citizen's pension. Details were sketchy but the idea is to have a scheme that abandons means testing to simplify the system and to avoid any disincentives to save. If set at a decent level the system will be expensive, and it remains to be seen whether it will become policy.

Taxing assets in the UK

Much of the literature on asset-based welfare and even broader policies on assets generally relates to various schemes that might encourage people to accumulate assets. Relatively little is said about how the tax system influences the amount that people save and the form in which they do so. A recent review of the tax system by Mirrlees et al (2010) has provided a thorough and authoritative account of the taxation system in relation to household savings. As part of this review, Adam et al (2010) have pointed out that the income tax treatment of saving has changed significantly over the last 30 years, largely due to the following:

- reforms of income tax during the 1980s that reduced the top marginal rate on savings income from 98 to 40 per cent;
- abolition of Mortgage Interest Tax Relief (MITR) in April 2000;
- introduction of personal pensions in 1988 bringing the same tax treatment for individual-based pensions as for employer-based occupational pensions;
- introduction of the Personal Equity Plan (PEP) and the Tax-Exempt Special Savings Account (TESSA) in 1987 and 1991 respectively. These have now been replaced by the ISA, which is similar in most important respects.

Assets are not only taxed on investment income and capital gains, but also by stamp duty and by Inheritance Tax on bequests. The current form of Inheritance Tax was introduced in 1986 to replace Capital Transfer Tax. Capital Transfer Tax not only taxed bequests but also gifts made during the donor's lifetime. But, as Adam et al (2010) have pointed out, differences in treatment were soon introduced and then widened, until Inheritance Tax was introduced and once again exempted lifetime gifts (except in the seven years before death) in an attempt to prevent people avoiding the tax by giving away their assets shortly before death.

Capital taxes have been extremely complex. For example, Adam et al (2010) have pointed out that in 1978 Capital Transfer Tax had 14 separate rates. The 1980s saw attempts to simplify the system and so when Inheritance Tax was introduced in 1988 it had a single rate (40 per cent) above a tax-free threshold. Capital Gains Tax was charged at the individual's marginal income tax rate from 1988. Four rates of stamp duty on properties were replaced by a single 1 per cent rate in 1984. Stamp duty on shares and bonds was almost abolished entirely: the rate fell from 2 to 0.5 per cent during the 1980s, and in 1990 the then Chancellor, John Major, announced that stamp duty on shares and bonds would be abolished in 1991/92 when the London Stock Exchange introduced a paperless dealing system known as TAURUS. However, this system was never introduced and stamp duty on shares and bonds remained.

Simplification always sounds like a good thing but it can have a negative side as it can often lead to blunt policy instruments that are not, perhaps, as fair and progressive as they might be. Other factors, such as house price inflation, can also lead to changes in thresholds. There was rapid growth in house prices from 1997 to 2005, far higher than any increases in both the Inheritance Tax threshold (which has typically increased in line with general price inflation) and the stamp duty zero-rate threshold (which has typically been frozen in cash terms). In 1997, Labour announced the reintroduction of graduated rates of stamp duty on properties. They are now 1, 3 and 4 per cent.

As a result of the rise in house prices after 1997, Adam et al (2010) have shown that the proportion of property transactions that attracted stamp duty grew from around half in 1997 to almost three quarters by 2003. Partly in response to this, the government doubled the stamp duty land tax threshold in 2005, and then increased it by a further £50,000 for one year only from 3 September 2008. We might also expect the rise in house prices to raise more Inheritance Tax and there was certainly concern expressed in some newspapers that 'ordinary' people would now be subject to Inheritance Tax rather than the privileged few. But the links between house prices and Inheritance Tax are less direct because housing wealth only makes up a proportion of all wealth left in bequests. Nevertheless, the proportion of estates liable for Inheritance Tax more than doubled in a decade – increasing from 2.3 per cent of the total in 1996/97 to 5.9 per cent in 2006/07 (Adam et al, 2010). This is a big increase, but the percentage is still very small. And in October 2007 the government effectively doubled the inheritance threshold for married couples and civil partners, reducing the number of estates liable to tax by a third (Adam et al, 2010). Property prices have also fallen substantially from their autumn 2007 peak.

Assets can be taxed in different ways. For example, the income used to accumulate savings may or may not be taxed. This is the case with savings in bank and building society accounts where people typically save from income that has been subject to income tax. In the case of pension wealth, however, contributions to pension pots made from income are exempt from income tax. This tax relief effectively means that higher rate taxpayers are subsidised more, by the state, than basic rate taxpayers who, in turn, are subsidised more than non-taxpayers. Thus, tax reliefs advantage people who are better off. Mortgage payments used to attract tax relief (through MIRAS) but this was abolished in 2000.

Tax allowances, breaks and reliefs are sometimes referred to as fiscal welfare (Mann, 2001; Sinfield, 2007), and these forms of welfare are sometimes referred to as the 'hidden welfare state' (Howard, 1997) because whereas expenditure on state benefits is easy to measure and publicise, the effective costs of fiscal and occupational welfare are much more obscure. Nevertheless, they add up to a considerable sum which goes to the better off. As we saw in Chapter Five, this tax relief on pensions is a 'hidden' form of welfare costing the public purse over £20 billion in 2008/09, with 60 per cent of this going to higher rate taxpayers (PPI, 2010). This is a considerable sum that in 2007/08 would have easily covered the entire cost of Pension Credit, winter fuel payments and free television licences for the over-75s.

As well as taxing the income used to accumulate assets, it is also possible to tax the returns/interest from accumulating assets. For example, interest from ordinary savings accounts is taxed at the same rate of income tax that the saver pays. So a higher rate taxpayer will currently pay 40 per cent tax on interest while a standard rate taxpayer will pay 20 per cent. An ISA, however, is exempt from income tax on interest. Pensions are also exempt from tax on investment returns. Housing is treated very differently if the house is the main or only home (in which case it is exempt from capital gains. Second homes (including buy-to-let properties) are taxed on the rental income received and are also subject to Capital Gains Tax.

And, finally, assets can be taxed when money is withdrawn from them. Withdrawals from savings accounts, whether ordinary ones or ISAs, are not subject to tax. But pension income is subject to tax, although a one-off lump sum (up to 25 per cent of the pension's value) is tax-free. Equity released from housing (for example, when the house is sold, assuming it is the primary residence) is not subject to tax.

Table 6.1 summarises the tax treatment of different assets, and it is clear that some assets are more 'privileged' than others. Pension wealth is particularly advantageous, followed by financial savings. But there is much variation within this asset type as ISAs receive much better treatment than ordinary accounts. There is also a considerable difference in tax treatment between first and subsequent properties. Such tax differences may affect and/or reward people's saving behaviour (and certain groups of people) more than others. For example, high earners

Table 6.1: Tax treatments of different assets

Asset	Returns			
	Income tax and NICs on contributions	Income tax on interest/ dividends	Capital Gains Tax	Income tax on withdrawals
Pension (employee contributions)	Exempt from income tax, not exempt from employer and employee NICs	Exempt	Exempt	Taxed, except for a 25% lump sum
Pension (employer contributions)	Exempt from income tax, exempt from employer and employee NICs	Exempt	Exempt	Taxed, except for a 25% lump sum
ISA	Taxed	Exempt	Exempt	Exempt
Interest-bearing account	Taxed	Taxed at 10%, 20% or 40%	N/A	
Housing (main or only property)	Taxed	Exempt	Exempt	Exempt
Housing (second or subsequent property)	Taxed	Rental income taxed	Taxed	Exempt

Source: Adapted from Adam et al (2010)

paying into pensions and ISAs appear to benefit most whereas those on low incomes who save in ordinary savings accounts benefit much less.

The degree of 'fiscal privilege' can be calculated quite precisely and this is what Adam et al (2010) have done. Table 6.2 shows the effective tax rate (ETR) on saving in each of the different asset types. Adam et al (2010) have made these calculations for basic and higher rate taxpayers assuming that all assets earn a 3 per cent real rate of return before tax and inflation is 2 per cent. They note that the ETR on an interest-bearing account is 33 per cent for a basic rate taxpayer, not the statutory income tax rate of 20 per cent, because tax is charged on the nominal return, not the real return. With a 3 per cent real return and 2 per cent inflation, £100 of saving yields nominal interest of about £5; 20 per cent tax on this, £1, represents 33 per cent of the £3 increase in the real purchasing power of the deposit. Inflation does not, however, affect ETRs on pensions, ISAs and owner-occupied housing, where the return is tax-exempt.

The lowest effective tax rates are for employer contributions to pensions. Employee contributions to pensions come next, with higher rate taxpayers facing a much lower rate of tax than basic rate taxpayers. ISAs and owner-occupied housing come next in the fiscal

Table 6.2: Effective tax rates on saving in different assets

Asset		Effective tax rate (%) for:	
		Basic rate taxpayer	Higher rate taxpayer
Pension (employee contributions)	Invested 10 years	−21	−53
	Invested 25 years	−8	−21
Pension (employer contributions)	Invested 10 years	−115	−102
	Invested 25 years	−45	−40
ISA		0	0
Interest-bearing account		33	67
Housing (main or only property)		0	0
Housing (second or subsequent property)	Invested 10 years	30	50
	Invested 25 years	28	48

Source: Adapted from Adam et al (2010)

privilege league, with ETRs of zero. The ETRs on property represent a combination of income tax and Capital Gains Tax.[7] Higher rate taxpayers pay more tax on these, as they do on interest-bearing accounts. which face the highest tax rates. But people on low incomes are more likely than people on high incomes to have a high proportion of any assets in such accounts and so they pay quite a price for saving.

Mirrlees et al (2010) reviewed the tax system, arguing that any reforms need to consider the system as a whole and need also to consider issues of progressivity and neutrality. They accept, however, that there may sometimes be a good case to deviate from neutrality if we wish to encourage or indeed discourage certain types of activity. For example, we may wish to tax alcohol and cigarettes at high rates but keep taxes low on savings and pensions. In relation to savings, Mirrlees et al (2010) have also pointed out that there is a tension between preventing tax avoidance and minimising disincentives to save. If taxes on capital are lower than taxes on income, some (particularly wealthy) groups may try to convert income into capital to avoid paying a higher rate of tax. Mirrlees et al (2010) have proposed key reforms in relation to the taxation of savings:

- take interest on bank and building society accounts out of tax altogether;
- remove tax on the 'normal' return to savings,[8] taxing only 'excess' returns;

- apply the standard income tax schedule to income from all sources (including savings, capital gains etc) after an allowance for the normal rate of return on savings;
- maintain and simplify the current system of pensions taxation, ending the excessively generous treatment of employer contributions and replacing the tax-free lump sum with an incentive better targeted.

They have argued that:

> The current tax system treats most harshly those assets that are most important to individuals with smaller amounts of savings, particularly interest-bearing bank and building society accounts. (Mirrlees et al, 2010, p 14)

The taxation of assets has received very little attention from social science academics, with the exception of economists, but it is a very important, if relatively complex and hidden form of state support. The current system generally seems to penalise the poorest and could be reformed to provide more support for those on lower incomes.

This chapter has concentrated on the taxation of savings. The next chapter turns its attention to capital taxes, including Council Tax and Inheritance Tax.

Within-household distribution of assets

Policies around assets tend to assume that assets are shared equally within the household. Social security policy, for example, carries out couple-based means tests of assets, on the assumption that these are a joint resource. But Rowlingson and Joseph (2010) have shown that this is not necessarily the case, particularly in relation to couples with different levels of resources between them and to cohabiting couples. For example, in couples where one member has a better-paid, higher-status job, that member of the couple is likely to have greater assets and take more of a lead in decision making around assets. Cohabiting couples also seem more likely to keep any assets and debts to themselves and to make independent decisions about them, especially if they are in a second or subsequent cohabiting relationship. The length of a couple's relationship also seems relevant here, as couples tend to keep their assets separate at the start of a relationship but then share them more as time goes on.

But does it matter if assets and debts are not shared equally within a couple? While the couple is together, there may be relatively few problems with this. For example, if one member of a couple has a much better pension pot than the other, neither member can benefit from this until retirement, at which time the issue becomes one of how the income from this pot is shared. As far as housing wealth goes, while the couple are together and living under the same roof, does it matter who owns more of the equity in the home, if both are benefiting equally from the accommodation? Whether or not it matters for intact couples, problems can certainly arise when couples separate or when one member of a couple dies.

Divorce law contains various rules and guidance about the separation of assets and debts on divorce and these begin with a yardstick of equal division (once children's needs are addressed) unless there are reasons to do otherwise, such as: the marriage has been short; the different parties have brought different amounts to the marriage; and/or made different contributions. Rowlingson and Joseph (2010) suggested that women seemed to be trading housing wealth for pension wealth on divorce, but is this necessarily in their best interests? The rules around the division of assets and debts on divorce do not currently apply to cohabiting couples, and so when these couples split, the person who has formal ownership of most of the assets during the relationship is likely to leave with most. This is contrary to what many people assume, including many people in cohabiting couples.[9] There is, therefore, a need for greater public awareness of the current law in this field and/or changes in the law. But it is also contrary to what many people think is appropriate.

One way of dealing with this issue might be for cohabiting couples to draw up 'living together agreements'.[10] Templates for this are provided by Advicenow, an independent, not-for-profit website providing information on rights and legal issues (see www.advicenow.org.uk). The website admits that these agreements have a slightly odd status in law. They state that the courts will not let people sign away their existing legal rights but that they will generally follow the agreement if it still produces a fair result for both parties and is based on honest information. Furthermore, they state that courts are even more likely to uphold the agreement if both parties had legal advice or had a solicitor draw up a formal legal 'deed'.

Similar issues apply to the treatment of assets on the death of one partner in a couple. Knowledge of issues around inheritance law and taxation is poor. In a survey in 2004, almost two respondents in five thought, incorrectly, that a long-term cohabiting couple would receive equal treatment under inheritance law as a married couple (Rowlingson and McKay, 2005). People who were themselves cohabiting were no more knowledgeable on this matter. When asked about Inheritance Tax, most people either had no idea how the system worked or thought that more people paid it, and paid more, than is actually the case.

The Law Commission (2007) has recommended that certain cohabiting couples might be treated in the same way as married couples in law in relation to assets and debts but the government has so far not acted on this recommendation. Rowlingson and Joseph (2010) found that people generally did think that, after a certain point, and in particular if the couple have children, cohabiting couples should be treated in the same way as married couples. Indeed, people thought that this was already the case in law and practice. However, there was a minority view, among the participants, that marriage should be treated differently and that cohabiting couples should draw up their own legal arrangements if they wished to share their assets and debts.

The question remains, however, that if a couple stay together, does it matter if one member owns more and has more control over the assets and debts? As far as pension and housing wealth go, it seems difficult to see a problem here but there is a potential source of financial exclusion within couples related to savings and debts. Where one person has high levels of debt and is servicing these from their own income then this person will be at risk of financial exclusion even if their partner has no debts and perhaps also individual savings to draw on. Most of the couples in Rowlingson and Joseph's (2010) study said that, even if they kept their money separate, they would 'help each other out' from time to time. However, some couples, with the most independent forms of money management and decision making, knew little about their partner's financial situation and so financial exclusion within couples was a distinct possibility. Rowlingson and Joseph (2010) called for greater discussion about decision making and ownership of assets within couples, for example, within financial capability programmes in schools.

Conclusions

While there was much discussion about asset-based welfare from 1997 onwards, there was actually very little policy change in practice. Even the discussion, however, was limited to a focus on savings for people on low incomes rather than assets more broadly. The Coalition government's decision to abandon the two flagship asset-based welfare policies (Child Trust Fund and Saving Gateway) may appear to be a setback for asset policy but, on the other hand, it may now have created an opportunity to have a more fundamental discussion about the balance between different kinds of asset accumulation/decumulation and the role of government policy. What balance of different kinds of assets should people aspire to have? Are people putting too many resources into housing assets rather than pensions or in more liquid products such as ISAs? How should the government help people to achieve the right balance, for example, through provision of state pensions and/or setting different levels of taxation and/or subsidy for different forms of asset accumulation/decumulation? How does this relate to different stages of life and to different socioeconomic groups?

With the abolition of the Child Trust Fund and the Saving Gateway but the continuation of tax-free ISAs (and with new 'Junior ISAs'), policy on savings currently seems to favour the rich and needs to consider how it supports those on low and middle incomes to save. Policy on housing wealth still supports owner-occupation but changes in the housing and mortgage markets look set to put the expansion of home ownership on hold for some time to come. This will continue to leave a significant minority outside of home ownership and also put some low-income owner-occupiers at risk of losing their homes. Policy on housing wealth needs to consider how to respond to these issues and also how to support those who wish to release equity from their homes. Policy on using up assets to pay for long-term care also needs review as it is widely perceived to be unfair. Our ageing population is putting pressure on our pension system and the last 40 years have failed to find a solution through the private sector. There is a clear case here for the state to step back in to help support people in retirement.

Notes

[1] This is Part 4 of Clause IV which read, from the 1918 constitution, 'To secure for the workers by hand or by brain the full fruits of their industry and the most equitable distribution thereof that may be possible upon the basis of the common ownership of the means of production, distribution and exchange, and the best obtainable system of popular administration and control of each industry or service'. This became: 'The Labour Party is a democratic socialist party. It believes that by the strength of our common endeavour we achieve more than we achieve alone, so as to create for each of us the means to realise our true potential and for all of us a community in which power, wealth and opportunity are in the hands of the many, not the few, where the rights we enjoy reflect the duties we owe, and where we live together, freely, in a spirit of solidarity, tolerance and respect'.

[2] Although MIRAS was phased out under the Conservatives, who also reduced the payment of mortgage interest for buyers who became unemployed.

[3] www.communities.gov.uk/housing/homeownership/

[4] This may change with the introduction of Universal Credit, starting from 2013.

[5] There is a longer history of means-tested, and generally local, provision through the Poor Laws, and some earlier legislation dealing with industrial injuries.

[6] Although Beveridge was writing even at this time on social security issues and joined the Board of Trade in 1908, subsequently working on the implementation of the National Insurance Act 1911.

[7] For simplicity, Adam et al (2010) assume that asset price inflation matches general inflation and real returns are received as dividends or rental income. The ETRs are lower for longer holding periods because Capital Gains Tax is levied when an asset is sold rather than when there is a rise in value.

[8] Mirrlees et al (2010) define a normal return to savings as the nominal interest rate on medium-term government bonds.

[9] This applies to England and Wales. There is some redress for unmarried couples in Scotland following the Family Law (Scotland) Act 2006.

[10] See http://static.advicenow.org.uk/files/livingtogether-agreements-2010-867.pdf

SEVEN

Social policy and the wealthy

Introduction

As argued in Chapter Two, social policy researchers, along with social scientists more generally, have focused overwhelmingly on *poverty* as a social problem. Research has covered this from a number of angles, including what poverty is, what causes it, what the consequences are of poverty, what the experience is of living in poverty, how poverty changes over time (the dynamics of poverty) and the ways in which policy might tackle poverty. Social policy researchers, along with researchers in the social sciences more generally, have had rather less to say about the wealthy/rich because they have not generally been seen as a 'social problem'. But we have argued that the wealthy might be seen as a social problem, or associated with social problems, for a number of reasons. First, there is increasing evidence that the gap between rich and poor causes social problems throughout society. Second, a large gap between rich and poor may be considered unjust if those who become rich do so through luck of birth rather than merit and hard work. Third, even if people do become richer than average through merit, this may not justify an extensive gap between those at the top and those at the bottom. This chapter therefore focuses on how policy might address the 'problem of riches'.

As we saw in Chapter Two, public opinion appears to agree that the gap between rich and poor is too high and that something should be done about it. But if the current gap is too high, what level of inequality would be appropriate and/or acceptable? Some may argue that there should be no inequality at all, with everyone receiving exactly the same. However, we do not take this view, as we, along with the majority of the general public, support the idea that effort and important hard work deserve some level of extra reward or incentive. We also accept that some forms of wealth creation are important and so would want to reward/incentivise this. However, we do question whether the kind of work which receives the largest rewards/incentives currently is the most important and deserving of such rewards. And we also argue that existing levels of reward at the top are far too high and cannot be justified on grounds of merit or wealth creation. This chapter therefore considers what level of reward (and therefore inequality) might be considered fair and what action might therefore be taken to achieve it.

We might have expected a Labour government to promote policies around equality but New Labour's policy response was, at best, ambiguous. Tony Blair was famously unconcerned about David Beckham's salary, focusing more on the position of people at the bottom than those at the top (Orton and Rowlingson, 2007a). Furthermore, the term 'redistribution' became associated with 'Old Labour' and was not to be mentioned, let alone discussed in any serious way.

This chapter begins by considering what the goal of social policy in this field might be. We outline five possible goals:

- to promote equal opportunities so that those who become wealthy are more likely to do so through merit than 'brute' luck of birth;
- to ensure that any extra rewards for certain kinds of work reflect the real economic and social value of different kinds of work and are at an appropriate level;
- to limit the negative effects of inequality between rich and poor;
- to encourage real wealth creation;
- to support socially responsible behaviour among the wealthy that may aid cohesion such as philanthropic activities.

The chapter then focuses on three key areas of policy that can help achieve these goals:

- equal opportunity policy
- taxation policy
- original income and wealth policy.

The goals of policy on riches

The role of social policy in relation to riches or the wealthy will depend, as with all policy responses, on the nature of 'the problem'. We argued, in Chapter Two, that the nature of the problem is manifold. It is partly a problem of lack of equal opportunities. But it is also a problem of too great a difference between the rewards accruing to those at the top compared to those at the bottom. Before looking at the potential policy responses to each of these in more detail, it is interesting to consider the general public's view about policy responses to the gap between rich and poor.

Rowlingson et al (2010) posed new questions in the British Social Attitudes Survey[1] (BSAS) in 2009 to investigate people's views about how government should respond to inequality. People in the survey were asked the following question:

> 'Thinking overall about the gap in income between those on high incomes and those on low incomes, what if anything do you think should be done to reduce this gap?'

People were given a number of options and asked to pick all they agreed with. They were also asked to pick the one priority that they thought would be the best way to reduce the income gap (see Table 7.1). Some of the options focused on policies that would increase the resources of those at the bottom, some focused on policies that would reduce the resources of those at the top and some concerned all members of society. The most popular answer (given by 62 per cent of people) was to provide better education and training opportunities. There was also considerable support for helping those in low-paid work, not only by reducing taxes on low incomes but also by increasing the minimum wage (mentioned by 56 per cent and 54 per cent respectively). Concern for people at the bottom, however, was mainly directed at those in work, as there was very little support for benefits to be raised for people on low incomes (17 per cent). There was also support for policies that would reduce the incomes of those at the top. Forty per cent of the public supported an increase in taxes for those on high incomes and some 25 per cent supported an upper limit on very high incomes (a maximum wage).

The BSAS 2009 survey also asked people whether or not they supported redistribution from the better off to the less well off. 'Only'

Table 7.1: Public views about the best ways to reduce the income gap (%)

Government should do the following to reduce the income gap ...	All (several answers)	Top priority (one answer)
Better education or training opportunities should be provided to enable people to get better jobs	62	30
Taxes for those on low incomes should be reduced	56	21
The minimum wage should be increased	54	18
Taxes for those on high incomes should be increased	40	12
There should be an upper limit on very high incomes	25	7
The government should create jobs for those that need them	25	6
Benefits for those on low incomes should be increased	17	4
Other	2	*
Nothing should be done		2
Base	2,267	1,775

Source: Rowlingson et al (2010)

36 per cent of the public said they agreed with this, despite the fact that 78 per cent felt that the gap between those with high incomes and those with low incomes was too large. Rowlingson et al (2010) explored why relatively few people appeared to support redistribution given concerns about inequality, and have pointed out that while levels of support for redistribution are not particularly high, nor are levels of opposition. A substantial minority (28 per cent) sit on the fence, neither supporting nor opposing redistribution. This suggests that political leaders and lobby groups could play an important role in getting people off the fence by making a stronger case for redistribution.

We also know, from a range of studies of attitude data, that the public support progressive taxation (Sefton, 2005; Orton and Rowlingson, 2007b). This issue was explored further by Rowlingson et al (2010) when they asked people in the BSAS 2009 what they thought about the level of taxes for people on high and low incomes. For each group, respondents were asked:

'Generally, how would you describe taxes in Britain today?'

Table 7.2 shows that people thought that those on low incomes paid too much tax and there was little support for taxes to be raised on 'middle' incomes. Views about taxes for those on 'high' incomes were more mixed, but with more people saying they were too low than saying they were too high.

As we might expect, however, these views varied depending on whether or not people considered themselves to be on a low, middle or high income. Whereas 33 per cent of the population as a whole said that taxes for those on high incomes were either too low or much too low, only 12 per cent of those who considered themselves to be on high incomes said that taxes on high incomes were too low or much too

Table 7.2: Public views about levels of taxation for different income groups (%)

Views about levels of taxation	For those on low incomes	For those on middle incomes	For those on high incomes
Much too high	21	6	7
Too high	51	36	18
About right	21	48	37
Too low	2	4	28
Much too low	*	*	4
Can't choose/not answered	5	6	5
Base	967	967	967

low (although only 4 per cent of the population considered themselves to be on a high income, so this is a small minority of people).

Support for redistribution is lower than we might have expected given high levels of concern for the gap between rich and poor, and Rowlingson et al (2010) have suggested that there are three reasons for this. The first reason is self-interest. Those on higher incomes, who might lose out from redistribution, are less likely to support redistribution than those on lower incomes. But a quarter of those on higher incomes, who say, when asked, that they put themselves first over others, still support redistribution, and some of those on lower incomes, who are the likely beneficiaries of redistribution, oppose it. So self-interest cannot explain lack of support for redistribution entirely.

The second reason relates to people's underlying beliefs about inequality. Those who see inequality as caused by social injustice or bad luck are much more likely to support redistribution than those who see it as due to laziness on the part of 'the poor' and hard work on the part of 'the rich'.

The third reason is that people support other kinds of government intervention aimed at reducing income inequalities. As we have seen in Chapter Two and above, there is a strong concern about lack of equal opportunities for children, and strong support for policies that would promote more equality of opportunity. However, the public recognises that equal opportunities and equal outcomes are linked, and that government action is needed on both fronts. There is also particular concern for workers on the lowest incomes. There is strong support for a minimum standard of living for everyone and also strong support for lower taxes for those on low incomes.

The public's support for education and training reflects their concern about equal opportunities (also mentioned in Chapter Two), and later in this chapter we discuss the kinds of reforms to the education system that might improve equal opportunities.

Equal opportunities are clearly important but, as discussed in Chapter Two and as recognised by the general public, it is very difficult to provide equal opportunities when outcomes are so unequal because some children will have greater advantages than others from an early age. For example, some parents will be able to afford to buy their children books, computers and other educational equipment as well as provide access to educational trips and experiences. Some parents will also be able to afford more basic resources such as spacious accommodation (useful for doing homework) and healthy food (important for sustaining attention at school, for example, after breakfast). Income is not the only form of capital that is important here, of course. Parents with higher human, social and cultural capital can also pass these on to their children, to their advantage. Equality of opportunity cannot therefore be disentangled from equality of outcome. Children do not have an equal start in life and it is difficult, if not impossible, for some to make up the ground they never had in the first place.

But even if it were possible to ensure equal, or fair, opportunities for all, there are still strong arguments, as outlined in Chapter Two, why current levels of inequality are unjust regardless of the level of equal opportunities. This is for two reasons. First, the current size of the gap seems difficult to justify on the grounds of relatively small differences in effort and ability. And second, the size of the gap appears to be causing a range of social and economic problems. Social policies should therefore aim to ensure that the extent of the gap between rich and poor is at an appropriate level, reflecting both differences in effort and ability but also reflecting the level of inequality that may cause social and economic problems.

It is difficult to justify the current gap between rich and poor, but it is not necessarily easy to set a precise target on reducing this gap unless one is a pure egalitarian and simply wishes to eradicate all inequality. In relation to poverty, the Blair government set itself the target of eradicating all child poverty as poverty was seen as a wholly negative state whereas inequality was not viewed as wholly negative by New Labour – and perhaps not even a motive for policy intervention at all. But the poverty measure used was, in effect, a measure of inequality: 60 per cent of median income. This kind of measure is not affected by the incomes of those in the top half of the income distribution, let alone those in the top 10 per cent or 1 per cent, but it does recognise that relative income is an issue. So if the public and governments are unlikely to support total equality, what level of equality should be aimed at?

The public appear to support a ratio of 6:1 for earnings and the *Hutton Review* (2010b) has consulted on a 20:1 ratio. These give us some suggestions to consider. Kondo et al (2009) have tentatively suggested that inequality causes health and social problems in societies with a Gini coefficient of more than 0.3. In Chapter Two we saw that Britain had this level of inequality in the 1960s, 1970s and early 1980s so it is not a level that is impossible to achieve. It is also the same level as currently exists in many neighbouring countries, namely Denmark, France, Belgium and Germany.

As well as seeking to reduce the gap between rich and poor, policy can also do more to reduce its negative effects. For example, if inequality causes people more mental health problems or high blood pressure due to stress, then we could put more money into mental health services or treatment of high blood pressure. This would of course be dealing with the symptoms rather than the deep causes of these problems. It is something that we already do to some extent, but it is worth considering how we can do this more effectively by better understanding the consequences of inequality.

Discussion about policies to limit wealth at the very top often raise concerns about whether this would reduce incentives to create wealth and so harm society more generally (see Chapter Two). Policy on the wealthy should therefore distinguish between different types of wealth because some are more valuable to society than others. 'Real' wealth in the form of (new) companies that employ people in satisfying, well-paid jobs, is extremely valuable, particularly at the current economic time. Ways of encouraging such real wealth creation are therefore vitally important. Other forms of wealth such as those created when shares increase in value due to speculation (for example, during internet 'bubbles') may be considered less important. The social value of different kinds of wealth deserves much greater discussion and debate.

There is, however, an issue in relation to sustainability and wealth. As countries become wealthier, they consume more of the world's resources, some of which (for example, oil) are finite. As we saw in Chapter Two, the link between gross domestic product (GDP) and happiness/wellbeing is not very strong and so, rather than arguing for further growth in national wealth (GDP), the challenge is to change the nature of the wealth that we produce from unproductive forms to productive forms. Businesses which provide meaningful and well-paid work for people should be encouraged. With better education and training (as part of increasing equal opportunities), skills levels should increase, and so the economy could become a more highly paid, highly skilled economy rather than trying to compete with low-paid, low-skilled economies (Finegold and Soskice, 1988; Reich, 1991).

David Cameron has recently put the case for measures of social progress based on wellbeing rather than purely material measures, and the National Statistician has been consulted on this topic.

Finally, policy towards the wealthy should support and encourage responsible behaviour among the wealthy. Much is said about the (bad) behaviour of the poor, but if we are to focus on individual behaviour at all, as seems to be increasingly the case, then, that the rich, who have often inherited substantial amounts of wealth and/or built it up with the help of existing legal and welfare structures, should also be expected to behave responsibly (Rowlingson and Connor, 2011). One example of this is philanthropy/charitable giving which should be supported by policy.

The rest of this chapter focuses on three key areas of policy related to inequality: equal opportunity policy, particularly within education, taxation policy and original income and wealth policies.

Equal opportunity policy

There is almost universal public support for equal opportunity policies that give children from different backgrounds the same, or very similar, chances in life. In fact, it is difficult to argue against this because to do so suggests a lack of support for basic fairness. But, as mentioned earlier in this book, there is a tension between equal opportunities and unequal outcomes. If the playing field is not level then it is difficult to provide truly equal opportunities as some children are advantaged from the start.

The responsibility for providing equal opportunities is often laid mostly at the school door and this is a very heavy responsibility for schools to take on, especially when they are also under pressure to increase performance, which may actually come into conflict with providing equal opportunities. Others have argued that the 'race is already run' by the time that children enter school, so interventions need to begin before this point (see the evidence within the Field report, 2010).

The Panel on Fair Access to the Professions (2009) discussed ways to increase equal opportunities starting with maternal health and child poverty through early years care to family, parenting and community, education and school attainment, post-school qualifications and finally, opportunities to progress in work. As mentioned above, a major plank of policy by New Labour was intervention in early years (for example, through Sure Start local programmes and then Sure Start children's centres) to give children from more disadvantaged backgrounds extra help from a very early age – originally from birth to four, but then for children of all ages.

Some have been critical of the direction of reform over time – with an apparent shift from child development and family support to the provision of childcare to help mothers get into the labour market (Lewis, 2003; Glass, 2005). A key element was that Sure Start was provided in poor areas, around the bottom 30 per cent of areas, but was not restricted to poor parents. Richer parents living in poor areas were thus able to use the childcare and supportive services being provided. Research evidence suggests that Sure Start Local Programmes have had positive effects on child outcomes, probably operating via changes to parenting. More recent research finds no differences between sub-groups, although earlier research had found some negative outcomes in more deprived families (National Evaluation of Sure Start Team, 2008).

Labour's policy for primary, secondary and tertiary education was, arguably, more concerned with increasing educational performance overall than increasing equal opportunities, and there is, surprisingly perhaps, little evidence that schools make much difference in terms of levelling the playing field for children. In fact, in England, children from different backgrounds start school with different levels of ability and their attainment at every subsequent age and stage tends to reveal these same patterns (Gorard, 2000; Gorard and See, 2009). The Equalities and Human Rights Commission (2010, p 645) has recently concluded that:

> ... for students from lower socio-economic groups, the gap [in educational outcomes] widens during the school years.

This finding is not new. Bernstein (1970) encapsulated the point when he wrote the seminal paper entitled 'Education cannot compensate for society', and various studies over more than 50 years have come to the same conclusion in the UK and elsewhere (Glass, 1954; Sargant, 2000). Bernstein's explanation for the inability of schools to compensate for society was related to what Bourdieu (1977) terms 'cultural capital'. Bernstein argued that different social classes used different 'codes' in their language, and the middle/upper classes developed 'elaborate' codes which restricted access to the education system they devised and ran.

Whatever the explanation, Gorard (2010) has argued that while schools can make a difference to pupils' lives, as contrasted with pupils not going to school at all, there is no substantial difference in the effectiveness of different schools. Mortimore (1997, p 479), for example, found that the vast majority (75 to 90 per cent) of the 30 to 40 per cent of exam outcomes that could be explained was attributable to the prior and individual characteristics of the pupils. Pring (2009) suggested some of the reasons why schools cannot compensate (much) for other factors when he listed some of the challenges that schools face: changing family patterns, an increase in families in which no member has been employed and the mental health problems and reported unhappiness of many young people in the UK. To a very large extent, then, schools simply reflect the local population in their intakes and tend to be highly segregated socioeconomically (Gorard, 2010).

Despite the challenges faced by schools in this area, Gorard (2010) has argued that some changes over the past 50 years have moved in the right direction in terms of increasing equal opportunities. These include the move towards comprehensive schooling in the 1960s, the use of banding to de-stratify the intakes in the 1970s, the National Curriculum of the 1980s and the trend away from catchment schools in the 1990s.

The Coalition government are strong supporters of equal opportunities, with Education Secretary Michael Gove (2010) stating:

> Schools should be engines of social mobility. They should provide the knowledge, and the tools, to enable talented young people to overcome accidents of birth and an inheritance of disadvantage in order to enjoy greater opportunities.

> Children from poorer backgrounds, who are currently doing less well at school, are falling further and further behind in the qualifications race every year – and that in turn means that they are effectively condemned to ever poorer employment prospects, narrower social and cultural horizons, less by way of resources to invest in their own children – and thus a cycle of disadvantage and inequality is made worse with every year that passes. Last year of the 80,000 pupils who had been on free school meals just 45 made it to Oxbridge. Just 2 out of 57 countries now have a wider attainment gap between the highest and lowest achieving pupils.

Following on from this, the Coalition government introduced higher rates of funding for children from poorer backgrounds as they need greater resources – the 'pupil premium'. Before the introduction of the 'pupil premium', extra resources were allocated to areas or schools rather than children, so some schools in poor areas received extra support even if the children attending the school had travelled from affluent areas to do so. The 'pupil premium' was designed so that extra resources would follow the children who needed them. The aim was to prevent the phenomenon that had occurred with some academies where the extra resources they had received had changed the nature of their intakes, but they continued to receive the extra funding even when they were no longer (if they ever had been) the school with the most disadvantaged pupils in their area.

The 'pupil premium' may be a step in the right direction in terms of equal opportunities, but policy has more recently been moving in the opposite direction as schools are becoming more, rather than less, diverse. As part of this growing diversity, the National Curriculum is being weakened and greater flexibility allowed for vocationally oriented students. Selection by faith, 'aptitude' and ability to pay is increasing with the result that socioeconomic segregation looks set to increase still further between schools (Gorard, 2009). It seems, therefore, that equal opportunities will decline as schools are forced to concentrate more on the general level of attainment rather than educational equity.

Even if schools were uniform in terms of curriculum and character this is unlikely to be sufficient in the short term to lead to equality of intake and therefore opportunity. To achieve this, it may be necessary to go further and abolish catchment areas to reduce the ability of more affluent parents to buy homes near 'good' schools (Gorard et al, 2003). Other policy reforms could be implemented, such as requiring all schools to recruit a certain proportion of children on free school meals or bussing children to different schools rather than relying on catchment areas. 'Bussing', taking poorer children further distances to higher-achieving schools, would have the added advantage of reducing car usage. School places could also be allocated by lottery (at least temporarily, but for all schools in an area). Gorard (2010) has suggested going even further to abolish league tables. Some of these proposed reforms are cost-free but they are radical and may face opposition from affluent parents who might see their advantage in the current school system challenged.

There is no sign currently that the Coalition government (or any other possible government) is going to adopt such radical reforms. In the 2010 Comprehensive Spending Review, the schools budget received some protection with an increase by 0.1 per cent in real terms announced. But, at the same time, the Education Maintenance Allowance (EMA), given to poor 16- to 19-year-olds to encourage them to continue their schooling, was abolished. The policy allowing universities to charge up to £9,000 per year narrowly passed through the House of Commons in December 2010 and looks set to increase educational divisions yet further. Such divisions are already very wide, not just in relation to income and class but also other factors such as ethnicity. David Lammy MP used the Freedom of Information Act to discover that only one British black Caribbean student was admitted to Oxford in 2009 (Lammy, 2010).

Compulsory education is important, of course, but further and higher education and training at work are also relevant to equal opportunities. Higher education has expanded massively since the 1960s when there were approximately 200,000 undergraduates in the country to more than 2.5 million today, around 40 per cent of young people (Panel on Fair Access to the Professions, 2009). But social class remains a strong factor in determining whether or not someone goes to university, with young people with parents in professional or managerial jobs almost three times as likely to go to university than those with routine jobs. And the differences are much greater in the more elite universities (Panel on Fair Access to the Professions, 2009).

The Panel on Fair Access to the Professions (2009) made a number of recommendations in relation to widening access to higher education, but the main policy change here since then has been the lifting of the fees cap on university tuition. This looks set to worsen the relative position of young people from more disadvantaged backgrounds as they are more likely to be debt averse (Callendar, 2003). Universities are being asked to put in place bursaries and other measures to attract non-traditional students, but the outlook does not seem positive.

The labour market is another area to focus on in terms of equal opportunities, and the role of unpaid internships has recently been criticised as allowing young people from more affluent backgrounds the chance to gain experience that other young people cannot afford to take (Panel on Fair Access to the Professions, 2009). Fair recruitment and selection processes also need to be considered alongside fair progression routes including more flexible working patterns. The Equalities and Human Rights Commission also exist to monitor discrimination and unequal outcomes among a range of groups and within a range of fields. A recent review (EHRC, 2010) has suggested that, while progress is being made on some fronts, the outcomes for some people are not improving as fast as they might. They have also shared concerns that the current economic situation will disadvantage particular groups.

Berthoud (2010) has also suggested that past recessions have disproportionately affected disadvantaged groups, including those with disabilities and those from minority ethnic backgrounds. This recession has so far affected the private sector rather more than public sector workers, a pattern that may well have reversed during 2011 and beyond following the 2010 Comprehensive Spending Review.

The Equality Act 2010 formed part of another strand of policy to tackle equal opportunities and outcome issues. It introduced a new duty on certain public bodies to have regard to the desirability of reducing socioeconomic inequalities. The duty applies to decisions of a strategic nature, such as when deciding priorities, setting targets, allocating resources and commissioning services.

It seems that primary and secondary education currently does little to level the playing field so that all children have similar chances in life. It could do more but patterns of inequality are set at a very early stage. And they continue into higher education and the labour market beyond. More radical action is needed here but it is also necessary to recognise that the link between equal opportunities and equal outcomes is strong. It is difficult to have real or 'deep' equal opportunities in a country with such high levels of inequality.

Taxation policy

The previous section has suggested that education policy could make some difference in terms of equal opportunities but current education policy appears to be doing relatively little. A key plank of policy in relation to outcomes rather than opportunities is taxation, as progressive taxation can contribute to redistribution if the taxes raised are spent, at least equally on all groups, if not more on those from poorer backgrounds. Layard (2005) noted that, in the 1960s, economists such as James Meade, James Mirrlees and Amartya Sen argued that simply raising taxes could blunt incentives leading to a reduction in total wealth, or the 'size of the cake', as it is described. So the optimum position is argued to be where gains from further redistribution are just outweighed by the losses from the shrinking of the cake. However, empirical research has never examined where this optimum point might be nor at what level of individual wealth an increase in income ceases to bring additional benefit.

As we saw earlier in this chapter, there is some popular support for (more) progressive taxation but there is, not surprisingly, less support from those who may have to pay more themselves (see earlier in this chapter). Opposition to tax increases has a long history. For example, William Harcourt tried to introduce a more progressive, graduated income tax in 1894 but faced strong resistance from the Treasury and Inland Revenue that such reform would be counter-productive because those on high incomes would not comply with the law by providing the necessary information that would be needed. Alfred Milner, the chair of the Inland Revenue at the time, argued that:

> Would this extra million a year [that graduated income tax would raise] not be dearly bought if it involved setting up a feud, so long happily avoided, between the public generally and the vast body of persons, often not very well-mannered or very literate, who are concerned in the collection of taxes. (quoted in Daunton, 2007, p 324)

This quote is interesting in the way that it gives the impression that people on high incomes are simply part of 'the public generally'. It is also interesting that issues of non-compliance are used against the policy when such issues are rarely used against policies relating to the poor. Harcourt managed to introduce more progressive death duties in 1894 and the Liberals tried again with a progressive income tax in 1906. They encountered similar arguments from the chair of the Inland Revenue at that time, William Primrose, although he did not seek to imply that high earners were 'the public generally'. He admitted that they were a relatively small group but stressed that they were an extremely powerful one. Primrose doubted that:

> Some 15,000 of the most powerful of the community would tolerate tamely such an inquisition into their private affairs as would be inevitable with a system of Progressive Income Tax. (quoted in Daunton, 2007, pp 324-5)

Primrose was right that the rich would not 'tolerate tamely' major tax reform, and there was considerable resistance to the 1909 Budget, which Lloyd George called:

> A War Budget. It is for raising money to wage implacable warfare against poverty and squalidness. (quoted in Daunton, 2007, p 364)

This Budget sought to introduce a graduated super-tax but concessions were made to those on 'modest' middle-class incomes, particularly for men with children. Daunton (2007, p 365) pointed out that most of the tax increase fell on the wealthy and on unearned incomes. An element of land taxation was also introduced. The 'People's Budget', famously, led to a major battle between democracy and privilege when the House of Lords vetoed the Budget, leading to a general election in 1910, and the eventual passing of both the Budget and major constitutional reform limiting the power of the Lords.

From then on, until 1979, levels of taxes increased fairly relentlessly (as shown in Figure 7.1). Increases were particularly pronounced during and soon after the two world wars to pay both for the war efforts but also the 'peace efforts' in repaying public debt and implementing major social reforms. The ratcheting up of the role of central government following the world wars in the early and mid-20th century is made plain.

This figure also shows that taxes came down dramatically in the 1980s and continued to fall in the early 1990s. Figure 7.2 focuses more on recent decades, illustrating more clearly the dramatic drop in tax

Figure 7.1: Government receipts as a percentage of GDP, 1900–2007

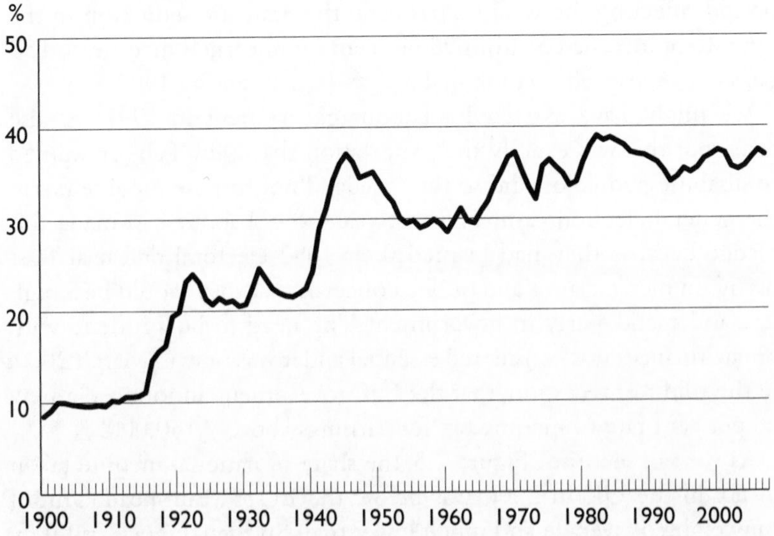

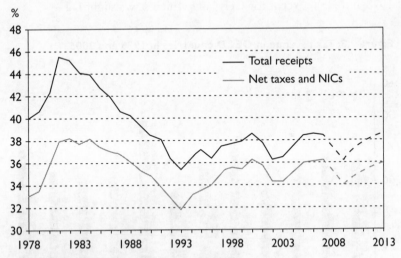

Note: Figures are for general government net receipts on a calendar-year basis.

Source: Clark and Dilnot (2002). Quoted in Adam and Browne (2009),

Figure 7.2: Government receipts as a percentage of GDP, 1978–2013

Note: Years are fiscal years, so 2008 means 2008/09.

Source: HM Treasury, Public Finances Databank (27 January 2009 version), www.hm-treasury.gov.uk/psf_statistics.htm

Quoted in Adam et al (2010, p 5), www.ifs.org.uk/mirrleesreview/dimensions/ch1.pdf

revenues in the 1980s. One of the key changes in taxation over this period, affecting the wealthy, has been the dramatic reduction in the top rate of income tax, from 98 per cent on unearned income and 83 per cent on earned income in 1978 to 40 per cent by 1992.

We might have expected a Labour government in 1997 to raise taxes, but this was exactly the expectation that New Labour wanted to disabuse people of, and so they pledged not to raise income tax in the general election campaign that year. New Labour had made this pledge because they had blamed their 1992 electoral defeat at least partly on media claims and public concerns that they would be a high 'tax and spend' party in government. The need to be 'prudent' with public finances was considered essential and it was only in March 2009, in the midst of recession, that the UK government announced a new 50 per cent rate of income tax for earnings above £150,000.

As we can see from Figure 7.3, the share of national income taken in tax in the UK in 2006 was below the EU15 (European Union) (unweighted) average and much lower than Sweden, France and Italy in 2006. But it was higher than in most of the new EU countries of Eastern Europe and higher than in the US, Japan and Australia. Figure 7.4 compares tax revenue in the UK with other OECD (Organisation for Economic Co-operation and Development) countries and also looks at changes over time. Taxes in most countries increased between 1978 and 2006 except for Germany, which saw a slight fall.

Figure 7.3: Tax revenue in OECD countries in 1978 and 2006

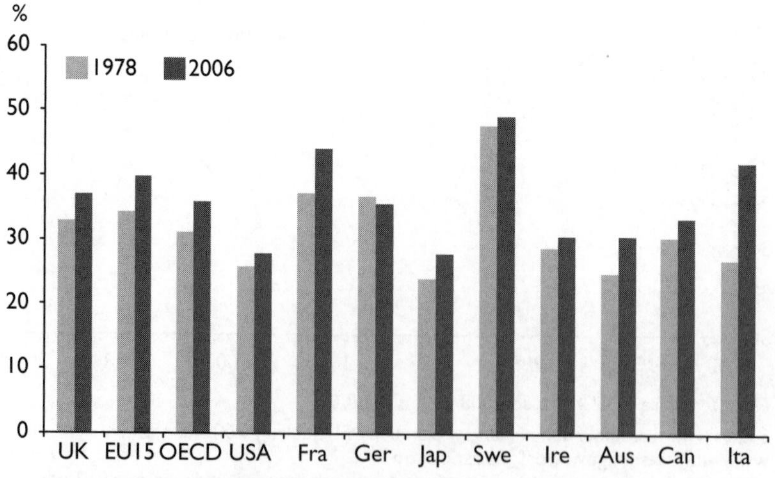

Note: All taxes and compulsory social security contributions.
Source: OECD (2008a). Quoted in Adam et al (2010, p 6),
www.ifs.org.uk/mirrleesreview/dimensions/ch1.pdf

Figure 7.4: Shares of direct and indirect tax paid by different quintiles (fifths) of the population

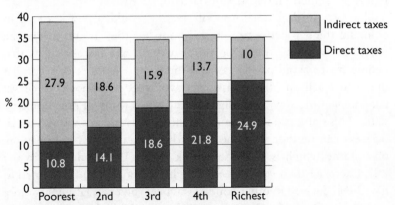

Source: Barnard (2008), www.statistics.gov.uk/downloads/theme_social/
Taxes-Benefits-2007-2008/Taxes_benefits_0708.pdf

As we saw earlier, resistance to increases in tax is often high, but it should not be exaggerated, and the public often shows support for higher taxes on wealthy groups. In a poll undertaken on behalf of *The Times* 57 per cent of those questioned stated that the 50 per cent tax on income for those earning over £150,000 was a positive measure. Only 22 per cent opposed it, and other polls suggested as many as 70 per cent supported the new tax (*New Statesman*, 2009). Further redistributive reforms to the income tax and National Insurance systems, such as removing the cap on National Insurance Contributions (NICs) for higher earners and making them payable on investment income, would also help redistribute income and close the gap in the public finances.

Higher rate taxpayers sometimes defend their position by pointing out that they contribute a substantial proportion of total income tax revenue: 56 per cent in 2008/09, according to Mirrlees et al (2010). This seems a considerable sum given that they make up only 12 per cent of all income taxpayers. However, this group receive more than half of all income so, in this sense, 56 per cent is a fair share. In fact, we might argue that it is not high enough. The top 1 per cent pay 23 per cent of all income tax and, once again, this reflects the fact that they receive about a quarter of all income (Mirrlees et al, 2010). These shares have risen substantially since 1978/79 due to growing inequality, despite reductions in the higher rates of income tax.

Direct taxation (largely income tax) is progressive although we could argue it should be even more so. Indirect taxes (such as custom and excise duties), however, are highly regressive, and the overall effect is actually that the bottom quintile currently pay *more* in taxes than any other group, including the top quintile, as a share of their income (see Figure 7.4, based on statistics in Barnard, 2008).

The rates of different forms of taxation could play a key role in reducing the gap between rich and poor but they are no means the only way of doing this. One problem with the tax system is that people try to avoid paying tax and there are a number of ways that they can legally do this. This is tax avoidance as opposed to illegal tax *evasion*. One way of legally avoiding tax is through non-domicile status. This status is one method by which UK residents who are born overseas can register with the tax authorities and then only pay tax on income which is either sent back to the UK or derived in the UK. There are then various ways in which income can be claimed to have been derived in other countries where the tax treatment is more favourable (Orton, 2008). Orton (2008) gives the high profile example of Mohammed Al-Fayed who had non-domicile status and negotiated with the Inland Revenue to pay a fixed sum of £240,000 tax per year. This is a considerable sum, but his wealth at the time was estimated at over £500 million, and while he claimed he had no income from his ownership of Harrods, tens of millions of pounds were being paid into an offshore account in Bermuda.

The Coalition government backed away from confronting wealthy 'non-doms' in 2010. There had been some expectation in the media that measures would be introduced to clamp down on this group but, instead, the government announced that it would launch a review of the taxation of non-domiciled individuals. The government is also considering a controversial General Anti-Avoidance Rule (GAAR), abandoned by Labour in 1999 as unworkable. This issue has sparked public protests, for example, at branches of Top Shop and other retail premises in December 2010 against Philip Green, the owner of Top Shop, who avoids paying tax by putting his assets in his wife's name and since she is resident in Monaco, she does not have to pay UK tax on them.

Tax avoidance is by no means limited to 'non-doms'. The Spending Review in October 2010 (HM Treasury, 2010) made explicit reference to reducing tax avoidance in the banking sector: It said that:

> The Government will continue to monitor tax receipts from the banking sector. As part of this, the Government expects the banking sector to comply with both the letter and the spirit of the law and not to engage in or promote tax avoidance. (HM Treasury, 2010, p 30)

Rowlingson (2011) has characterised Coalition policy towards the wealthy as a very 'softly-softly' approach, particularly when compared with the government's hard-line policies towards those on benefit, where people who do not take up job offers could lose their benefits for up to three years.

The 2010 Comprehensive Spending Review also confirmed that the government would not be continuing with Labour's one-off bonus tax but would, instead, introduce a banking levy (HM Treasury, 2010). Few concrete details were provided but the Spending Review suggested that the levy would generate around £2.5 billion per year, rather less than the £3.5 billion raised by the bonus tax the previous year. Bankers' bonuses in Britain in 2009 were £7.3 billion and expected to be about £7 billion in 2010.[2] This is considerably lower than the £11 billion paid out at the height of the financial boom in 2007 but still a considerable sum of money going to a relative handful of people at a time of major welfare cuts and reductions in spending on public services.

Nick Clegg, Leader of the Liberal Democrats and Deputy Prime Minister, said, at the Liberal Democrat conference in September 2010, that the government would introduce a super-tax if bankers failed to show restraint on bonuses. Speaking on BBC Radio 4's Today programme on 21 September 2010, Clegg warned bankers:

> 'If you abuse the generosity of taxpayers, who have provided both directly and indirectly, a massive infusion of public funds by awarding yourselves bonuses that appear almost gratuitously offensive at a time when other people are having to make sacrifices in terms of their pay and pensions, then clearly this government will not be able to stand by.'

In February 2011, the government agreed a deal with the banks that committed them to lending more money in 2011(especially to small businesses), to pay less in bonuses than they had in the previous year and to be more transparent about their pay packages. The deal led to the resignation of the Liberal Democrat peer Lord Oakeshott, who had been a Treasury spokesman. He said that the agreement was far too generous to the banks and should not have been signed.

While the Spending Review said relatively little about wealth and the wealthy, the Emergency Budget in June 2010 had witnessed some strong rhetoric. Even George Osborne, Chancellor of the Exchequer, pointed out that:

> Some of the richest people in this country have been able
> to pay less tax than the people who clean for them.

He claimed that they had managed this partly through turning some
of their income into capital and paying a lower rate of tax through
Capital Gains Tax than they would have to pay in income tax. Capital
Gains Tax is an important wealth tax. It is levied when people sell or
give away 'chargeable assets' which have increased in value. There is
an annual exemption threshold (£10,100 in 2009/10). Entrepreneurs'
relief gives an additional relief of £1 million on the sale/gift of company
shares or business assets. A key exemption from Capital Gains Tax is
the principal private residence, costing the public purse an estimated
£6.5 billion in 2007/08 (Wilcox, 2008).

Osborne's solution to the problem of tax avoidance in relation to
Capital Gains Tax was to increase it, currently 18 to 28 per cent for
higher earners (Boadway et al, 2009). Low and middle-income savers
would continue to pay 18 per cent. But this was a very small change
and the government is still effectively giving tax breaks to the wealthy
who can transfer income into capital gains. Crawshaw (2009) has called
for Capital Gains Tax to be charged on the gains arising from the sale
of principal private residences to capture windfall gains from housing
sales and level the playing field somewhat between the benefits of
owner-occupation and private renting.

Just prior to the Spending Review, the government also announced
some changes to Alistair Darling's previous proposals on non-state
pension tax relief. As we saw in Chapter Six, this form of tax relief is
a 'hidden' form of welfare costing the public purse over £20 billion
in 2008/09, with 60 per cent of this going to higher rate taxpayers
(PPI, 2010). Orton (2008, p 268) has pointed out that the 'injustice'
of pension tax relief is compounded by the fact that contributions to
the state retirement pension's fund (the National Insurance Fund) do
not qualify for tax relief and so the poorest have to pay the most into
their pension pot which is, on the whole, less generous than private
pensions. This serves to highlight the hidden forms of welfare (including
the fiscal privileges) enjoyed by the wealthy (Titmuss, 1958; Mann,
2001; Orton, 2008).

The government's 2010 proposals on non-state pension tax relief
were fairly modest, restricting the annual amount of tax-free income
from £255,000 to £50,000 that savers can put into pensions. The
Treasury expected that this would largely affect those on incomes of
over £100,000 and hopes that the changes will eventually save it more
than £4 billion a year. But it could have gone much further and either

abolished non-state pension tax relief altogether or reduced it to the standard rate for all workers.

Taxes on income are always unpopular because they largely tax work, and work is seen as something to be encouraged rather than discouraged. Taxes on unearned income and wealth are arguably easier to justify, and the particularly unequal distribution of wealth might also provide another reason for taxing it more heavily. There are a number of possible mechanisms for taxing wealth, and Chapter Six reviewed how the tax system treats savings. This chapter looks in more detail at taxes of people's stocks of wealth and taxes of flows of wealth.

In the UK, Council Tax is, effectively, our main tax on people's stock of wealth. It is a tax on property levied by local authorities. Properties are placed in one of eight bands (A–H) with a different amount of tax payable in each band – amounts also vary between local authorities. The highest tax rate in band H is three times the lowest, and there are fixed rates of payment between the bands. Orton (2002) has shown that Council Tax is very regressive as it accounts for 5.2 per cent of income for households in the bottom quintile and only 1.7 per cent of income for households in the top quintile.

Council Tax is a very regressive tax but it is more progressive than the Poll Tax (Community Charge) that it replaced after major public protests (former Prime Minister Margaret Thatcher also being replaced). But, given the economic situation and persistent wealth inequality, it is time for the tax to be made more progressive. This could be done through a number of reforms, including, adding extra bands at the top and bottom of the scale, changing the ratios between each band and removing Council Tax discounts for owners of second and long-term empty homes (Crawshaw, 2009).

An alternative to reforming Council Tax would be to replace it with an annual property or land value tax (Maxwell and Vigor, 2005; Lloyd, 2009) or, even more radically, to replace it with a more comprehensive wealth tax. Such a tax has been proposed at various points in the past by politicians, policy makers and academics. For example, Labour had proposed introducing a wealth tax in 1975 following on from its manifesto pledge to do so. But this was never introduced, and Denis Healey (1989, p 404, quoted in Boadway et al, 2009) later reflected:

> ... you should never commit yourself in Opposition to new
> taxes unless you have a good idea how they will operate in
> practice. We had committed ourselves to a Wealth Tax; but
> in five years I found it impossible to draft one which would

yield enough revenue to be worth the administrative cost and the political hassle.

Meade (1978), however, continued to argue for a wealth tax in the late 1970s and in 1981 the French introduced their 'Solidarity Tax' along similar lines.

Boadway et al (2009) have argued that the case for a tax on people's stock of wealth is that people benefit directly from holding rather than just spending wealth and derive both status and power from it. But they argue that it is expensive to administer, it might raise relatively little (presumably because of tax avoidance?) and it might be both unfair and inefficient. There might also be difficulties in making it work well with capital that is mobile. Furthermore, many OECD countries, like Austria and the Netherlands, have abolished their wealth tax due to issues of complexity, compliance and cost. But wealth taxes do still exist in France, Spain, Norway and Switzerland as of 2010 (Boadway et al, 2009).

Boadway et al (2009) do suggest that an annual tax on very high value property might be appropriate perhaps through an additional Council Tax that would affect only occupiers of very high value properties.

There are a number of issues that wealth taxes, of all kinds, have to consider. For example, what should the taxable unit be: individuals, couples, families? Should the tax be levied only on individuals or include trusts? Which assets would be charged (housing, savings, pensions, possessions)? How would wealth be valued, annually? And who would pay for this? What would be the threshold, if any, and rates?

The debate on this has most recently been revived by Mirrlees et al (2010) who have argued that the government should consider replacing Council Tax and stamp duty with a more progressive tax:

> Council tax is based on valuations almost 20 years out of date, it is highly regressive with respect to property values and it gives a discount for sole occupancy – features that are unfair and encourage inefficient use of housing stock. Stamp duty land tax, as a transaction tax is highly inefficient ... its 'slab' structure – with big cliff edges in tax payable at certain thresholds – creates particularly perverse incentives. Replacing these two taxes on a revenue neutral basis with a simple tax proportional to up-to-date consumption values of properties ... is a much-needed step forward. (Mirrlees et al, 2010, p 12)

Alongside taxes of the stock of wealth, there are also taxes of the flow, particularly from one generation to another. In the UK, Inheritance Tax is one of the most unpopular taxes, with half the population supporting total abolition in 2000 (Hedges and Bromley, 2001). This is surprising, perhaps, because Inheritance Tax is levied on unearned windfalls rather than earned income, and so might be thought fairer than income tax in some ways. It certainly provides less of a disincentive to work because it is not levied on the proceeds of earned income and it is relatively difficult to avoid. It may therefore seem logical to have high rates of Inheritance Tax.

But the tax is unpopular, partly at least because it is seen as a 'double tax' and one that penalises saving (Prabhakar et al, 2008). Until recently, it appeared to be in decline in many developed countries although the recession may put on hold or even reverse that decline. For example, the Labour government in October 2007 actually reduced rather than increased Inheritance Tax – benefiting the top 5 per cent of wealth holders (Prabhakar et al, 2008). It does, however, raise a significant if small amount of revenue, with the Treasury expecting to get £4 billion from Inheritance Tax in 2007/08, £4.6 billion from Capital Gains Tax and £14.3 billion from stamp duty (70 per cent of this from property transactions and 30 per cent from business transactions) (Boadway et al, 2009). It would be possible to abolish Inheritance Tax and raise the same amount through a 1p increase in basic rate of income tax (20p to 21p) or 3p increase in higher rate (40p to 43p). Prabhakar (2008) suggests, however, that opposition to Inheritance Tax falls when people are confronted with stark choices, for example, to raise income tax in its place.

Given all the issues with Inheritance Tax it is no surprise that a number of suggestions for reforming or replacing it have been put forward. Atkinson (1971, p 184) argued that:

> The lifetime capital receipts tax would be the most effective way in which wealth-transfer taxation could contribute towards bringing about greater equality in inherited wealth. Most importantly, it would provide a clear incentive for donors to spread their wealth widely.

More recently, Prabhakar et al (2008) suggested a capital receipts tax so that when people receive some inherited wealth they are taxed on it at the same rate as they pay income tax. Boadway et al (2009) have suggested abolition of Inheritance Tax in favour of a Capital Gains Tax on death imposed only on the gains in value, not the entire value.

The rate would be 18 per cent on all gains (that is, there would be no threshold). The Mirrlees Review (Mirrlees et al, 2010) recently also suggested abolishing the tax. But they only suggested that this should be done if it could be replaced with a more progressive and comprehensive lifetime wealth transfer tax.

> Recent increases in wealth inequality, coupled with increases in housing wealth for particular groups, increase the case for taxing wealth transfers on both equity and efficiency grounds ... we do not think that a tax on estates at death is the best way to approach these issues – there is a stronger case, in principle, for a tax on lifetime receipts, taxing transfers received on an ongoing and cumulative basis. There are important administrative and transition challenges to be addressed in bringing such a proposal to fruition. However, as a long-term proposition, the case for moving in this direction is persuasive. (Mirrlees et al, 2010, p 16)

These are radical proposals coming from a highly eminent economist and should be taken seriously by the government.

Ackerman and Alstott (1999) have proposed higher rates of Inheritance Tax if parents have already given their children a good start in life: a 'privilege tax'.

At a time of major cuts to basic benefits and services, the government could do much more to raise contributions from those who have benefited massively from tax cuts and economic changes from the 1980s onwards. It is, so far, pursuing a 'softly-softly' approach to this in relation to Capital Gains Tax and non-state pension tax relief, but it could go much further with both of these. It could take a much tougher stance against tax avoidance and 'non-doms'. It could also consider a range of alternative policies, as suggested by the Mirrlees review.

Policies for original income and wealth

Tax rises are rarely popular, even, it seems, among people who will *not* be directly subject to them. As we saw earlier in this chapter, redistribution is also relatively unpopular as it raises issues about the justice of taking away from one group and the deservingness of the group who receive more as a result. But redistribution would not be necessary if 'original' levels of income and wealth of different groups were fair from the start. Rather than seeking to correct this through unpopular tax increases, another way of dealing with this inequality would, therefore, be to ensure a fairer allocation of original income and wealth.

The inequality of 'original' incomes (that is, incomes before taxation and social transfers) is much larger than that of final incomes. Data for the mid-2000s for the OECD nations finds an overall average Gini coefficient of around 45 per cent before the operation of taxes and transfer, and 31 per cent after. The fiscal systems of different countries may make greater or lesser attempts at changing the inequality of people's incomes – and Figure 7.5 shows the overall effects using OECD data. Nations such as Finland, Iceland and Denmark tended to have relatively low levels of income inequality before redistribution. Some countries, such as Germany, France, Belgium and the Czech Republic, have higher levels of pre-tax inequality than those of the UK, but are rather more equal once taxes and benefits have had their effects. Surprisingly, perhaps, Sweden has one of the lowest rates of inequality after taxes and transfers but the level of inequality before these is rather high.

So how can we regulate original income and wealth? The government already plays a role in the allocation of original income in the form of the National Minimum Wage. This was introduced in 1999 as a way of ensuring that employers paid a certain minimum depending on the age of the employee – and was originally set at £3.60 per hour for those aged 22+, and £3 for those aged 18–21. Its introduction was opposed by the Conservatives at the time and there was some concern that it would lead to wage inflation and job loss. But such fears were unfounded partly, perhaps, because it was set at a low level (Metcalf, 2008; Brown, 2009). While it has been increased over time the rate of £5.93 per hour[3] is still very low and is not enough for a worker, working a 40-hour week, to avoid poverty. There are therefore calls for the National Minimum Wage to be set at a 'living wage' level. The level of the living wage in London is currently regarded as £7.85 per hour. Some organisations, including the Greater London Authority (GLA) and KPMG ensure that all workers receive this level of pay.[4] Rates are calculated by the GLA in London and by the Joseph Rowntree Foundation for the rest of the country.

As we have just seen, the government currently sets a National Minimum Wage. It could also, in theory, set a National Maximum Wage. This may seem like a very radical policy but we saw above that one quarter of the public in 2009 supported the policy of an upper limit on very high earnings. And we also saw that the public consistently support a ratio of 6:1 earnings from top to bottom. Ramsay (2005) called her ideas for a maximum wage a *'modest proposal'*, setting the

Figure 7.5: Income inequality before and after taxes and transfers

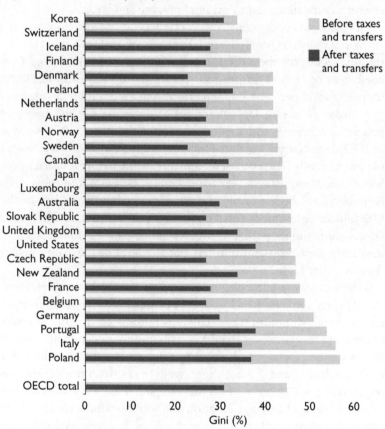

Source: OECDStatExtracts, December 2010,
http://stats.oecd.org/Index.aspx?DataSetCode=INEQUALITY

maximum wage at 10 times the minimum wage. She argued that this ratio would reflect different rewards for skills, ability and effort. In cash terms, this proposal would have set a maximum wage at just over £100,000 which would only affect the top 1 per cent. Ramsay (2005) argued that her proposal was modest because it does nothing to tackle wealth inequality or the ability of people to accumulate wealth, which, as we have seen, is more unequal than income.

One potential problem that a maximum wage policy may face is that employers would find other ways to give rewards to highly paid workers such as bonuses or company cars etc. High-paid workers already benefit from various 'perks' and occupational welfare (May, 2007).

So the policy would have to work hand-in-hand with taxes on other kinds of rewards. There is also, perhaps, a disadvantage with this policy compared with introducing higher taxes on this group as higher taxes would produce revenue that could be used to increase the incomes of those lower down the income ladder and/or pay for services. It is not clear what organisations would do with any money 'saved' by introducing a maximum wage. Some might redistribute it to other workers but some might hand it out in dividends to shareholders, thus benefiting more affluent groups. Pizzigati (2005) has argued that a sufficiently high rate of tax on incomes above a certain threshold is an alternative to simply mandating a maximum wage.

It might seem unlikely that any of the main political parties, particularly the Conservative Party, would support a maximum wage policy, but David Cameron did ask Will Hutton to set up the Review of Fair Pay in the Public Sector. His interim report (Hutton, 2010b, p 7) stated that:

> There is a strong case for a maximum pay multiple, such as 20:1, which would demonstrate fairness by reassuring public opinion, addressing the collective action problem and benefiting productivity.

Nevertheless, despite increases in top pay in the public sector, pay inequality remains highest in the private sector. Indeed it may well be this inequality of rewards in the market sector that is partly responsible for driving the level of earnings within the public sector.

The interim report from the Hutton Review (Hutton, 2010b) gave previous examples of maximum pay multiples, going back to Plato, who argued for a 4:1 ratio to ensure that excessive inequality would not damage social cohesion. More recently, J.P. Morgan introduced a 20:1 wage ratio between executives and junior bank employees in his company. And more recently still, Ben and Jerry's ice cream company had a 7:1 ratio between the highest and lowest paid employees although this was abandoned in 1995. Finally, the John Lewis Partnership had a 25:1 ratio in its original constitution although this was also revised, up to 75:1 ,when the constitution was revised in 2000.

There are also some practical examples of maximum wages in the world of sport. Maximum wages currently exist in the form of salary caps for either teams or players (or both), although their levels tend to be extremely high. The level is currently around US$14 million a year for a player in the National Basketball Association, for instance. Until 1961 players in the English football league were also subject to a maximum wage – set at £20 per week, with some players immediately having rises to £100 once the cap was lifted. And in the much more distant past, the Statute of Artificers 1558–63 established maximum wages for labourers in England, attempting to keep a lid on the wage inflation resulting from plague deaths and the resulting adverse demography (Woodward, 1980).

One of the issues with a maximum wage is what the base case for setting the multiple might be. Hutton (2010b) reviews a number of possible bases including the National Minimum Wage, the living wage, the lowest-paid employee, the lowest-paid 'core' employee, the average employee (using either the mean or median wage) and so on. The problem with setting the maximum in relation to the national minimum or living wage would be that this is a national figure and local labour markets vary considerably. Furthermore, organisations vary considerably and the same figure may be excessive for one small organisation and constraining for another larger and more complex organisation. It may therefore make some sense to set a pay maximum for each organisation separately. Hutton (2010b) was also not convinced about setting the maximum pay in relation to the average worker because this would lose the link to the lowest-paid worker. Furthermore, the mean is not independent of senior salaries whereas the median is less easily understood. Hutton's (2010b) initial thoughts were therefore to link the maximum pay with the pay of the lowest earner. Hutton did, however, suggest a possible pay structure which incorporated a ratio of 18.5:1 from top to bottom along with 10 pay bands, with pay increasing more as one moves up the pay structure.

Hutton's (2010b) interim conclusion was to support the idea of a maximum pay ratio, noting that pay for high earners had been increasing at a much faster rate than for low earners with no evidence that this extra pay is a result of 'due desert' or merit. He also pointed to the restricted labour market for senior positions as a mechanism fuelling wage inflation at that end rather than, once again, any merit. A maximum pay multiple could, he suggested, ensure greater fairness and restore the respect for civil servants among the public. But he did admit some potential problems such as potential adverse effects on recruitment and retention, perverse incentives to contract out the lowest paid work, setting the maximum as a target which organisations try to reach, the growth of alternative forms of pay (for example, bonuses or other benefits), inflexibility over pay and definitional issues.

So Hutton was supportive of the idea of a maximum pay ratio in his interim report but by the publication of his final report in March 2011 he had decided against the idea, at least in the short term, and recommended, instead, greater transparency and self-regulation, for example, through 'Fair Pay Reports' and 'Fair Pay Codes'. Hutton (2011, p 10) explained that he had decided against a single maximum

Table 7.3: Illustrative example of pay levels and ratios

Pay band	Salary (£)	Increase from previous band	Ratio to base level
1 Staff	13,000	–	1
2 Staff	16,000	23	1.2
3 Staff	20,000	24	1.5
4 Staff	25,000	24	1.9
5 Staff	32,500	30	2.5
6 Management	44,000	35	3.4
7 Management	61,500	40	4.7
8 Executives	92,000	50	7.1
9 Executives	143,000	55	11
10 Chief executive	240,000	68	18.5

Source: Hutton (2010b, p 96)

pay ratio because it would be 'unfair, hitting some organisations more than others, and create perverse incentives'. He also pointed out that a 20:1 maximum multiple would only affect 70 senior managers in the public sector. He argued, instead, for greater analysis of top pay in the public sector to contribute to an informed debate and to ensure that pay reflects performance. Government departments were being given until July 2011 to consider their response to the Hutton Review.

In the US, Barack Obama initially proposed to limit pay of employees within companies receiving state aid, such as AIG (to US$500,000). But such policies often face substantial opposition as the rich have considerable power to resist them, and this power may present a better explanation than any flaws in arguments considering the undeserving nature of their wealth.

Alongside discussion of pay in the public sector, Compass established a more general High Pay Commission with funding from the Joseph Rowntree Charitable Trust (see http://highpaycommission.co.uk/) in November 2010 for a year. Its interim report (High Pay Commission, 2011) reviewed the growth in high pay and put forward arguments for why this was a problem. It also established three principles that its future recommendations will be based around: transparency, accountability and fairness.

One of the arguments against a maximum wage is that it involves 'interfering' with the rates that 'the market' is willing to pay. However, top executive pay is not currently determined by the market. Remuneration committees, described by the Treasury Select Committee (2009b) as 'cosy clubs', decide on top executives' pay. Ramsay (2005) cites evidence from a *Guardian* survey that, in 2001, just 392 people sat on the remuneration committees of 98 of the largest UK companies. This small group belong to similar networks and groups. She argues that reciprocity rather than a real assessment of contribution or performance plays the major role in setting pay.

The Treasury Select Committee (2009b) has argued for a widening of the pool of people sitting on these committees. It could go much further in recommending companies to introduce voluntary ratios limiting earnings differentials. Some Japanese and European companies already do this (quoted in Lansley, 2006). Walker (2009) has made a number of recommendations in relation to corporate governance and remuneration in the banking sector such as forcing banks to disclose how many employees earn more than £1 million per year and giving non-executive directors more power to monitor pay deals.

One of the advantages of having some kind of maximum wage or required ratio for earnings, however, would be that original income would be set in a fair way rather than relying on tax to redistribute from rich to poor. Once taxes are required to achieve social justice, issues of tax avoidance and evasion become difficult and people can feel aggrieved that 'their' money is being taken and given to another group who may then be considered 'undeserving'. Such objections are more difficult to make if original income is fair. Although some will claim that a maximum wage is a step too far in terms of interfering with 'the market', this principle has been widely accepted in terms of the minimum wage, so it is difficult to reject the idea of a maximum wage on this principle alone.

We have focused on original income policies in the form of maximum and minimum wages but we could also consider a Basic Income (or Citizen's Income) to ensure an income floor below which people cannot fall. This could also be considered alongside an original wealth policy such as a citizen's inheritance or capital grant (as suggested by Ackerman and Alstott, 1999; and Nissan and Le Grand, 2000; and discussed in Chapter Six, at p 157).

In addition to direct regulation of wages or income, there are other means of trying to affect people's 'original' income outside of the tax system.[5] Various anti-discrimination legislation has attempted to reduce the inequalities of pay between men and women in particular. More recent legislation has sought to bring down the barriers to equal participation by gender, age, sexual orientation, disability, religious identity and 'race'. These relate to the question of (more) equal opportunities already discussed.

Other barriers to participation in the labour market include childcare, with many parents with caring responsibilities (mothers, typically) working part-time hours at lower rates of pay. Strategies to improve childcare availability and quality, while not at too great a cost, may enable some people to increase their working hours and opportunities.

The success of such legislation is open to question, although it seems unlikely that gaps at the very top of the distribution can have been much affected.

Conclusions

The wealthy have benefited greatly from tax cuts and other economic changes in (and since) the 1980s. It is time for them to make a fairer contribution to the public purse. The government is currently taking a very 'softly-softly' approach towards this group while at the same time taking a hard line against people on benefit. This chapter has considered policies that will produce a fairer system (and a more level playing field) from the start, in terms of original income and wealth policy, and then equal opportunities policies which will allow people to gain rewards due to merit rather than luck of birth. Finally, the chapter has discussed tax policies that ensure that those who can afford to do so contribute more.

The chapter began with a discussion about the goals of policy in relation to the wealthy, arguing that these would depend on the nature of the 'problem'. It also reviewed public attitudes to this question and showed high levels of support for better education and training opportunities as well as for reducing taxes for those on low incomes and increasing the minimum wage. Overt support for redistribution was relatively low although people did back a progressive tax and benefit system. This part of the chapter also considered what level of inequality might be aimed at through policy and highlighted different possible approaches to this. But there has been very little discussion about this and more thinking and research would be very useful here.

As far as equal opportunities go, schools are key institutions, but we argue that, to date, the gap in educational outcomes by socioeconomic group only widens during the school years. So there is very little evidence that schools give everyone an equal chance. Radical reforms of education might help here (for example, abolishing catchment areas, introducing lotteries for popular schools, bussing children from poorer areas to higher-achieving schools, etc), but even these policies, which are likely to be highly unpopular with certain groups, are unlikely to tackle the broader issues of disadvantage faced by children growing up in poorer families. The role of further and higher education alongside training opportunities in adulthood is also important to consider here.

Taxation is one way of redistributing income and wealth from rich to poor although it is generally unpopular, particularly by those paying most. Tax receipts declined quite dramatically in the 1980s and this was partly responsible for the increase in inequality at that time. The share of national income taken in tax in the UK in 2006 was lower than the EU15 (unweighted) average and much lower than Sweden, France and Italy. And while those on the highest incomes pay the greatest amount of tax, they actually pay a lower proportion than the very poorest (due to indirect taxes). The Coalition government (like Labour before it) has taken a 'softly-softly' approach to tax issues such as non-domiciles, tax avoidance and bankers' bonuses. Much of the discussion about tax focuses on income tax but a recent review (by Mirrlees and others) has suggested a major overhaul of wealth taxes.

Taxation can clearly be used redistribute the income and wealth that people have, but other original income and wealth policies can affect the amount of income and wealth people have in the first place. Such policies can therefore mean that redistribution is unnecessary (or less necessary). The minimum wage is an existing original income policy and discussion has turned to whether some kind of maximum wage or salary ratio could be introduced although it looks unlikely that any government would do so without considerable public pressure. In terms of original wealth policies, a citizen's inheritance could provide all adults with a stock of wealth, potentially funded by a higher Inheritance Tax.

Notes

[1] The BSAS is carried out by the National Centre for Social Research (NatCen), Britain's largest independent social research organisation. The survey is funded by a range of charitable and government sources. Further information about NatCen and the British Social Attitudes series of surveys can be found at www.natcen.ac.uk

[2] BBC News, 5 October 2010 (www.bbc.co.uk/news/business-11473352).

[3] This applies for those aged 21+. There are other rates of £4.92 for those aged 18–20, £3.64 for those aged 16–17 and £2.50 for apprentices under 19, or 19 or over and in the first year of their apprenticeship.

[4] A list of employers signed up to this policy is listed at: www.citizensuk. org/campaigns/living-wage-campaign/living-wage-employers/

[5] Recognising that tax systems can have both direct effects, and indirect effects through changing incentives to work.

Conclusions

Since the 1980s, there has been a major shift in responsibility for welfare from the state to the individual, driven by both Conservative and Labour governments. During this same period, there has also been a major shift in the distribution of income and wealth such that the gap between the rich and poor has grown steadily wider. The two trends are linked together as policy changes which have reduced the role of the state have favoured the better off. This book has explored these trends and presented new evidence and arguments in relation to them. But our main conclusion is that there has been insufficient thinking, empirical research and policy discussion in this field. We need a major review of wealth and the wealthy, a new Royal Commission on the Distribution of Income and Wealth as took place in the 1970s. In the meantime, this book serves to highlight some key issues and policy ideas.

A major mechanism for achieving a shift from collective to individual welfare has been a range of government policies which have encouraged people to build up their own personal assets in the form of financial savings ('asset-based welfare policies' and financial inclusion policies), housing wealth and private pension wealth. 'Asset-based welfare' for those on lower incomes has been much discussed, but the two flagship policies, the Child Trust Fund and the Saving Gateway, were fairly small scale in practice and, indeed, the Saving Gateway was extensively piloted but then abandoned before it was introduced nationwide. The Child Trust Fund has also been abolished by the Coalition government. And although various financial inclusion policies have increased the number of people with bank accounts and provided more advice to people with debt problems, the number of people on low incomes who have savings to fall back on remains very small.

There has been greater success, it seems, in relation to housing wealth, where more and more people have become owner-occupiers. Some have benefited greatly from this and seen their housing wealth soar, up to 2007 at least. However, the outlook is not so positive as the economic situation and related job losses may cause increasing numbers of owner-occupiers to struggle with their mortgages, and negative equity may become an increasing problem if house prices continue to fall. And some owner-occupiers, perhaps particularly older people, may be on very low incomes and have homes that need repairs that they cannot afford. But there is also an issue for those who are not home owners as the social rented sector has shrunk and become residualised. The private sector also has its problems and there appears to be insufficient housing supply to meet demand. Thus, the shift towards more individual responsibility for welfare through housing has not achieved its desired ends.

There has been even less success in relation to private pension wealth. The number of people with private pensions has actually fallen in recent years, despite a raft of government policies to encourage non-state provision. Private sector employers are increasingly reluctant to support occupational pensions and people are wary of investing in the stock market through personal pensions.

We argue, therefore, that the shift towards more individual responsibility for welfare has run out of steam and it is time for the state to step back in to ensure financial security. This is not to say that individuals should play no part in this as they will need to make contributions to state pensions, social housing and savings schemes. And they can also make contributions, on top, if they wish to do so, to more private schemes. But we need to develop a more holistic policy on assets which starts by outlining the goals of such a policy and takes into account the appropriate balance between: state and individual; assets, incomes and services; housing, pensions and financial wealth; and accumulation and decumulation.

We also argue for a fundamental review of policy responses to the growing concentration of income and wealth which has occurred since the 1980s. Once again, this review needs to start with an analysis of the nature of any 'problem' caused by this trend, and we outline five key problems here. First, there is evidence that a large gap between rich and poor is likely to cause health and social problems irrespective of poverty. Second, the rise in wealth at the very top looks likely to have contributed to, if not caused, the economic crash we have witnessed in the first decade of the 21st century. Third, there is evidence that those who get to the top do not generally do so because of their own talent and hard work but, in many cases, because they were lucky to be born to rich parents. Fourth, even if people succeed on their own merit, there are strong arguments that the *degree* of reward that those at the top receive is difficult to justify. And finally, the kind of work which is rewarded by the market (albeit a very imperfect one at the moment) is not necessarily the kind of work which people place most social value on. Each of these 'problems' leads to different policy responses although each is linked by a need to reduce the current level of inequality.

In this book, we have considered three main policy areas: equal opportunity policies, taxation policy and original income and wealth policies. We argue that equal opportunities are almost impossible to guarantee when outcomes are so unequal. Even with the right policies, schools, universities and employers cannot entirely make up for the differential advantages of children born to rich families as opposed to poor ones. And we are a long way from having the right policies with primary and secondary schools with increasing diversity of schooling and segregation by social class. Early years intervention looks set to make some difference and the Equality Act 2010 may also help improve equality in the workplace, but the chances of someone from a poor family going to a top university or entering one of the professions are slim and may indeed be reducing relative to children from better-off families.

So how can we give everyone a fair chance of succeeding? One way is to level the playing field through a more progressive tax system. It is no coincidence that levels of taxation declined substantially in the 1980s just as inequality rose. Britain now has lower rates of taxation than many other European countries. While some may see this in a positive sense as providing incentives and rewards for hard work, we have already seen that people reach the top in life at least partly through luck of birth rather than individual hard work, and there are many other rewards from working in top jobs. Also, the argument about rewarding hard work cannot be made in relation to inherited wealth and so there are particularly strong arguments for more progressive, and higher, taxes of this kind of unearned wealth.

While taxation can redistribute income and wealth from rich to poor (or from the rich to those in the middle as well as people in poverty), it does nothing to tackle the original distribution of income and wealth. Other policies, such as a minimum and maximum wage, can ensure a fairer starting point. The introduction of a National Minimum Wage was opposed by the Conservatives when it was first introduced but now seems accepted by all political parties. The introduction of a National *Maximum* Wage is not supported by any political party at present but the Conservative/Liberal Democrat Coalition did ask Will Hutton to review the idea of a wage ratio of 20:1 in the public sector. So there are tentative moves in this direction. Original income and wealth policies also encompass basic income and capital grants ideas. Once again, these might seem quite radical but proposals for a 'universal pension' are currently being floated in the government, and capital grants appeal to those on the left and right of the political spectrum even if they have not yet been adopted by mainstream politicians.

The current gap between rich and poor is too great and it needs to be reduced. But to what level? There has been very little discussion of this question but some recent research has suggested that if we were to return to the level of inequality we had in the 1970s and the level which currently exists in many European countries, such as France, the Netherlands and Germany, then the problems caused by inequality would be significantly reduced. The public also have a view on this question and consistently support a wages ratio of 6:1, far lower than the 20:1 ratio discussed recently for the public sector.

The main argument against reducing the gap between rich and poor is that this would involve interfering with 'the market', but markets are imperfect, as we have seen with dramatic and devastating consequences over the last few years. And in any case, we already 'interfere' with the market in many ways to ensure a certain level of welfare. As a democracy, it is the public, not the market, which should have ultimate power to direct policy. But the public are sometimes presented with a very stark choice: between a 'pure' liberal market economy with an unfettered market on the one hand versus a completely controlled command economy in which the market is subordinated to the state on the other. There are, however, many 'varieties of capitalism' and different 'welfare state regimes' to be considered (Esping-Andersen, 1990; Hall and Soskice, 2001). There should be much greater discussion about the range of policy directions on offer, and we hope that the arguments and evidence in this book will contribute to this discussion and provide stronger grounds for policies which will lead both to a more equal distribution of wealth and to a closing of the gap between rich and poor.

References

Abel–Smith, B. and Townsend, P. (1965) *The poor and the poorest*, London: Bell.

Acheson, D. (1998) *Independent inquiry into inequalities of health*, London: HMSO.

Ackerman, B. and Alstott, A. (1999) *The stakeholder society*, New Haven, CT: Yale University Press.

Adam, S. and Browne, J. (2009) *A survey of the UK tax system*, IFS Briefing Note 9, London: Institute for Fiscal Studies.

Adam, S., Browne, J. and Heady, C. (2010) 'Taxation in the UK' in J. Mirrlees et al (eds) *Dimensions of tax design: The Mirrlees Review*, London: Institute for Fiscal Studies (www.ifs.org.uk/mirrleesreview/dimensions/ch1.pdf).

Adonis, A. and Pollard, S. (1997) *A class act: Myth of Britain's classless society*, London: Hamish Hamilton.

Aleroff, C. and Knights, D. (2008) *The link between income, savings and property in funding retirement*, Financial Services Research Forum, Nottingham: Nottingham Business School.

Alesina, A. and Rodrick, D. (1992) 'Distribution, political conflict and economic growth: a simple theory and some empirical evidence', in A. Cuckierman, C. Hercowitz and L. Leiderman (eds) *Political economy, growth and business cycles*, Cambridge: MIT Press.

Appleyard, L. and Rowlingson, K. (2010) *Home ownership and the distribution of personal wealth*, York: Joseph Rowntree Foundation.

Arneson, R. (1989) 'Equality and equal opportunity for welfare', *Philosophical Studies*, vol 56, pp 77-93.

Aron, R. (1950) 'Social structure and the ruling class', *British Journal of Sociology*, vol I, no 1, March, pp 1-16 (part 1) and June, pp 126-43. (part 2)

Atkinson, A.B. (1971) 'The distribution of wealth and the individual lifecycle', *Oxford Economic Papers*, vol 23, no 2, pp 239-54.

Atkinson, A. (1997) *Public economics in action*, Oxford: Oxford University Press.

Atkinson, A.B. (2007) 'The distribution of top incomes in the United Kingdom 1908-2000', in A.B. Atkinson and T. Piketty (eds) *Top incomes over the twentieth century: A contrast between Continental European and English speaking countries*, Oxford: Oxford University Press, pp 82-140.

Atkinson, A.B. and Harrison, G. (1978) *The distribution of personal wealth in Britain*, Cambridge: Cambridge University Press.

Atkinson, A.B. and Piketty, T. (2007) *Top incomes over the twentieth century: A contrast between European and English speaking countries*, Oxford: Oxford University Press.

Atkinson, A.B. and Salverda, W. (2003) *Top incomes in the Netherlands and the United Kingdom over the twentieth century*, Mimeo, Oxford: Nuffield College.

Atkinson, A.B., Gordon, J. and Harrison, J. (1986) *Trends in the distribution of wealth in Britain 1923–1981*, STICERD Discussion Paper 70, London: London School of Economics and Political Science.

Bamfield, L. and Horton, T. (2009) *Understanding attitudes to tackling economic inequality*, York: Joseph Rowntree Foundation.

Banks, J., Emmerson, C. and Tetlow, G. (2005) *Estimating pension wealth of ELSA respondents*, IFS Working Papers, W05/09, London: Institute for Fiscal Studies.

Banks, J., Marmot, M., Oldfield, Z. and Smith, J. (2006) 'Disease and disadvantage in the United States and in England', *Journal of the American Medical Association*, vol 295, no 17, pp 2037-45.

Banks, J., Marmot, M., Oldfield, Z. and Smith, J. (2007) *The SES health gradient on both sides of the Atlantic*, IZA Discussion Paper No 2539, Bonn: IZA.

Barnard, A. (2008) *The effects of taxes and benefits on household income, 2007/08*, London: Office for National Statistics (www.statistics.gov. uk/downloads/theme_social/Taxes-Benefits-2007-2008/Taxes_ benefits_0708.pdf).

Barnard, M., Taylor, J., Dixon, J., Purdon, S. and O'Connor, W. (2007) *Researching the very wealthy: Results from a feasibility study*, London: NatCen.

Bartels, L. (2008) *Unequal democracy: The political economy of the new gilded age*, Princeton, NJ: Princeton University Press.

Batra, R. (1987) *The Great Depression of 1990*, New York: Simon & Schuster.

Beaverstock, J.V. (2010) *The privileged world city: Private banking, wealth management and the bespoke servicing of the global super-rich*, GaWC Research Bulletin 338, Loughborough: Globalization and World Cities Network (www.lboro.ac.uk/gawc/rb/rb338.html).

Beaverstock, J.V., Hubbard, P.J. and Short, J.R. (2004) 'Getting away with it? Exposing the geographies of the super-rich', *Geoforum*, vol 35, pp 401-7.

Begum, N. (2004) *Analysis in brief – The Labour Force Survey: Employment by occupation and industry*, London: Office for National Statistics.

Bernard, J. (1982) *The future of marriage*, New Haven, CT: Yale University Press.

Bernstein, B. (1970) 'Education cannot compensate for society', *New Society*, vol 15, no 387, pp 344-7.

Berthoud, R. (2010) *Patterns of non-employment, and of disadvantage, in a recession*, ISER Working Paper 2009-23, Colchester: University of Essex.

Besley, T. and Coate, S. (1991) 'Public provision of private goods and the redistribution of income', *American Economic Review*, vol 81, no 4, pp 979-84.

Beveridge, W. (1942) *Social insurance and allied services*, Cmd 6404, London: HMSO.

Bishop, M. and Green, M. (2008) *Philanthrocapitalism: How the rich can save the world*, New York: Bloomsbury Press.

Blair, T. (1998) *The Third Way*, Fabian Pamphlet 588, London: Fabian Society

Blanden, J. (2009) 'How much can we learn from international comparisons of social mobility?', Paper presented at Carnegie Corporation of New York and Sutton Trust Conference on Social Mobility and Education, New York, June.

Blanden, J., Gregg, P. and Machin, S. (2005) *Intergenerational mobility in Europe and North America*, London: The Sutton Trust.

Blond, P. (2010) *Red Tory*, London: Faber & Faber.

Blond, P. and Gruescu, S. (2010) *Asset building for children*, London: ResPublica.

Blunkett, D. (2001) *Politics and progress: Renewing democracy and civil society*, London: Demos and Politico's.

Blunkett, D. (2005) 'The asset state: the future of welfare', A keynote speech by Rt Hon David Blunkett MP, Secretary of State for Work and Pensions, 5 July, given at the Institute for Public Policy Research, London (www.ippr.org.uk/events/54/6161/the-asset-state-the-future-of-welfare-a-keynote-speech-by-rt-hon-david-blunkett-mp-secretary-of-state-for-work-and-pensions).

Boadway, R., Chamberlain, E. and Emmerson, C. (2009) 'Taxation of wealth and wealth transfers', in J. Mirrlees, S. Adam, T. Besley, R. Blundell, S. Bond, R. Chote, M. Gammie, P. Johnson, G. Myles and J. Poterba (eds) (2010) *Dimensions of tax design: The Mirrlees Review*, Oxford: Oxford University Press.

Bourdieu, P. (1977) 'Cultural reproduction and social reproduction', in J. Karabel and A.H. Halsey (eds) Power and ideology in education, New York, NY: Oxford University Press, pp 487-511.

Bourdieu, P. (1986) 'The forms of capital', in J. Richardson (ed) *Handbook of theory and research for the sociology of education*, New York: Greenwood.

Breen, R. and Goldthorpe, J. (1999) 'Class inequality and meritocracy: a critique of Saunders and an alternative analysis', *British Journal of Sociology*, vol 50, no 1, pp.1-27.

Breeze, B. (2010) 'More than money: the social meaning of philanthropy in contemporary UK society', Unpublished PhD thesis, Canterbury: Kent University.

Brewer, M. and Browne, J. (2009) *Can more revenue be raised by increasing income tax rates for the very rich?*, IFS Briefing Note 84, London: Institute for Fiscal Studies.

Brewer, M., Sibieta, L. and Wren-Lewis, L. (2008) *Racing away? Income inequality and the evolution of high incomes*, IFS Briefing Note 76, London: Institute for Fiscal Studies (web publication only).

Brewer, M., Muriel, A., Phillips, D. and Sibieta, L. (2009) *Poverty and inequality in the UK: 2009*, Commentary 109, London: Institute for Fiscal Studies.

Brewer, M, Goodman, A., Shaw, J. and Sibieta, L. (2006) *Poverty and inequality in Britain 2006*, London: IFS.

Brown, W. (2009) 'The process of fixing the British National Minimum Wage, 1997–2007', *British Journal of Industrial Relations*, vol 47, pp 429-43.

Butler, T. and Savage, M. (eds) (1995) *Social change and the middle classes*, London: UCL Press.

Bull, J. (1993) *Housing consequences of relationship breakdown*, London: HMSO.

Burchardt, T. and Propper, C. (1999) 'Does the UK have a private welfare class?', *Journal of Social Policy*, vol 28, no 4, pp 643-65.

Burgoyne, C. and Morison, V. (1997) 'Money in remarriage: keeping things simple – and separate', *The Sociological Review*, vol 45, no 3, pp 363–95.

Butler, T. and Lees, L. (2006) 'Super-gentrification in Barnsbury, London. Globalization and gentrifying global elites at the neighbourhood level', *Transactions of the Institute of British Geographers*, vol 31, pp 467-87.

Butler, T. and Savage, M. (eds) (1995) *Social change and the middle classes*, London: UCL Press.

Bynner, J. and Despotidou, S. (2001) *Effect of assets on life chances*, London: Institute of Education.

Bynner, J. and Paxton, W. (2001) *The asset effect*, London: Institute for Public Policy Research.

Cabinet Office (2009) *New opportunities: Fair chances for the future*, White Paper, London: Cabinet Office.

Callendar, C. (2003) *Attitudes to debt: School leavers and further education students' attitudes to debt and their impact on participation in higher education*, London: Universities UK.

Cameron, D. (2009) 'The Big Society', Hugo Young Lecture, 10 November.

CASE (Centre for the Analysis of Social Exclusion) and HM Treasury (1999) *Persistent poverty and lifetime inequality: The evidence*, CASEPaper 5, London: London School of Economics and Political Science.

Castles, F. (1998) *Comparative public policy*, Cheltenham: Edward Elgar.

CEBR (Centre for Economics and Business Research) (2009a) 'City bonuses bounce back by fifty per cent – but still far lower than 2007/08 peak', Press release, 21 October, London: CEBR.

CEBR (2009b) 'City jobs increasing in 2010 but will remain below peak levels for at least a decade', Press release, 15 October, London: CEBR.

Chua, B. (2003) 'Maintaining house values under the condition of universal ownership', *Housing Studies*, vol 18, no 3, pp 765-80.

Clark, T. and Dilnot, A. (2002) *Long-term trends in British taxation and spending*, IFS Briefing Note 25, London: Institute for Fiscal Studies (www.ifs.org.uk/bns/bn25.pdf).

Clarke, J. and Newman, J. (1997) *The managerial state*, London: Sage Publications.

Clarke, J., Langan, M. and Williams, F. (2001) 'Remaking welfare: the British welfare regime in the 1980s and 1990s', in A. Cochrane, J. Clarke and S. Gewirtz (eds) *Comparing welfare states* (2nd edn), London: Sage Publications.

Clarkwest, A. (2008) 'Neo-materialist theory and the temporal relationship between income inequality and longevity change', *Social Science & Medicine*, vol 66, no 9, pp 1871-81.

Clegg, N (2010) 'Inequality becomes injustice when it is passed on, generation to generation', *The Guardian*, 22 November (www.guardian.co.uk/commentisfree/2010/nov/22/inequality-injustice-nick-clegg).

CLG (Communities and Local Government) (2007) *Risk assessment*, New Horizons Research Summary No 5, London: CLG.

CLG (2008) *The Pomeroy review of prospects for private sector shared equity*, London: CLG.

Coates, K. and Silburn, R. (1970) *Poverty: The forgotten Englishmen*, Harmondsworth: Penguin.

Cohen, G. (1989) 'On the currency of egalitarian justice', *Ethics*, vol 99, pp 906-44.

Collard, S. and McKay, S. (2005) 'Closing the savings gap? The role of the Saving Gateway', *Local Economy*, vol 21, no 1, pp 25-35.

Collinson, P. (2010) 'House prices "will go nowhere for years"', *The Guardian*, 12 January. Available at: www.guardian.co.uk/money/blog/2010/jan/12/house-prices-go-nowhere (accessed 20 July 2010).

Commission on Funding of Care and Support (2011) *Fairer care funding: The Report of the Commission on Funding of Care and Support*, London: Commission on Funding of Care and Support.

Conley, D. (2009) 'Don't blame the billionaires: who cares about the excesses of the rich? It's the fate of the poor that matters', *The American Prospect*, December, vol 20, no 10, pp 37-9.

Corry, D. and Glyn, A. (1994) 'The macroeconomics of equality, stability and growth', in A. Glyn and D. Miliband (eds) *Paying for inequality: The economic costs of social justice*, London: Institute for Public Policy Research.

Costa-Font, J. and Jofre-Bonet, M. (2008) 'Is there a "secession of the wealthy"? Private health insurance uptake and national health system support', *Bulletin of Economic Research*, vol 60, no 3, pp 265-87.

Crawford, C., Johnson, P., Machin, S. and Vignoles, A. (2011) *Social mobility: A literature review*, London: Department for Business Innovation and Skills.

Crawshaw, T. (2009) *Re-thinking housing taxation: Options for reform*, London: Shelter.

Crosland, A. (1956) *The future of socialism*, London: Cape.

Daunton, M. (2007) *Trusting Leviathan: The politics of taxation in Britain, 1799–1914*, Cambridge: Cambridge University Press.

Davey, J. (1997) *Equity release: An option for older home-owners*, York: Centre for Housing Policy.

Dean, H. (2006) 'Activation policies and the changing ethical foundations of welfare', ASPEN/ETUI Conference: Activation Policies in the EU, 20-21 October, Brussels.

Dean, H. with Melrose, M. (1999) *Poverty, riches and social citizenship*, Basingstoke: Macmillan.

Deaton, A. (2003) 'Health, inequality, and economic development', *Journal of Economic Literature*, vol 41, no 1, pp 113–58.

De Botton, A. (2005) *Status anxiety*, London: Penguin.

DETR (Department of the Environment, Transport and the Regions) (2000) *Quality and choice: A decent home for all: The way forward for housing*, White Paper, London: The Stationery Office.

DH (Department of Health) (2009) *Shaping the future of care together*, Green Paper, London: DH.

DHSS (Department of Health and Social Security) (1980) *Inequalities in health: Report of a working group* [The Black Report], London: DHSS.

Doling, J. (1997) *Comparative housing policy*, Basingstoke: Macmillan.

Doling, J. (2010) 'Housing and demographic change', in M. Elsinga and R. Ronald (eds) *Beyond home ownership: New perspectives on housing tenure, policy and society*, London: Routledge.

Doling, J. and Ford, J. (2007). 'A union of home owners', Editorial. *European Journal of Housing and Planning*, vol 7, no 2, pp 113–27.

Doling, J. and Ronald, R. (2010a) 'Property-based welfare and European homeowners: how would housing perform as a pension?', *Journal of Housing and the Built Environment*, published online: 12 February.

Doling, J. and Ronald, R. (2010b) 'Home ownership and asset-based welfare', *Journal of Housing and the Built Environment*, vol 25, no 2, pp 165-73.

Doling, J. and Ronald, R. (2011) 'Meeting the income needs of older people in East Asia: using housing equity', *Ageing & Society*, published online, May.

Donovan, N. and Halpern, D. (2002) *Life satisfaction: The state of knowledge and implications for government*, London: Cabinet Office (http://webarchive.nationalarchives.gov.uk/+/http://www.cabinetoffice.gov.uk/media/cabinetoffice/strategy/assets/paper.pdf).

Dorling, D. (2010) *Injustice: Why social inequality persists*, Bristol: The Policy Press.

Dorling, D., Rigby, J., Wheeler, B., Ballas, D., Thomas, B., Fahmy, E., Gordon, D. and Lupton, R. (2007) *Poverty, wealth and place in Britain, 1968 to 2005*, York: Joseph Rowntree Foundation.

DTI (Department of Trade and Industry) (2005) *Tackling over-indebtedness*, London: DTI.

du Gay, P. (2008) 'Keyser Suze elites: market populism and the politics of institutional change', in M. Savage and K. Williams (eds) *Remembering elites*, Oxford: Wiley Blackwell.

Dworkin, R. (2000) *Sovereign virtue: The theory and practice of equality*, Cambridge, MA: Harvard University Press.

DWP (Department for Work and Pensions) (1998) *A new contract for welfare: Partnership in pensions*, Green Paper, London: The Stationery Office.

DWP (2005) *Women and pensions: The evidence*, London: DWP.

DWP (2006) *Security in retirement: Towards a new pensions system*, White Paper, London: The Stationery Office.

DWP (2010a) *Impact of changes to Local Housing Allowance from 2011* (www.dwp.gov.uk/local-authority-staff/housing-benefit/claims-processing/local-housing-allowance/impact-of-changes.shtml).

DWP (2010b) *The abstract of statistics for benefits, national insurance contributions, and indices of prices and earnings, 2009 edition*, London: DWP.

Dwyer, P. (2002) 'Making sense of social citizenship', *Critical Social Policy*, vol 22, no 2, pp 273-99.

Dwyer, P. (2010) *Understanding social citizenship: Themes and perspectives for policy and practice*, Bristol: The Policy Press.

Edwards, L. (2002) *A bit rich? What the wealthy think about giving*, London: Institute for Public Policy Research.

Edwards, M. (2010) *Small change: Why business won't save the world*, San Francisco, CA: Berrett-Koehler.

EHRC (Equalities and Human Rights Commission) (2010) *How fair is Britain? Equality, human rights and good relations in 2010*, The First Triennial Review, London: EHRC.

Emmerson, C. and Wakefield, M. (2001) *The Saving Gateway and the Child Trust Fund: Is asset-based welfare 'well fair'?*, London: Institute for Fiscal Studies.

Esping-Andersen, G. (1990) *Three worlds of welfare capitalism*, Cambridge: Polity Press.

Field, F. (2010) *The Foundation Years: Preventing poor children becoming poor adults. The report of the Independent Review on Poverty and Life Chances*, London: Cabinet Office.

Finegold, D. and Soskice, D. (1988) 'The failure of training in Britain: analysis and prescription', *Oxford Review of Economic Policy*, vol 4, no 3, pp 21-53.

Forbes (2010) *Bill Gates no longer world's richest man* (www.forbes. com/2010/03/09/worlds-richest-people-slim-gates-buffett-billionaires-2010-intro.html).

Ford, J. (2006) 'UK home ownership to 2010 and beyond – risks to lenders and borrowers', in J. Doling and M. Elsinga (eds) *Home ownership: Getting in, getting from, getting out, Part III*, Delft: IOS Press.

Forrest, R. (2008) 'Risk, governance and the housing market', *Housing Finance International*, September, pp 3-13.

Forrest, R., Kennett, P. and Leather, P. (1999) *Home ownership in crisis? The British experience of negative equity*, Aldershot: Ashgate.

Forrest, R., Murie, A. and Williams, P. (1990) *Home ownership: Differentiation and fragmentation*, London: Unwin Hyman.

Frank, R. (2007) *Richi$tan. A journey through the 21st century wealth boom and the lives of the new rich*, New York: Piatkus.

Fraser, D. (1973) *The evolution of the British welfare state: A history of social policy since the industrial revolution*, London: Macmillan.

Friedman, M. (1957) *A theory of the consumption function*, Princeton: Princeton University Press.

Gabaix, X. and Landier, A. (2008) 'Why has CEO pay increased so much?', *Quarterly Journal of Economics*, vol 123, no 1, pp 49-100.

Galbraith, J. (1961) *The Great Crash 1929*, London: Pelican.

Gamble, A. and Prabhakar, R. (2006) 'Assets and capital grants: the attitudes of young people to capital grants', in W. Paxton and S. White (eds) *The new politics of ownership*, Bristol: The Policy Press.

Garland, D. (1996) 'The limits of the sovereign state: strategies of crime control in contemporary society', *British Journal of Criminology*, vol 36, pp 445-71.

Giddens, A. (1974) 'Elites in the British class structure', in P. Stanworth and A. Giddens (eds) *Elites and power in British society*, Cambridge: Cambridge University Press.

Giddens, A. (1998) *The third way*, Cambridge: Cambridge University Press.

Gilbert, N. (2004) *The transformation of the welfare state*, Oxford: Oxford University Press.

Giles, C. and Pimlott, D. (2009) 'House prices are too high, say economists', *Financial Times*, 3 January. Available at: www.ft.com/cms/s/0/ade2abbe-f8a9-11de-beb8-00144feab49a,_i_email=y.html (accessed 20 July 2010).

Ginn, J. (2003) *Gender, pensions and the lifecourse*, Bristol: The Policy Press.

Gladstone, D. (ed) (1999) *Before Beveridge: Welfare before the welfare state*, Choice in Welfare No 47, London: Civitas.

Glass, D. (1954) *Social mobility in Britain*, London: Routledge.

Glass, N. (2005) 'Surely some mistake?', *The Guardian*, 5 January (www.guardian.co.uk/society/2005/jan/05/guardiansocietysupplement.childrensservices).

Glyn, A. and Miliband, D. (eds) (1994) *Paying for inequality: The economic cost of social injustice*, London: Rivers Oram Press/IPPR.

Goldthorpe, J. and Mills, C. (2008) 'Trends in intergenerational class mobility in modern Britain: evidence from national surveys, 1972–2005', *National Institute Economic Review*, vol 205, no 1, pp 83-100.

Gorard, S. (2000) *Education and social justice*, Cardiff: University of Wales Press.

Gorard, S. (2008) 'Research impact is not always a good thing: a reconsideration of rates of "social mobility" in Britain', *British Journal of Sociology of Education*, vol 29, no 3, pp 317-24.

Gorard, S. (2009) 'Does the index of segregation matter? The composition of secondary schools in England since 1996', *British Educational Research Journal*, vol 35, no 4, pp 639-52.

Gorard, S. (2010) 'Education can compensate for society – a bit', *British Journal of Educational Studies*, vol 58, no 1, pp 47-65.

Gorard, S. and See, B.H. (2009) 'The impact of SES on participation and attainment in science', *Studies in Science Education*, vol 45, no 1, pp 93-129.

Gorard, S., Taylor, C. and Fitz, J. (2003) *Schools, markets and choice policies*, London: Routledge Falmer.

Gordon, D. and Pantazis, C. (eds) (1998) *Breadline Britain in the 1990s*, Aldershot: Ashgate.

Gordon, D., Adelman, L., Ashworth, K., Bradshaw, J., Levitas, R., Middleton, S., Pantazis, C., Patsios, D., Payne, S., Townsend, P. and Williams, J. (2000) *Poverty and social exclusion in Britain*, York: Joseph Rowntree Foundation.

Gove, M. (2010) 'Government announces pupil premium to raise achievement', Press release, 26 July, London: Department for Education.

Granovetter, M. (1973) 'The strength of weak ties', *American Journal of Sociology*, vol 78, May, pp 1360-80.

Gravelle, H. (1998) 'How much of the relation between population mortality and unequal distribution of income is a statistical artefact?', *British Medical Journal*, vol 316, no 7128, pp 382-5.

Green, F., Machin, S., Murphy, R. and Zhu, Y. (2010) *The changing economic advantage from private school*, CEE discussion papers, CEEDP0115, London: Centre for the Economics of Education, London School of Economics and Political Science (http://eprints.lse.ac.uk/28288/).

Gregg, P., Harkness, S. and Machin, S. (1999) 'Poor kids: child poverty in Britain, 1966–96', *Fiscal Studies*, vol 20, pp 163-87.

Gregg, P., Jewell, S. and Tonks, I. (2005) *Executive pay and performance in the UK 1994–2002*, Xfi Centre Paper No 05/05, Exeter: Xfi Centre for Finance and Investment.

Gregg, P., Jewell, S. and Tonks, I. (2010) *Executive pay and performance in the UK*, AXA Working Paper Series No 5, Discussion Paper No 657.

Gregory, J. (2011) *Does housing work for the workers?*, Touchstone: Trades Union Congress.

Guardian (2010) 'Fears of mass UK banking exodus prove unfounded', 18 February (www.guardian.co.uk/business/2010/feb/18/uk-banker-exodus-exaggerated).

Hall, P. and Soskice, D. (2001) *Varieties of capitalism: The institutional foundations of comparative advantage*, Oxford: Oxford University Press.

Hall, S. (2009) 'Financialised elites and the changing nature of finance capitalism: investment bankers in London's financial district', *Competition & Change*, vol 13, pp 173-89.

Hamnett, C. (1997) 'Housing wealth, inheritance and residential care in Britain', *Housing Finance*, no 34, pp 35-8.

Hancock, R. (2000) 'Estimating the housing wealth of older home owners in Britain', *Housing Studies*, vol 15, part 4, pp 561-79.

Harbury, C. and Hitchens, D. (1979) *Inheritance and wealth inequality in Britain*, London: George Allen & Unwin.

Harvey, P., Pettigrew, N., Madden, R., Emmerson, C., Tetlow, G. and Wakefield, M. (2007) *Final evaluation of the Saving Gateway 2 pilot: Main report*, London: HM Treasury/Department for Education and Skills.

Haseler, S. (1999) *The super-rich: The unjust new world of global capitalism*, London: St Martin's Press.

Healey, D. (1989) *The time of my life*, London: Michael Joseph.

Heath, A., Dirk de Graaf, N. and Li, Y. (2010) 'How fair is the route to the top? Perceptions of social mobility', in A. Park, J. Curtice, E. Clery and C. Bryson (eds) *British Social Attitudes: The 27th report: Exploring Labour's legacy*, London: Sage Publications.

Hedges, A. and Bromley, C. (2001) *Public attitudes to taxation*, London: Fabian Society.

Hewitson, B., Seale, B. and Joyce, L. (2011) *Public engagement exploring care and support funding options*, London: Commission on the Funding of Care and Support.

Hewitt, M. (2002) 'New Labour and the redefinition of social security', in M. Powell (ed) *Evaluating New Labour's welfare reforms*, Bristol: The Policy Press.

High Pay Commission (2011) *More for less: What has happened to pay at the top and does it matter?*, Interim report, London: High Pay Commission.

Hills, J. (1995) *Income and wealth: The latest evidence*, York: Joseph Rowntree Foundation.

Hills, J. (2002) 'Following or leading public opinion? Social security policy and public attitudes since 1997', *Fiscal Studies*, vol 23, no 4, pp 539-58.

Hills, J. (2004) *Inequality and the state*, Oxford: Oxford University Press.

Hills, J. (2007) *Ends and means: The future roles of social housing in England*, CASEReport 34, London: London School of Economics and Political Science.

Hirsch, D. (2006) *Paying for long-term care: Moving forward*, York: Joseph Rowntree Foundation.

HM Government (2010) *State of the Nation report: Poverty, worklessness and welfare dependency in the UK*, London: Cabinet Office.

HM Treasury (2000) *Helping people to save: The modernisation of Britain's tax and benefit system*, Number 7, London: HM Treasury.

HM Treasury (2001) *Savings and assets for all: The modernisation of Britain's tax and benefit system*, Number 8, London: HM Treasury.

HM Treasury (2004) *Delivering stability: Securing our future housing needs, Barker Review of Housing Supply – Final Report: Recommendations*, London: HM Treasury.

HM Treasury (2010) *Spending Review 2010*, London: HM Treasury.

Hobcraft, J. (1998) *Intergenerational and life-course transmission of social exclusion*, CASEPaper 15, London: London School of Economics and Political Science.

Holliday, I. (2000) 'Productivist welfare capitalism: social policy in East Asia', *Political Studies*, vol 48, pp 706-23.

Holmans, A. (1997a) 'Housing and inheritance revisited', *Housing Finance*, vol 33, pp 14-23.

Holmans, A. (1997b) *Housing inheritance: Current tends and future prospects*, London: Council of Mortgage Lenders.

Holmans, A. (2008) *Prospects for UK housing wealth and inheritance*, London: Council of Mortgage Lenders.

Holmans, A., Stephens, M. and Fitzpatrick, S. (2007) 'Housing policy in England since 1975', *Housing Studies*, vol 22, no 2, pp 147-62.

Howard, C. (1997) *The hidden welfare state*, Princeton, NJ: Princeton University Press.

HSE (Health and Safety Executive) (2009) *Work related injuries and ill health in construction* (www.hse.gov.uk/statistics/industry/construction/index.htm).

Humphrey, A., Mills, L., Morrell, G., Douglas, G. and Woodward, H. (2010) *Inheritance and the family: Attitudes to will-making and intestacy*, London: NatCen.

Hutton, J. (2010) *Independent Public Service Pensions Commission: Interim report*, London: HM Treasury.

Hutton, W. (2010a) *Them and us*, London: Little, Brown & Co.

Hutton, W. (2010b) *Hutton review of fair pay in the public sector: Interim report*, London: HM Treasury.

Hutton, W. (2011) *Hutton review of fair pay in the public sector: Final report*, London: HM Treasury.

Iannelli, C. and Paterson, L. (2006) 'Social mobility in Scotland since the middle of the twentieth century', *The Sociological Review*, vol 54, no 3, pp 520-45.

IDS (2009a) 'Pay increases for FTSE – 100 NEDs averaged 15% increase in 2008', Press release, 13 February, London: IDS.

IDS (2009b) 'FTSE directors' earnings defy gravity', Press release, January, London: IDS (www.incomesdata.co.uk/news/press-releases/ftse_directors.pdf).

Irvin, G. (2008) *Super rich: The rise of inequality in Britain and the United States*, Cambridge: Polity Press.

Isles, N. (2003) *Life at the top: The labour market for FTSE-250 chief executives?*, London: The Work Foundation.

Izuhara, M. (2009) *Housing, care and inheritance*, Abingdon: Routledge.

James, O. (2007) *Affluenza*, London: Vermillion.

Jencks, C. (2002) 'Does inequality matter?', *Daedalus*, Winter, vol 131, no 1, pp 49-65.

Jenkins, S. (1990) 'The distribution of wealth: measurement and models', *Journal of Economic Surveys*, vol 4, no 4, December, pp 329-60.

Jensen, M. and Murphy, K. (1990) 'Performance pay and top management incentives', *Journal of Political Economy*, vol 98, no 2, pp 225-64.

Johnson, P. and Reed, H. (1996) *Two nations? The inheritance of poverty and affluence*, London: Institute for Fiscal Studies.

Johnstone, S. (2005) *Options for financing private long-term care*, York: Joseph Rowntree Foundation.

Judge, K. (1995) 'Income distribution and life expectancy: a critical appraisal', *British Medical Journal*, vol 311, no 7015, pp 1282-5; discussion pp 1285-7.

Judge, K., Mulligan, A. and Benzeval, M. (1998) 'Income inequality and population health', *Social Science & Medicine*, vol 46, nos 4–5, pp 567–79.

Juster, T., Smith, J. and Stafford, F. (1999) 'The measurement and structure of household wealth', *Labour Economics*, vol 6, pp 253-75.

Karabel, J. and Halsey, A.H. (eds) (1977) *Power and ideology in education*, New York: Oxford University Press.

Kelly, G. and Lissauer, R. (2000) *Ownership for all*, London: Institute for Public Policy Research.

Kemeny, J. (1981) *The myth of homeownership*, London: Routledge & Kegan Paul.

Kempson, E. (2002) *Over-indebtedness in Britain*, London: Department of Trade and Industry.

Kempson, E., Atkinson, A. and Collard, S. (2006) *Saving for children: A baseline survey at the inception of the Child Trust Fund*, HMRC Research Report 18, London: HM Revenue & Customs.

Kempson, E., McKay, S. and Collard, S. (2005) *Incentives to save: Encouraging saving among low-income households. Evaluation of the Saving Gateway pilot scheme*, London: HM Treasury.

Kempson, E., McKay, S. and Willitts, M. (2004) *Characteristics of families in debt and the nature of indebtedness*, DWP Research Report No 211, London: The Stationery Office.

Keynes, J. (1936) *The general theory of employment, interest and money*, London: Macmillan.

Klein, R. and Millar, J. (1995) 'Do-it-yourself social policy: searching for a new paradigm?', *Social Policy & Administration*, vol 29, no 4, pp 303-16.

Kodz J., Davis S., Lain D., Strebler M., Rick J., Bates P., Cummings J. and Meager, N. (2003) *Working long hours: A review of the evidence: Volume 1 – Main report*, Employment Relations Research Series ERRS16, London: Department of Trade and Industry.

Kondo, N., Sembajwe, G., Kawachi, I., van Dam, R., Subramanian, S. and Yamagata, Z. (2009) 'Income inequality, mortality and self-rated health: meta-analysis of multilevel studies', *British Medical Journal*, vol 339, b4471.

Labour Party (2001) *Ambitions for Britain: General Election Manifesto*, London: Labour Party.

Lammy, D. (2010) 'The Oxbridge whitewash', *The Guardian*, 6 December (www.guardian.co.uk/commentisfree/2010/dec/06/the-oxbridge-whitewash-black-students).

Lansley, S. (2006) *Rich Britain: The rise and rise of the new super-wealthy*, London: Politico's.

Lansley, S. (2009) *Unfair to middling: How Middle Income Britain's shrinking wages fuelled the crash and threaten recovery*, London: TUC Touchstone Extras.

Law Commission (2007) *Cohabitation: The financial consequences of relationship breakdown*, No 307, London: Law Commission.

Law Commission (2009) *Intestacy and family provision on death*, Consultation Paper 191, London: Law Commission.

Layard, R. (2005) *Happiness: Lessons from a new science*, London: Allen Lane.

Leigh, A. (2007) 'How closely do top income shares track other measures of inequality?', *Economic Journal*, vol 117, no 524, pp F619-F633.

Leigh, A., Jencks, C. and Smeeding, T. (2009) 'Health and economic inequality' in W. Salverda, B. Nolan and T. Smeeding (eds) *The Oxford handbook of economic inequality*, Oxford: Oxford University Press.

Leon, D.A., Vagero, D. and Olausson, P.O. (1992) 'Social class differences in infant mortality in Sweden: comparison with England and Wales', *British Medical Journal*, vol 305, pp 687-91.

Levin, E.J. and Pryce, G. (2011) 'The dynamics of spatial inequality in UK housing wealth', *Housing Policy Debate*, vol 21, no 1, pp 99-132.

Lewis, J. (2003) 'Developing early years childcare in England, 1997–2002: the choices for (working) mothers', *Social Policy & Administration*, vol 37, no 3, pp 219-38.

Lister, R. (2004) *Poverty*, Cambridge: Polity Press.

Lloyd, T. (2009) *Don't bet the house on it: No turning back to housing boom and bust*, London: Compass.

Lowe, S. (2004) *Housing policy analysis*, Basingstoke: Palgrave.

Lynch, J.W., Davey Smith, G., Kaplan, G.A. and House, J.S. (2000) 'Income inequality and mortality: importance to health of individual income, psychosocial environment, or material conditions', *British Medical Journal*, vol 320, pp 1200-4.

Lynch J.W., Davey Smith, G., Harper, S., Hillemeier, M., Ross, N., Kaplan, G. and Wolfson, M. (2004) 'Is income inequality a determinant of population health? Part 1: A systematic review', *Milbank Quarterly*, vol 82, no 1, pp 5-99.

MacInnes, T., Kenway, P. and Parekh, A. (2009) *Monitoring poverty and social exclusion*, York: Joseph Rowntree Foundation.

McElwee, M. (2000) *The great and the good: The rise of the new class*, London: Centre for Policy Studies.

McKay, S. (1992) *Pensioners' assets: A review of the evidence*, London: Policy Studies Institute.

McKay, S. (2009) 'Reforming pensions – investing in the future', in J. Millar (ed) *Understanding social security* (2nd edn), Bristol: The Policy Press.

McKay, S. (2010) 'Where do we stand on inequality? Reflections on recent research and its implications', *Journal of Poverty and Social Justice*, vol 18, no 1, February, pp 19-33.

McKay, S. and Kempson, E. (2003) *Savings and life events*, London: Department for Work and Pensions.

McKay, S., Kempson, E., Atkinson, A. and Crame, M. (2008) *Debt and older people: How age affects attitudes to borrowing*, London: Help the Aged.

McKay, S. and Rowlingson, K. (1998) *Social security in Britain*, Basingstoke: Macmillan.

McKay, S. and Rowlingson, K. (2008) 'Social security and welfare reform', in M. Powell (ed) *Modernising the welfare state: The Blair legacy*, Bristol: The Policy Press.

Machin, S., Dearden, L. and Reed, H. (1997) 'Intergenerational mobility in Britain', *Economic Journal*, vol 107, pp 47-66.

Mack, J. and Lansley, S. (1985) *Poor Britain*, London: Allen & Unwin.

Macmillan, L. (2009) *Social mobility and the professions – For submission to the Panel for Fair Access to the Professions*, Bristol: Centre for Market and Public Organisation.

Majima, S. and Warde, A. (2008) 'Elite consumption in Britain, 1961–2004: results of a preliminary investigation', in M. Savage and K. Williams (eds) *Remembering elites*, Sociological Review Monograph Series, Oxford: Blackwell.

Malpass, P. (2008) 'Housing and the new welfare state: wobbly pillar or cornerstone?', *Housing Studies*, vol 23, no 1, pp 1-19 (January).

Mann, K. (2001) *Approaching retirement*, Bristol: The Policy Press.

Marmot, M. (2004) *Status syndrome*, London: Bloomsbury.

Marmot, M. (2010) *Fair society: Healthy lives: The Marmot Review*, London: UCL.

Marshall, T.H. (1950) *Citizenship and social class and other essays*, Cambridge: Cambridge University Press.

Maxwell, D._(2005) *Using housing wealth: Is there a role for government?*, JRF Discussion Paper, York: Joseph Rowntree Foundation.

Maxwell, D and Vigor, A. (eds) (2005) *Time for land value tax*, London: Institute for Public Policy Research.

May, M. (2007) 'Occupational welfare', in M. Powell (ed) *Understanding the mixed economy of welfare*, Bristol: The Policy Press.

Meade, J. (1978) *The structure and reform of direct taxation*, London: George Allen & Unwin.

Mellor, J. and Milyo, J. (2001) 'Re-examining the ecological association between income inequality and health', *Journal of Health Politics, Policy and Law*, vol 26, no 3, pp 487–522.

Mellor, J. and Milyo, J. (2002) 'Income inequality and health status in the United States: evidence from the current population survey', *The Journal of Human Resources*, vol 37, no 3, pp 510-39.

Menchik, P. (1979) 'Intergeneration transmission of inequality: an empirical study of wealth mobility', *Economica*, vol 46, pp 349-62.

Merrill Lynch Capgemini (2009) *World wealth report* (www.ml.com).

Metcalf, D. (2008) 'Why has the British National Minimum Wage had little or no impact on employment?', *Journal of Industrial Relations*, vol 50, pp 489-512.

Milanovic, B. (2009) *Two views on the cause of the global crisis*, YaleGlobal online, New Haven, CT: Yale University.

Miliband, E. (2010) 'The new generation', Speech to Labour Party conference, 28 September.

Mills, C. Wright (1959) *The power elite*, New York: Oxford University Press.

Ministry of Justice (2009) *Judicial and court statistics*, Cm 7467, London: The Stationery Office.

Mirrlees, J., Adam, S., Besley, T., Blundell, R., Bond, S., Chote, R., Gammie, M., Johnson, P., Myles, G. and Poterba, J. (eds) (2010) *Reforming the tax system for the 21st century*, London: Institute for Fiscal Studies, April (www.ifs.org.uk/mirrleesReview).

Modigliani, F. and Brumberg, R. (1954) 'Utility analysis and the consumption function: An interpretation of cross-section data' in K.K Kurihara (ed) *Post-Keynesian economics*, New Brunswick, NJ: Rutgers University Press.

Moran, M. (2008) 'Representing the corporate elite in Britain: capitalist solidarity and capitalist legitimacy', in M. Savage and K. Williams (eds) *Remembering elites*, Oxford: Wiley Blackwell.

Mortimore, P. (1997) 'Can effective schools compensate for society?', In A.H. Halsey, H. Lauder, P. Brown and A. Stuart Wells (eds) *Education, culture, economy, society*, Oxford: Oxford University Press, pp 476-87.

Mosca, G. (1939) *The ruling class*, New York: McGraw-Hill.

Moss, D.A. (2009) 'An ounce of prevention: financial regulation, moral hazard, and the end of "too big to fail"', *Harvard Magazine*, September-October (http://harvardmagazine.com/2009/09/financial-risk-management-plan).

Murray, C. (2006) *In our hands: A plan to replace the welfare state*, Washington, DC: The American Enterprise Institute.

NAO (National Audit Office) (2011) *The Mortgage Rescue Scheme*, London: Department for Communities and Local Government.

National Equality Panel (2010) *An anatomy of economic inequality in the UK*, London: Government Equalities Office (www.equalities.gov.uk/pdf/NEP%20Report%20bookmarked.pdf).

National Evaluation of Sure Start Team (2008) *The impact of Sure Start local programmes on three year olds and their families*, London: Institute for the Study of Children, Families and Social Issues, Birkbeck, University of London.

Nationwide (2009) *UK house price data* (www.nationwide.co.uk/hpi/historical.htm).

nef (New Economics Foundation) (2009) *A bit rich: Calculating the real value to society of different professions*, London: nef (www.neweconomics.org/sites/neweconomics.org/files/A_Bit_Rich.pdf).

New Statesman (2009) 'Tax but no spend', 30 April, www.newstatesman.com/uk-politics/2009/05/tax-rate-labour-party-brown

Nicoletti, C. and Ermisch, J. (2007) 'Intergenerational earnings mobility: changes across cohorts in Britain', *The B.E. Journal of Economic Analysis and Policy*, vol 7, pp 1-36.

Nissan, D. and Le Grand, J. (2000) *A capital idea: Start-up grants for young people*, London: The Fabian Society.

North, R.D. (2005) *Rich is beautiful. A very personal defence of mass affluence*, London: The Social Affairs Unit.

Observer, The (2008) 'Why the new rich are different: they give away billions to charity', 22 June (www.guardian.co.uk/society/2008/jun/22/voluntarysector.charitablegiving).

ODPM (Office of the Deputy Prime Minister) (2005) *Homebuy: Expanding the opportunity to buy*, London: ODPM.

Oliver, M., Shapiro, T. and Press, J. (1993) '"Them that's got shall get": inheritance and achievement in wealth accumulation', *Research in Politics and Society*, vol 5, pp 69-95.

ONS (Office for National Statistics) (2008) *Pension trends*, London: ONS.

ONS (2009) *Wealth in Great Britain: Main results from the Wealth and Assets Survey 2006/08* (www.statistics.gov.uk/downloads/theme_economy/wealth-assets-2006-2008/Wealth_in_GB_2006_2008.pdf).

ONS (2010) *Social Survey Division, Wealth and Assets Survey, Wave 1, 2006–2008: Special Licence Access* (computer file) (4th edn), Colchester, Essex: UK Data Archive (distributor), November, SN: 6415.

Orton, M. (2002) 'Council tax: who benefits?', *Benefits*, vol 10, no 2, pp 251-65.

Orton, M. (2006) 'Wealth, citizenship and responsibility: the views of better-off citizens in the UK', *Citizenship Studies*, vol 10, no 2, pp 251-65.

Orton, M. (2008) 'State approaches to wealth', in T. Ridge and S. Wright (eds) *Understanding inequality, poverty and wealth*, Bristol: The Policy Press.

Orton, M. and Rowlingson, K. (2007a) 'A problem of riches: towards a new social policy research agenda on the distribution of economic resources', *Journal of Social Policy*, vol 36, no 1, pp 59-78.

Orton, M. and Rowlingson, K. (2007b) *Public attitudes to inequality*, York: Joseph Rowntree Foundation.

Overton, L. (2010) *Housing and finance in later life: A study of UK equity release customers*, London: Age UK.

Palier, B. (2009) *A long goodbye to Bismarck? The politics of welfare reforms in Continental Europe*, Amsterdam: Amsterdam University Press.

Panas, J. (1984) *Mega gifts: Who gives them, who gets them?*, Chicago, IL: Bonus Books Inc.

Panel on Fair Access to the Professions (2009) *Unleashing aspiration: The final report of the Panel on Fair Access to the Professions*, London: Cabinet Office.

Parkinson S., Searle, B.A., Smith, S.J., Stokes, A. and Wood, G. (2009) 'Mortgage equity withdrawal in Australia and Britain: towards a wealth-fare state?', *European Journal of Housing Policy*, vol 9, no 4, pp 363-87.

Paton, G. (2009) 'Lord Mandelson launches tuition fee review', *The Telegraph*, 9 November (www.telegraph.co.uk/education/6530502/ Lord-Mandelson-launches-tuition-fee-review.html).

Payne, G. and Roberts, J. (2002) 'Opening and closing the gates: recent developments in male social mobility in Britain', *Sociological Research Online*, vol 6, no 4.

Paxton, W. (2001) 'Assets: the third pillar of welfare?', in S. Regan (ed) *Assets and progressive welfare*, London: Institute for Public Policy Research.

Pemberton, H. (2006) 'Politics and pensions in postwar Britain', in H. Pemberton, P. Thane and N. Whiteside (eds) *Britain's pensions crisis: History and policy*, London/Oxford: British Academy/Oxford University Press, pp 39-63.

Pen, J. (1971) *Income distribution*, London: Penguin.

Pensions Commission (2004) *Pensions: Challenges and choices. The first report of the Pensions Commission*, Norwich: The Stationery Office.

Pensions Commission (2005) *A new pension settlement for the twenty-first century: The second report of the Pensions Commission*, Norwich: The Stationery Office.

Pensions Commission (2006) *The final report of the Pensions Commission*, Norwich: The Stationery Office.

Pharoah, C. (2009) *Charity Market Monitor 2009*, London, Caritas Data.

Pizzigati, S. (2005) *Greed and good: Understanding and overcoming the inequality that limits our lives*, New York: Apex Press.

PPI (Pensions Policy Institute) (2009) *Retirement income and assets: How can housing support retirement?* (www.pensionspolicyinstitute.org.uk/ uploadeddocuments/2009/PPI_Retirement_income_and_assets_ report_2_-_Housing_Sept_2009.pdf).

PPI (2010) *Pensions facts*, London: PPI.

Prabhakar, R. (2008) *The assets agenda*, London: Palgrave Macmillan.

Prabhakar, R., Rowlingson, K. and White, S. (2008) *How to defend Inheritance Tax*, London: Fabian Society.

Price, D. (2003) 'Pension sharing on divorce: the future for women', in C. Bochel, N. Ellison and M. Powell (eds) *Social Policy Review 15*, Bristol: The Policy Press.

Pring, R. (2009) 'Education cannot compensate for society: reflections on the Nuffield Review of 14-19 Education and Training', *Forum*, vol 51, no 2, pp 197-204.

Putnam, R. (2000) *Bowling alone: The collapse and revival of American community*, New York: Simon & Schuster.

Ramsay, M. (2005) 'A modest proposal: the case for a maximum wage', *Contemporary Politics*, vol 11, no 4, December, pp 201–15.

Rawls, J. (1971) *A theory of justice*, Cambridge, MA: Belknap Press of Harvard University Press.

Regan, S. and Paxton, W. (2001) *Asset-based welfare: International experiences*, London: Institute for Public Policy Research.

Reich, R. (1991) *The work of nations: Preparing ourselves for 21st-century capitalism*, New York: Vintage Books.

Reich, R. (2010) 'The roots of economic fragility and political anger', blog posted on Tuesday, 13 July (http://robertreich.org/post/805148061).

Ring, P. (2003) 'Risk and UK pension reform', *Social Policy & Administration*, vol 37, part 1, pp 65–81.

Rodgers, G. (1979) 'Income and inequality as determinants of mortality: an international cross-section analysis', *Population Studies*, vol 33, no 2, pp 343–51.

Rowlingson, K. (2006) '"Living poor to die rich"? or "spending the kids' inheritance"? Attitudes to assets and inheritance in later life', Journal of Social Policy, vol 35, no 2, pp 175–92.

Rowlingson, K. (2008) 'Wealth', in T. Ridge and S. Wright (eds) *Understanding poverty, income and wealth*, Bristol: The Policy Press.

Rowlingson, K. (2011a) *Does income inequality cause health and social problems?*, York: Joseph Rowntree Foundation.

Rowlingson, K. (2011b) 'All in this together? Reflections on wealth, the wealthy and fairness', in N. Yeates, T. Haux, R. Jawad and M. Kilkey (eds) *In defence of welfare: The impacts of the spending review*, Social Policy Association.

Rowlingson, K. and Connor, S. (2011) 'The "deserving" rich? Inequality, morality and social policy', *Journal of Social Policy,* vol 40, pp 437–52.

Rowlingson, K. and Joseph, R. (2010) *Assets and debts within couples: Ownership and decision-making*, London: Friends Provident Foundation.

Rowlingson, K. and McKay, S. (2005) *Attitudes to inheritance in Britain*, Bristol: The Policy Press.

Rowlingson, K., Orton, M. and Taylor, E. (2010) 'Do we still care about inequality?', in A. Park, J. Curtice, E. Clery and C. Bryson (eds) *British Social Attitudes: The 27th report: Exploring Labour's legacy*, London: Sage Publications.

Rowlingson, K., Whyley, C. and Warren, T. (1999) *Income, wealth and the lifecycle*, York: Joseph Rowntree Foundation (www.jrf.org.uk/publications/income-wealth-and-lifecycle).

Rowntree, S. (1901) *Poverty: A study of town life*, London: Macmillan; (2001 reprint, Bristol: The Policy Press).

Royal Commission on Long-Term Care for the Elderly (1997) *With respect to old age: Long term care – Rights and responsibilities*, London: Department of Health.

Royal Commission on the Distribution of Income and Wealth (1975) *Report Number 1: Initial report on the standing reference*, Cmnd 6171, London: HMSO.

Runciman, W. (1966) *Relative deprivation and social justice: A study of attitudes to social inequality in twentieth-century England*, London: Routledge & Kegan Paul.

Sampson, A. (2004) *Who runs this place? The anatomy of Britain in the 21st century*, London: John Murray Publishers.

Sargant, N. (2000) *The learning divide revisited: A report of the findings of a UK-wide survey on adult participation in education and training*, Leicester: The National Institute of Adult Continuing Education.

Saunders, P. (1986) 'Comment on Dunleavy and Preteceille', *Society and Space*, vol 4, no 2, pp 155-63.

Saunders, P. (2010) *Beware false prophets: Equality, the good society and the spirit level*, London: Policy Exchange.

Savage, M. and Williams, K. (2008) 'Elites remembered in capitalism and forgotten by social sciences', in M. Savage and K. Williams (eds) *Remembering elites*, Oxford: Wiley Blackwell.

Scott, J. (1982) *The upper classes: Property and privilege in Britain*, London: Macmillan.

Scott, J. (1994) *Poverty and wealth: Citizenship, deprivation and privilege*, Longman: Harlow.

Scott, J. (2008) 'Modes of power and the reconceptualisation of elites', in M. Savage and K. Williams (eds) *Remembering elites*, Oxford: Wiley Blackwell.

Sefton, T. (2005) 'Give and take: attitudes to redistribution', in A. Park, J. Curtice, K. Thomson, C. Bromley, M. Phillips and M. Johnson (eds) *British Social Attitudes: The 22nd Report*, London: Sage Publications.

Sefton, T. (2009) 'Moving in the right direction? Public attitudes to poverty, inequality and redistribution', in J. Hills, T. Sefton and K. Stewart (eds) *Towards a more equal society?*, Bristol: The Policy Press, pp 223-44.

Sefton, T., Hills, J. and Sutherland, H. (2009) 'Poverty, inequality and redistribution', in J. Hills, T. Sefton and K. Stewart (eds) *Towards a more equal society?*, Bristol: The Policy Press, pp 21-46.

Shelter (2009) *Rethinking housing taxation: Options for reform*, London: Shelter.

Sherraden, M. (1991) *Assets and the poor: A new American welfare policy*, New York: M.E. Sharpe, Inc.

Sinfield, A. (2007) 'Tax welfare', in M. Powell (ed) *Understanding the mixed economy of welfare*, Bristol: The Policy Press, pp 129-48.

Sklair, L. (2001) *The transnational capitalist class*, Oxford: Blackwell.

Smith, J. (2005) 'Mortgage equity withdrawal and remortgaging activity', in P. Boelhouwer, J. Doling and M. Elsinga (eds) *Home ownership: Getting in, getting from, getting out*, Delft: IOS Press.

Smith, S.J. and Searle, B. (2008) 'De-materialising money? Observations on the flow of wealth from housing to other things', *Housing Studies*, vol 23, part 1, pp 21-43.

Smith, S.J., Searle, B.A. and Cook, N. (2009) 'Rethinking the risks of home ownership', *Journal of Social Policy*, vol 38, no 1, pp 83-102.

Snowdon, C. (2010) *The spirit level delusion*, Ripon: Little Dice.

Sodha, S. (2005) *Housing-rich, income-poor*, London: Institute for Public Policy Research.

Stephens, M. (2007) 'Mortgage market deregulation and its consequences', *Housing Studies*, vol 22, no 2, pp 201-20.

Stephens, M., Wilcox, S. and Dailley, M. (2008a) *Developing safety nets for home-owners*, York: Joseph Rowntree Foundation.

Stephens, M., Ford, J., Spencer, P., Wallace, A., Wilcox, S. and Williams, P. (2008b) *Housing market recessions and sustainable home-ownership*, York: Joseph Rowntree Foundation (www.jrf.org.uk/publications/housing-market-recessions-and-sustainable-home-ownership).

Stewart, K. (2009) 'Labour's record on inequality and the new opportunities White Paper', *The Political Quarterly*, vol 80, no 3, pp 427-33.

Sunday Times, The (2009) 'Football stars plan to dodge 50p tax rate', 31 May (www.timesonline.co.uk/tol/sport/article6395778.ece).

Sunday Times, The (2010) *The Sunday Times Rich List 2010*, 18 July (www.thesundaytimes.co.uk/sto/public/article346801.ece?CMP=KNGvccp1-sunday%20times%20rich%20list%20 2010%20full%20list).

Sunday Times, The (2011) *The Sunday Times Giving List 2009/10*, 8 May.

Taylor-Gooby, P. (2000) *Risk, trust and welfare*, Basingstoke: Macmillan.

Thane, P. (1982) *The foundations of the welfare state*, London: Longman.

Thorndike, J. (1980) *The very rich: A history of wealth*, New York: Crown.

Titmuss, R. (1958) *Essays on the welfare state*, London: Allen & Unwin.

Townsend, P. (1979) *Poverty in the United Kingdom*, Harmondsworth: Penguin.

Townsend, P., Davidson, N. and Whitehead, M. (1986) *The Black Report and the health divide*, Harmondsworth: Penguin.

Toynbee, P. and Walker, D. (2008) *Unjust rewards: Exposing greed and inequality in Britain today*, London: Granta Books.

Treasury Select Committee (2009b) *Banking crisis: Reforming corporate governance and pay in the city*, London: TSO (www.publications. parliament.uk/pa/cm200809/cmselect/cmtreasy/519/519.pdf).

Turok, I. (2010) 'Book review of Wilkinson, R. and Pickett, K. *The Spirit Level*', *New Agenda*, vol 37, p 60.

Veblen, T. (1899 [1985]) *A theory of the leisure class*, London: Allen & Unwin.

Vogler, C. (2009) 'Managing money in intimate relationships: similarities and differences between cohabiting and married couples', in J. Miles and R. Probert (eds) *Sharing lives, dividing assets*, Oxford: Hart Publishing.

Walker, D. (2009) *A review of corporate governance in UK banks and other financial industry entities, Final recommendations*, 26 November, London: Canary Wharf.

Wanless, D. (2006) *Securing good care for older people: Taking a long-term view*, London: The King's Fund.

Warren, T., Rowlingson, K. and Whyley, C. (2001) 'Female finances: gender wage gaps and gender asset gaps', *Work, Employment and Society*, vol 15, pp 465-88.

Wakefield, M. (2003) *Is middle Britain middle-income Britain?*, IFS Briefing Note 38, London: Institute for Fiscal Studies.

Wallace, A. (2010) *Public attitudes to housing*, York: Joseph Rowntree Foundation.

Wedgwood, J. (1929) *The economics of inheritance*, London: Pelican Books.

Westaway, J. and McKay, S. (2007) *Women's financial assets and debts*, London: Fawcett Society.

Wheary, J., Shapiro, T. and Draut, T. (2007) *By a thread: The new experience of America's middle class*, New York: Demos.

White, S. (2003) *The civic minimum: On the rights and obligations of economic citizenship*, Oxford: Oxford University Press.

White, C and Edgar, G (2010) 'Inequalities in healthy life expectancy by social class and area type: England, 2001–03', *Health Statistics Quarterly*, vol 45, Spring 2010, London: Office for National Statistics.

Wilcox, S. (2008) *Housing Review 2008/9*, London: Chartered Institute of Housing.

Wilhelm, M. (1997) 'Inheritance, steady-state consumption inequality and the lifetime earnings process', *Manchester School of Economic and Social Studies*, vol 65, no 4, pp 466-76.

Wilkinson, R. (1996) *Unhealthy societies: The afflictions of inequality*, London: Routledge.

Wilkinson, R. (2005) *The impact of inequality*, Abingdon: Routledge.

Wilkinson, R. and Pickett, K. (2009a) *The spirit level: Why more equal societies almost always do better*, London: Penguin.

Wilkinson, R. and Pickett, K. (2009b) 'Income inequality and social dysfunction', *Annual Review of Sociology*, vol 35, pp 493-511.

Willetts, D. (2010) *The pinch: How the baby boomers took their children's future – And why they should give it back*, London: Atlantic Books.

Williams, H. (2006) *Britain's power elites: The rebirth of a ruling class*, London: Constable & Robinson.

Williams, P. (2007) 'Home-ownership at the crossroads?', *Housing Finance*, vol 2, pp 1-14.

Williams, P. (2010) *Home equity: Accumulation and decumulation through the lifecycle*, London: Resolution Foundation.

Williams, T. (2004) *The impact of household wealth on child development*, Working Paper No 04-07, Washington, DC: Centre for Social Development, Washington University in St Louis.

Wind-Cowie, M. (2009) *Recapitalising the poor: Why property is not theft*, London: Demos.

Wittenberg, R., Comas-Herrera, A., Pickard, L. and Hancock, R. (2004) *Future costs of long-term care for older people*, York: Joseph Rowntree Foundation.

Wolff, E. (2002) 'Inheritances and wealth inequality, 1989-1998', *American Economics Association Papers and Proceedings*, Bequests, Saving and Wealth Inequality, vol 92, no 2, pp 260-4.

Woodward, D. (1980) 'The background to the Statute of Artificers: the genesis of Labour policy, 1558-63', *The Economic History Review*, New Series, vol 33, no 1, pp 32-44.

World Economic Forum (2010) *Global competitiveness report 2010–2011*, Geneva: World Economic Forum.

Young, M. (1958) *The rise of the meritocracy*, London: Transaction Publishers.

Zwaniecki, A. (2008) 'More US companies led by foreign-born executives', America.gov Press release, 28 February.

Z/Yen Group (2010) *The Global Financial Centres Index 8*, September (www.zyen.com/GFCI/GFCI%208.pdf).

Index

Page references for tables and figures are in *italics*; those for notes are followed by n